MW00416617

AMERICAN MERCENARY

AMERICAN MERCENARY

THE RIVETING, HIGH-RISK WORLD OF AN ELITE SEAL TEAM OPERATOR TURNED HIRED GUN

DANIEL CORBETT

CENTER
STREET

New York • Nashville

Center Street
Hachette Book Group
1290 Avenue of the Americas, New York, NY 10104
centerstreet.com
X.com/CenterStreet

First Edition: August 2024

Center Street is a division of Hachette Book Group, Inc.
The Center Street name and logo are trademarks of Hachette Book Group, Inc.

The publisher is not responsible for websites (or their content) that are not owned by the publisher.

The Hachette Speakers Bureau provides a wide range of authors for speaking events. To find out more, go to hachettespeakersbureau.com or email HachetteSpeakers@hbgusa.com.

Center Street books may be purchased in bulk for business, educational, or promotional use. For information, please contact your local bookseller or the Hachette Book Group Special Markets Department at special.markets@hbgusa.com.

Library of Congress Cataloging-in-Publication Data
Names: Corbett, Daniel D., III, author.
Title: American mercenary : the riveting, high-risk world of an elite SEAL team operator
  turned hired gun / Daniel Corbett.
Other titles: Riveting, high-risk world of an elite SEAL team operator turned hired gun
Description: First edition. | New York : Center Street, 2024.
Identifiers: LCCN 2023056639 | ISBN 9781546006190 (hardcover) | ISBN
  9781546006213 (ebook)
Subjects: LCSH: Corbett, Daniel D., III, 1984– | Mercenary troops—United
  States—Biography. | Mercenary troops—Serbia—Biography. | United States. Navy.
  SEALs— Reserves—Biography. | Special operations (Military science)—United
  States—History—21st century. | Afghan War, 2001-2021—Veterans—Biography. |
  Operation Enduring Freedom, 2001–2014.
Classification: LCC UB148 .C67 2024 | DDC 355.3/54—dc23/eng/20240212
LC record available at https://lccn.loc.gov/2023056639

ISBN: 9781546006190 (hardcover), 9781546006213 (ebook)

Printed in the United States of America

LSC

Printing 1, 2024

To Mom and Dad

CONTENTS

PART I

1. Gun in My Face   3
2. "Dirty"   6
3. An $85,000 Oversight   9
4. Quitting Time   13
5. Shotguns and Go-Fast Boats   15
6. Familiar Waters   20
7. Asim   24
8. The *Maersk Kentucky*   29
9. Pirates?   35
10. Sniper, Shooter, Linguist   38
11. "We Need Dirty"   42
12. ██████ Level Three   46
13. The Pony Room   49
14. LAX>>>AUH   54
15. Reservoir Dogs   59
16. Brian Bourne   64
17. Going in Black   71
18. Rule of Three   76
19. The Range   79
20. Accommodations   83
21. Time to Hunt   88
22. Camel Crushing It!   93
23. Tech Guy   99
24. Partner Force   102
25. Rolling Solo   108
26. Camp Yemen   112
27. False Extract   117
28. Terminated   122
29. Hank and Kerry   128
30. The Modern Mercenary   134
31. Does Serbia Count as a Western Country?   137

PART II

32. Welcome to Belgrade 143
33. Sveti Sava 147
34. Daniel Corbett Number Three 150
35. Vučić, aka the Wolf 152
36. Familiar Friends, Familiar Faces 160
37. Centralni Zatvor 163
38. They Call Me Foka 166
39. Roomies 168
40. The State Department 174
41. Room 311 180
42. CZ99 185
43. A Flash of Silver 188
44. Small Court 190
45. Milosh's News 196
46. Fucking Serbia, Man 199
47. Dragoslav 202
48. The Doldrums 205
49. Change of Command 208
50. Court Date! 212
51. The Stench 216
52. Happy Birthday to Me 218
53. New Fish 220
54. The Glasses 223
55. Turns Out I Am Fluent 226
56. Foka Legende! 229
57. Derby Day 233
58. Closing Arguments 237
59. The Verdict 239
60. Bowl, Spoon, Blanket, Kiro 241
61. Home Again, Home Again 245
62. Yallah, Brother 251

PART I

1

GUN IN MY FACE

Here I am in Belgrade, Serbia. Here I am at my friend Nikola's apartment, helping him get ready for a party he's having later in the day. I've been in this strange, not-quite-European, kind-of-Russian country for a couple of months working a human intelligence gathering job—a "humint" gig—for a client in the Middle East. In my past life, I was a top-tier Navy SEAL, and while I'm still technically a reservist with the SEAL Teams, what I've been for the last few years is politely known as a "contractor."

I prefer "mercenary."

We'll get to the particulars of what this means, but on this day in Serbia, I'm busy at my friend Nikola's apartment. I'm looking forward to the party. A woman is coming whom I've been eager to meet. Not like that. You see, I've been hired to get dirt on a non-Serb who lives in Belgrade, a money guy for a network of terrorists on the Arabian Peninsula, and this young woman happens to work at my target's firm. This is what my humint gig consists of—meeting people, chatting them up, taking notes, reporting back to my client. Shit, this Serbia gig doesn't even call for a gun. Like I said, I've been here two months, and I haven't touched a single firearm.

Remember this point.

At the moment, this job calls for, of all things, cooking.

That afternoon, I help Nikola make his mother's lamb stew recipe. Mostly I chop vegetables and scrape them into a pot. Around lunchtime, he takes a call. It's all in Serbian and I have no idea what he's talking about. He hangs up and tells me he has to step out for a few and that I can just chill. Fine by me.

After some channel surfing—a short game in Serbia, since there's only a handful of watchable channels, one of which shows nonstop garbage reality

3

TV—I grab my backpack to change clothes. Nikola isn't back yet, but people are going to show up soon. I've got a pair of nice jeans and a collared shirt folded neatly in my bag. I peel off my hoodie. As I reach for my shirt, the apartment door swings open and Nikola flies into the room, slamming into the living room wall. He's immediately followed by four men all wearing—are those police uniforms? If they are, they look cheap as hell. Is this some kind of prank?

Standing there shirtless, I notice that Nikola's hands are handcuffed in front of him. Before I can process any more information, a black mass appears in my periphery. I rotate my head to the left.

It's a pistol, pointed directly at my forehead.

———

As a Navy SEAL who's operated in places like Iraq and Afghanistan, I've been around a lot of guns and have been shot at countless times. Done my fair share of shooting too. But never has anyone put a gun point-blank in my face. Mostly because no one could ever get the drop on me. Mostly because in those instances I was expecting a gun and had one of my own.

Again, just to be extra clear, I did *not* have a gun on me that day in Belgrade.

Let's back up. What is a mercenary? Someone who gets paid to do things other people don't want to do, basically. Someone who travels the world on someone else's dime, but on their own passport. Mercenaries never carry more than $10,000 in cash because that would tip off the FBI and/or Interpol. They never travel with weapons—if a weapon is needed, they figure out how to get one. Sometimes the client provides them. Some jobs are boring, some exciting, some fun. Some hurt. Mercenaries take meetings in high-end restaurants in Abu Dhabi and low-end strip malls in Anywhere, USA. They use encrypted comms, dead drops, and surveillance detection routes (SDRs), among other techniques. Many have friends in the military or three-letter agencies. Many are loners, many more are family men. Almost all mercenaries are men.

What *isn't* a mercenary is what you see on TV and in the movies. We don't travel with aliases on fake passports. We don't drive Porsches or Land Rovers, we drive Kia Sorentos, Nissan Pathfinders, Toyota Hiluxes. We don't have access to drones or air support. And our liaisons are not sexy Bond girls with names like Vesper Lynd and Pussy Galore but instead are ugly, world-weary men with names like Omar and Herbert.

Are there people in the world who are as good at killing as James Bond or Jack Reacher? Yes, better even. Are there people in the world who do the things they do? Absolutely. Do some of them actually wear Paul Smith blazers? Guilty as charged. But a lot of the rest of what we've been trained to accept through the media is bullshit.

All that follows, however, is *not* bullshit. Well, nearly all. A man in my position has to keep *some* secrets.

As you know, I am a mercenary, and I got here courtesy of the US Navy SEAL Teams.

Let's get this out of the way: I love the navy. I love what they taught me how to do. I love how they taught me. I love where they sent me to work. I love the people I worked with. I love the mission—I did at the beginning of my career, anyway. I love the direction, the discipline, the challenge. I love what the navy revealed to me about myself, about my capabilities, about my limitations, about my tendencies. The navy helped make me a better person, and I will be forever grateful for that.

But—you knew there was a "but" coming—that's not to say it was all roses and champagne on smooth seas. One thing I don't love is that the navy is so good at turning otherwise interesting, intelligent, motivated men into people whose identity eventually becomes only "I am in the navy, and I serve the United States, and that's it." The main problem with this is that when the work is done, what's a man to do? Many of my friends have no earthly clue. Some drink, others drug. Some work, others fade away. Some end it all early by staring down one of their own guns and pulling the trigger. This is a problem for many vets, across all the services. What are we supposed do now that we're not doing what we were trained for? What does the US military owe us?

It's a real question, one I've grappled with mightily. I'm one of the lucky ones, though. I always felt fully formed, even when I enlisted in the navy at the tender age of seventeen. Of course, I was not fully formed. But I was secure enough in who I was to know that I would never lose myself to the navy, its rules, or its expectations. I have my parents to thank for that. I proudly defended the United States and did what I was asked to do with professionalism and efficiency, but now that I'm on the other side of my service, I realize that I didn't serve the navy so much as the navy served me. Like I said: one of the lucky ones.

Let's back up a little more. It all started one sunny afternoon in California's Central Valley...

2

"DIRTY"

Daniel D. Corbett III, born 1984, Honolulu, Hawaii. Mom, Debbie. Dad, Daniel Corbett II. Brother, Joseph. Tough, loving family. *Lots* of love. Mom was the toughest of us all. She grew up poor. Had a brother in supermax on a twenty-year bid for grand larceny. Military family, Dad was an HVAC technician in the army. After a year in Hawaii, we bounced around. Arizona, Germany, Northern California. Mom had to put up with Dad when he lost an eye to a brain tumor. I was eleven at the time. Dad developed a five-year opioid addiction. More than anything, he loved Vicodin and self-pity. When he looked in the mirror during that time, he and his one good eye seethed with hate and remorse. He made us live with the shades drawn and the lights off. If he was going to be half-blind, we were too. Mom nearly left him. But she didn't. She led him out of the darkness, and love eventually returned to our family. Mom used to walk around the house back then reciting her personal motto: "Love is the antagonist of fear." I was too young to really get that, but I still liked it. I was not too young to hate my dad's self-pity, which I rejected, swearing I'd never go that route. Anyway, he got better. His recovery coincided with my abandonment of the religion known to most all Americans as "football." I'd started playing in sixth grade, the year Dad lost his eye. Those first teams sucked. I was usually put on the line of scrimmage, on either side of the ball. Our mantra was, "We aren't fast, and we probably won't win, but we hit ten times harder." Coach didn't even do speed drills or run routes in practice, he just had us hit. I snapped off a wicked growth spurt after sixth grade and was five-ten and 170 pounds by the middle of junior high. (Don't get too excited: I am still five-ten and 170 pounds. OK, maybe 175.) I also got faster. I moved from lineman to running back and middle linebacker. Decent punter too. This was when Dad was at his worst, and those years were tough, with Dad moping around the house like a zombie. I was mostly a good kid, but I had a big chip on my shoulder. I didn't take shit from anyone, I couldn't even deal with *others* taking shit from *other* anyones. I regularly picked fights with bullies who were older and stronger than I, usually in order to stand up for other kids who were younger and weaker. I got roughed up now and then, but not often. By early high school, I was known as a bully of bullies. A good guy, if a little complicated. By junior year, I was on track for a D-I football scholarship, but I was tired of football. That was the year dad kicked pills, love returned to our home, and I rejected self-pity. Thankfully, he is still with us. The August before school started, I left the team. I would miss my teammates and our crazy coach who doubled as an English teacher, but it had to be done. (I've met some salty guys since high school, but even now High School Coach stands out for his tirades, his tendency to violently whip his whistle on your helmet, his intolerance for stupidity and imperfection, his flying tobacco spit, and his creative use of profanity that always left me both confused and entertained.) I ran cross-country instead, kind of like Dad, who had run track. Now *those* kids were fast. I could manage a six-minute-per-mile pace, but the fast kids were running 5:15s on race day. Still, I loved the exertion, the challenge of running hell-bent over open country for 2.5 kilometers, turning around, and retracing my route with the task of hitting a negative split. I'd run a lot for football, but never had I sustained an elevated heart rate like this. I was hooked. And even though I wasn't the fastest, our assistant coach noticed me. He was getting ready to go into BUD/S, aka Basic Underwater Demolition/SEAL training, the first step on a training program that turns navy men into elite SEALs. I had no idea what any of that meant. He gave me a VHS copy of a SEAL recruiting video. This is the aforementioned "sunny afternoon in California." Tape in hand, I went home. Popped it in. And sat there, rapt. I must have watched that tape fifty times, holed up in my little room in our single-level ranch. The video had all the rote shit: the live-fire training session, the pyrotechnics, the gravelly Sam Elliott voice-over making everything so *serious*. But what I liked most were the guys they interviewed. They were all so matter-of-fact. At one point, the interviewer asked, "What makes you so good?" The interviewee answered, "It's not that we're that good, it's that everyone else sucks." Welp, that was that. Where do I sign? The football posters came down, the navy posters went up. I soon received a BUD/S warning order from the local recruiter and got accepted to the Delayed Entry Program. I had to negotiate with my parents some, but a year later, in July 2002, at only eighteen years of age, I was off to join the US Navy. Basic training, followed by a navy "A school"—in my case a four-week-long parachute rigger course. I packed parachutes into bags for ejecting pilots and learned to sew. I took this course in Pensacola, Florida. I'd never been to Florida, so I thought I was headed to Miami. Miami it was not. Everyone there called it "LA," not for "Los Angeles" but for "Lower Alabama." By November I was in BUD/S. It was hard, but I didn't think it was *that* hard. Still, a lot of guys dropped out. Not me. After that, I went to SEAL Qualification Training, graduating in November 2003. I then received orders to SEAL Team 5 and deployed twice with them. We went to Iraq and kicked down doors. We went to the Philippines and lived in the wild, learning Tagalog, betting on cockfights, training Filipino special forces to fight their own Islamic extremists. I was then selected to screen for SEAL Team 6. At twenty-three, I became one of the youngest operators to make it. Most of my teammates were in their early thirties, many with over ten years in the Teams. We hunted Taliban and other terrorists in the plains and orchards and mountains of Afghanistan. I never went to sniper school, but with most any other rifle I was deadeye. My Heckler & Koch HK416 assault rifle was my best friend. Now and then I cheated on it with a belt-fed machine gun, the MK 46, aka "the SAW." We deployed at night, with dogs, in helos. I usually fell asleep on the way to targets, the heavy drone of the Chinook shaking out a lullaby just for me. We fast-roped, we climbed, we crouched, we crawled. My specialty became close quarters combat (CQC). I could see things better than the enemy and even better than some of my teammates. When the shooting began, I rarely missed. The fight was never fair. We had night vision, A-10 Warthogs, AC-130 gunships, drones, suppressors, infrared laser sights, dedicated satellite comms. Most of all, we had each other. The best of the best, all willing to do whatever was needed to get the job done and come home. My nickname was Dirty, not because of what I did in the field, but because of one night at a strip club when I was first brought into the Teams. Through it all, I didn't just learn to shoot or be a good operator, I learned to be responsible and mature. I learned to be a man.

And then, in 2011, everything changed. Just like with football, I was tired. America felt tired. The mission *was* tired. We'd had enough.

I was out.

3

AN $85,000 OVERSIGHT

Let me give you an example of how tired things had gotten.

When we first deployed to Afghanistan, we operated alone—meaning no Afghan counterparts on missions. Then we were asked to bring along five or so Afghan special forces so we could get them up to speed on modern warfare. Officially we accepted this, and just threw the Afghans in the back while we conducted business as usual. Unofficially we couldn't help but wonder: Why are we, an elite unit, doing bilateral missions with a fighting force that has a history of turning on Americans? This wasn't common, but it happened often enough that we had a term for when a partner force turned on us—green on blue. And then, within what felt like a matter of months, we were conducting missions with five of *us* and twelve or more of *them*. The roles had reversed. That was the red line.

This is when I leave SEAL Team 6 to become a close quarters combat (CQC) instructor in the SEAL Qualification Training school in Coronado, near San Diego, California. This doesn't mean I teach hand-to-hand or how to gut an enemy with a Mark III tactical knife, but that I teach prospective SEALs how to enter buildings and kill enemies inside without getting killed or wounded in turn. This was practically all we did at SEAL Team 6, so I know I'll be good at teaching CQC.

Only it turns out—not so much.

On day one of CQC, I and another former SEAL Team 6 operator turned instructor are asked to give a room-clearing demo for seventy-two students. There are various kinds of CQC training grounds, aka kill houses. Some mimic villages of single-room huts, others consist of warrens of interlocking apartments and offices on multiple levels, but basically a kill house is a structure with rooms, doors, windows, hallways, and various points of concealment, access, and escape. The rooms have no ceilings but instead are covered by "rafters"—metal catwalks prowled by instructors and sometimes students. We use live 5.56 rounds, shooting photorealistic paper targets. These are mounted on bullet-absorbing ballistic walls, meaning that guys can shoot in rooms right next to each other and not have to worry about getting hit.

My partner and I do the demo. It only takes us eight seconds. We kill everyone.

As soon as the kill house is called cold, the lead instructor on the rafter above barks, "All right, gentlemen—do *not* do anything Instructor Corbett just did."

I'm heated. Who the fuck is this guy? I hold my tongue as he tells another instructor to take my place. The room is reset, I go to the rafters, he calls the house hot. As soon as the action begins, I see where I went wrong.

I'm so used to working with top-level operators that I forgot some things. Mostly I forgot that these students aren't top-level operators. Shit, for most of them, this is their first time in a kill house. I have tons of real-world experience and know what to do by reflex, and the way I clear rooms is something these kids will only experience if they make it to SEAL Team 6. Some will make it there, but most won't. That's not my problem. My problem is learning—quickly—how to become a good instructor.

For the next couple of weeks, I shadow instructors, relearning the basics of CQC that have been stripped from me in actual battle. I put in the work and get better. After a few months, I'm up there in the rafters teaching young guys how to stay alive—because that's really what we're doing. We're not teaching how to kill, necessarily, but how to stay alive through the act of killing.

They have to know how to do this, even if they might not be as active as my generation of operators was.

By 2011 the war on terror is changing. There are fewer direct-action raids. The drone is ascendant. Hellfire missiles are cheaper to develop and deploy than SEALs or any other special operators. Yes, there tends to be more collateral damage with drone warfare, but that's considered acceptable. What becomes painfully obvious to me and my peers is that we practiced our trade during a golden era. The enemy back then was a diffuse guerrilla force. They hid, they appeared, they attacked, they disappeared. They didn't stand up lines of soldiers or use artillery and armor—they fought on the ground, locally. So we did too.

We attacked at night, with silent, lethal force. There were long stretches of boredom and training and practice, but the active part of our job was downright cinematic. Here, what you see on TV and in the movies is pretty accurate.

But by September 2011, the active part of our job has become much less so. Over the span of just a few years, we've gone from conducting capture-kill night raids on Taliban positions to working with three-letter liaisons to train Afghan special forces. Or worse, we're tasked with doing village stability operations (VSOs). No offense, but this is not what SEALs train for—this is what army Green Berets train for. My peers and I have zero interest in dropping off food, water, fuel, and ammunition to village elders in broad daylight, hoping that when we leave the village, we won't get hit by an ambush. More and more, we find ourselves sitting on bunks at forward operating bases (FOBs) twiddling our highly trained thumbs and rewatching every movie on our laptops for the nth time.

This is my headspace when, in mid-2011, I head to the career counselor's office to talk about reenlistment. Despite my misgivings, I'm fifty-fifty on re-upping. I'm ten years into a naval career that, after ten more years, will net me a full retirement package at the ripe old age of thirty-eight. Even if I just teach CQC for the rest of my time, I can deal with that.

Also, I know that I'm up for an $85,000 reenlistment bonus, which is well over a year's salary.

I make an appointment to see the career counselor, Yeoman Petty Officer First Class Velasquez, one of the many non-SEAL support personnel on base. I've only had one interaction with her, and all I can remember is that we don't get along. I also remember that she's pretty, and seems a little on the heavy side, but to be fair, our guacamole-green camouflage uniforms don't flatter anyone.

I'm right on time. She sits behind her desk playing a game on her phone. She doesn't say a word, I take a seat. It takes about thirty seconds for her to get to a break in her game. She looks up. I'm mildly shocked to see that her makeup is fit for a night of clubbing. More power to her. I understand the need for conformity in the military, but it's not my favorite part of the job. As a SEAL who is able to take advantage of "relaxed grooming standards," who am I to judge? Personally, I feel like if you're doing your job, then who cares what you look like?

"Petty Officer Corbett, what do you want?" she asks. If she were chewing gum, she'd smack it.

"Hey, Velasquez," I say, opting for a more casual mode. "I'm here to chat about my reenlistment."

"What reenlistment?"

"At my last command, I figured out that I can dissolve my extension and reenlist, meaning I can get this big bonus everyone but me seems to be getting."

She squints. She clearly couldn't give two shits. She asks for my Social Security number and punches it into her computer. "Looks like you needed to dissolve that extension a long time ago." She picks up her cell phone and glances at some notification from whatever game she's playing.

"How long ago?"

"Like a year, Petty Officer Corbett."

"*Exactly* how long ago?"

She wheels her mouse and leans toward her computer's screen, rattling off a date for when I was deployed in Afghanistan. When you're on deployment it's hard enough to remember which day of the week it is, let alone the date.

"Does that mean I can't get the bonus?"

"Affirmative, Petty Officer Corbett." It's almost like she's enjoying this.

"What if I reenlist next February?"

"You'll qualify for a bonus, yes. But it won't be significant."

She keeps talking, but I can't hear anything but my own silent rage. I know in that instant that my naval career has effectively ended.

"Corbett! Hey, Corbett!" YN1 Velasquez barks.

I snap out of it. "Yes?"

"You all right?"

"Yup! All good." I stand. "Thanks, Velasquez."

She says nothing as I turn and leave. Behind me, I hear her gaming session resume.

I already know that I'll just serve out my current contract and bounce. I'll stay quiet about my plans, but February 24, 2012, will be my last day in the US Navy.

As that date approaches, I think about what I'll do next. I've been in the navy since the age of eighteen, and I really only know how to do one thing: work on a team to kill the enemies of the United States. Naturally, I conclude that being a mercenary is the thing for me.

4

QUITTING TIME

WHEN I PICTURE A MERCENARY, I SEE A SPECIFIC GUY IN IRAQ STANDING NEAR a gray water truck at FOB al-Asad in Haditha. He was thirty-five-ish, muscle-bound, had on 5.11 tactical pants in tan or desert camouflage. Black wraparound sunglasses. A beard, a black ball cap. An earpiece radio. A bulky GPS watch, a rigger's belt with a 9 mm pistol, extra magazines, and a Cold Steel knife. He wore body armor with no shirt underneath. He was sleeved in prison-style tattoos—spiderwebs, "Trust No One," a set of weighted scales. For hair he rocked a mohawk, black hair, bleached tips.

No shit.

It was in 2005 that I first started seeing guys like this, all in Iraq, nearly all employed by Blackwater, a company founded by the ex-SEAL Erik Prince. The men were all ex-military, and many were ex–special forces. Shirtless Mohawk might have been a SEAL. I hoped not. He looked ridiculous.

We crossed paths with mercenaries all the time, and whenever I spoke with one who'd been in the Teams, they'd ask the same thing: "When are you getting out, Dirty? Contractor pay is five times what you're making. I'll put in a good word."

Universally, these men and their employers continued the military tradition of using jargon to skirt the true nature of a thing. Like using "neutralize" for "kill," these people called themselves "contractors," never "mercenaries."

Whatever. I'm going with "mercenary." The word itself says money, and I don't have a problem with that. I've been doing a lot more for a lot less for a long time.

My last day in the navy arrives in February 2012. That week I come to work in civilian clothes, making the rounds from department to department to secure signatures on my discharge paperwork. On my final day, I go to my CO's office at 1300. I make sure to dress to the nines—gray three-piece suit, Italian shoes, matching belt. I don't have a plan for my post-SEAL life, but he doesn't need to know that. And I'm not about to share it with him.

"Corbett," he says when I enter his office.

"Sir."

He takes my papers and barely registers my clothing. Either he's happy for me or he doesn't care about my plans. Fine by me.

He stands when he's finished signing and hands everything over. He offers his hand. "Best of luck, Corbett."

"Thank you, sir."

And that's that.

I have some drinks with friends at Shore Club in Pacific Beach, and the next morning send an email to an outfit I've heard a lot about—Trident Group America, out of Virginia. They only hire former SEALs, and the job entails antipiracy work on cargo ships plying the Indian Ocean. It pays about $20,000 per month, meaning that in three months, I'll make more than a full year in the navy.

Also, I'll get to fight pirates.

5

SHOTGUNS AND GO-FAST BOATS

A WEEK LATER, I'M ON A PLANE TO VIRGINIA TO TRY OUT FOR TRIDENT. AS I ride in the cab from Norfolk airport, I'm reminded of one of the things I hate about Virginia: the grass and weeds devouring the sidewalks. (I was stationed in Virginia Beach from 2007 to 2010.) I don't know why, but it bugs the shit out of me.

Other things in Virginia bug the shit out of me too. The AC in my room at the Comfort Inn isn't on—it's only April, but in Virginia that's not too early for some heat and a lot of humidity. The guy at the front desk is rude. The cab on the way to Trident smells like the bottom of an ashtray mixed with cat piss. This feels like the most Virginia part of all the little Virginia annoyances.

The cab pulls up to a low-slung business complex, I pay and get out. Trident doesn't have a sign, but it might as well: there's a garage at one end of the complex, and standing in front of it is a jacked dude covered in tattoos. He holds a clipboard. I can't see his eyes behind his—you guessed it—wraparound sunglasses. I walk up to him.

"Name?" he asks before I reach him.

"Daniel Corbett."

"Roger. Stand by for the physical screening. Two-mile run, minimum of twelve pull-ups."

I peer inside the garage and see a dozen other guys milling around. I go and join them. We don't do much talking.

The run is easy, but not my best—I post mile splits of 6:54 and 7:13. I guess the days of negative splits are gone. The pull-ups are more difficult. Normally I can peel off twenty, but somehow I fucked up my shoulder on the flight and struggle to reach twelve. Tattooed Wraparounds ticks some box on his form. "Good enough." After that it's time to shoot.

We're loaded into a bus and driven out to a small, overgrown field. Maybe I'm not in the best shape, but I can shoot. We're each lined up fifty meters from an E-type silhouette target—a white sheet of paper with a black shape that looks kind of like a giant bottle but is supposed to be the head and upper torso of a person. Each of us is given an M4 rifle with iron sights and a single thirty-round magazine.

Tattooed Wraparounds gives a quick range brief and then barks, "All right, fuckers. I don't want to be out here all day, so you guys only get three volleys to sight in. It ain't gotta be gnat's ass, the test is easy." We throw on our eyes and ears and lie prone for the first course of fire. Prone is the most stable shooting position, but with this grass I can barely see the center of my target.

I raise my hand. "Can we call the range cold to make some bowling alleys?"

Tattooed Wraparounds says, "Good idea."

We get up and march slowly toward our targets, mashing down the grass. We come back, lie prone again, and the range is called hot. I send three solid shots, same sight picture and clean breaks.

"Range is cold, down range!" Tattooed Wraparounds hollers.

I stomp more grass as I walk to my target. My shots are tight but high and right. I don't remember what the per-click adjustments are on iron sights, but I've done this so many times that I just say to myself, "Six down, four left." Range is hot, second volley, range is cold. A tight group right where it needs to be. I don't need a third volley, so I stand back. A couple others do the same.

Range is cold, Tattooed Wraparounds checks the targets. "Good enough. Take five, then we shoot the qualification. It's going to be three iterations of three shots, center mass."

Several minutes later, we're prone in the grass again. Range is hot, I squeeze three quick shots. When everyone's finished, we go to see how we did.

As we're walking, the guy to my left—the youngest-looking guy there, Latino, mustache, an In-N-Out Burger T-shirt, vaguely familiar—asks, "You a good shot?"

"We're about to find out."

As we get closer, I can't see any holes on my target. This means they're either all in the black or I completely missed the paper. Odds are the former, but if it's the latter, this is going to be a *short* trip.

I reach my target and see one pinkie-size hole dead center. Keyholing three rounds at fifty meters with iron sights is no small feat, and I'd be hard pressed to do it again.

"Goddamn!" the kid whistles. "Nice shooting, Dirty!"

Fuck, he knows me. Were we in the Teams together? It takes a second, but then I place him—we go to the same gym in San Diego. For the life of me, I can't remember his name. I go with the standard, "Hey, bro, thanks." I'm fooling no one. He can tell I don't know his name. He doesn't remind me of it, but he also doesn't seem to care. "You're not bad either," I add. I'm being nice. His shots all hit the target, but each is separated by four or five inches. If that's what he can do from a prone position on the ground at only fifty meters, how's he going to shoot pirates at a hundred meters or more from the bridge wings of a cargo ship where everything is moving?

"Eh, I can tighten up," he says, as if he can hear my thoughts.

We shoot two more volleys, the rifles are collected. I eventually snag his name—Tony. We're taken back to the bus, where Tattooed Wraparounds informs us, "All right, gents. We are now headed out in our go-fast boats with some shotguns so we can see how you do from a moving platform." A chorus of "Woo-hoo!" and "Hell yeah!" echoes through the small bus.

I stay quiet.

Sure, I guess that will be a cool thing to do, but it makes zero sense. One, we are going to be on massive ships that don't get jostled by the sea anywhere near as much as go-fast boats, and two, shotguns?!

When we get to the marina, I ask the instructor, "Why shotguns?"

"Local ordinance. We're not going very far out, and we can't have a stray 5.56 impacting a random sailboat." Uh, OK. Shotguns it is.

The group is divided, we board the boats—two rigid hull inflatable boats (RHIBs) with twin outboard engines. Tony is on the other boat. Within minutes, we're out of the marina and headed to the chop of the Atlantic. It's ironic, since I'm a navy man, but I hate being on the water unless I'm on a lazy river with some tequila. Helicopters and on foot, those are my comfort zones. Big boats like the one I'm signing up to fight pirates from don't irk me—they get tossed like any other ship, but they're so big they feel less like a boat and more like a building.

As soon as our boat passes the breakwater, the shotgun is taken out of its case and handed to the first shooter. He immediately puts the butt on his hip to strike a pose while some other dude snaps a picture of him. This is repeated again and again. It's like they turn into eighteen-year-old Instagram influencers who just found a trendy set of fairy wings painted on the side of some vegan cupcake shop on Rodeo Drive. Except they think they're badasses. Whatever.

Eventually it's my turn to shoot at an orange buoy that has been deployed by the lead instructor.

He hands me the shotgun. "You want a cool video, Corbett?"

"Nope, all good!" I pop off two shells from the pump-action shotgun as fast as I can. I hit the buoy once, not because I'm bad with the shotgun, but because it's a fucking shotgun loaded with buckshot.

We stay out for an hour, crisscrossing the ocean, shooting "cool videos," and having a good old time dumping metal pellets into the Atlantic.

We turn back to shore. Marina, bus, business complex. Tattooed Wrap-arounds hands out a packet with forms, including one for a Transportation Worker Identification Credential (TWIC). I'll fill them out on the plane back to San Diego. Tony wants to get drinks. No—he wants to "Burn it down!" I don't want to burn Norfolk or any other place down, and besides my flight is at 0642. Of course, he's on the same flight, which just gets him more amped. I tell him no thanks, and we part ways. It's my loss, according to Tony. Somehow I doubt it.

Shitty cab, pit stop at Popeyes, ten-piece dinner, Comfort Inn. I crush the entire dinner except for two wings and pass out before 2100. Up at 0428, two minutes before my alarm is set to go off. I order a cab. I throw on my travel clothes and pack up my carry-on and head to the lobby. The cab is already there. An older, heavyset woman is behind the wheel. I jump in. I'm so relieved she's not a smoker.

"ORF?"

"Yup."

"Which airline, honey?"

"United."

"Getcha getcha," she says, kind of like a variation on "You betcha." "Music?" she asks.

"Whatever you want."

We listen to Linda Ronstadt the whole way to the airport. Fine by me.

Check-in, Starbucks, venti Veranda no room. Head to the gate. No sign of Tony. Maybe he *did* burn it down.

I do the Trident paperwork on the plane. Two days later, I submit everything. One month after that, I get my TWIC.

In four days I'm headed to Cairo, Egypt, to fight pirates.

6

FAMILIAR WATERS

I'M USED TO FLYING COMMERCIAL, OR COMAIR, AS WE CALL IT. I'M ALSO USED to flying in C-17 Globemaster IIIs, C-130 Herculeses, and CH-17 Chinooks, but this job will have none of those. In fact, I would say that we military types are *too* used to flying COMAIR. The US military may have the world's largest defense budget, but that doesn't mean it's not cheap. We always flew economy. If we relied on navy travel agents, the seats were usually middles. And for some reason we never flew direct, often making stops in places that were in the opposite direction of our final destination.

As a contractor, Trident is a little better. To get to Egypt I'll fly from San Diego to Denver, Denver to Frankfurt, Frankfurt to Cairo. I even pay a little extra out of pocket to get window seats the whole way. Movin' on up!

I get to San Diego International an hour and a half early with a packed-to-the-gills black North Face duffel bag. In all my travels, I've never seen anyone else rocking this exact bag. Inside are running shoes, Lululemon workout gear (I love my Lululemon shit—deal with it), a couple of casual outfits for ports of call, toilet kit, laptop, a one-terabyte USB hard drive full of movies and TV shows. I hope that between this and my phone's Audible app that I'll have enough to entertain me during downtime on my twenty-four-day excursion.

After checking in and clearing security, I head to Hudson News. Sudoku magazine, new Uni-ball pen. I like doing sudoku in ink. It adds a level of consequence to any mistakes. I appreciate consequences, always have, always will. They make life more...interesting.

I don't know if it's because I've returned to this airport so many times or because it's just a nice place, but I love San Diego International. I usually run into a buddy here, and I've met more than a couple of girls while sipping some preflight concoction at one of the terminal bars. I find a seat near the gate and open the sudoku book. I alternate between fitting the numbers in place and people watching. I make up little stories, ask these strangers private questions they'll never answer. One couple looks like they'll be divorced within a week. A young kid with *way* too many bags, a neck pillow, an eye mask, and charging cords coming out of every pocket looks like he's never traveled before. Some other guy is a Lebowski Dude wearing Birkenstocks and socks. Why, man, why?

I turn back to the puzzle book and zone out. As the numbers drift around my brain and land on the page, I wonder about pirates. It won't be my

All of this runs through my mind while I fly east, toward troubled waters.

7

ASIM

DENVER, TWO-HOUR LAYOVER, LUFTHANSA FLIGHT TO FRANKFURT. Lufthansa! I must be doing something right. The plane is spotless, the seats are spacious, and the flight attendants are...gorgeous. The stewardesses wear little black pillbox hats throughout the boarding process. If I had an aisle seat, I would chat one up, but I'm in a window, and talking across two other people with the hope of getting a phone number is a bad look. I make a mental note to book aisles on Lufthansa from now on for this exact purpose. I take my seat and fall asleep as the plane takes off and flies east into the night.

I wake two hours before landing, somewhere over the west coast of Ireland. My neck stabs with pain from being crooked in one position for too long. Someday maybe I'll swallow my pride and get one of those travel neck pillows.

Actually, no. I won't ever do that.

Frankfurt airport, terminal Brauhaus, double schnitzel with extra sauerkraut. Food is excellent. After that I have three hours to kill. I wander around. Frankfurt Airport is huge. Before my final connection, I stop at a convenience store for some gum only to spot a thing I'd totally forgotten about: a Kinder Egg!

This is a hollow milk chocolate egg wrapped in foil, and it was my all-time favorite when I was a kid living in Germany. I pick one up and give it a gentle shake. Yep, they still have a little deconstructed toy inside. I buy it and head to my gate.

I find a seat near the check-in desk and open the egg. There's not a lot to the milk chocolate egg, the real prize is what's inside. My egg has parts for a little green truck. There's a piece of folded paper the size of a postage stamp. I take this out and flatten it on my thigh. Instructions. No words, like a set of IKEA assembly directions. If you think it's weird that a grown man enjoys putting together a toy from inside a chocolate egg, then you've never had a Kinder Egg. I forgive you.

The spell is broken by an announcement in Arabic, followed by a German translation, then English. My Egyptair flight to Cairo is boarding. I take my spot in line, but it's more like a scrum. I'm one of maybe half a dozen non-Arabs on the flight. We're still in Germany, but culturally we're already in Egypt, and queuing is not something Egyptians do.

The plane is not on the same level as Lufthansa. It's nice, but not that nice. I won't be chatting up any flight attendants on this leg. It has nothing to do with looks. As with the scrum outside, it has everything to do with cultural norms. Different countries play by different rules and customs. And I always play by the rules. Except for when I might not.

This is an important point, and one that I know makes mercenary sense even before I've technically worked as a mercenary. On occasion, mercenaries might have to break rules and customs over the course of a job. But up to that point, it's of paramount importance to be by the fucking book. The point is to be invisible, not to draw attention, to be a normal person by all accounts. Even if mercenaries are not normal at all.

I take my window seat on the plane's port side and get into the difficult part of the sudoku book. My mind is elsewhere. I keep making dumb mistakes, which, because I'm using ink, makes a mess of the pages. Consequences. Not deadly ones, at least.

I don't sleep. Don't want to.

Initial descent into Cairo. I've never been to Egypt. I peer out my window, scanning for Giza and the Pyramids, but the setting sun is too blinding. I lower my shade. We bump through some thermals—there are no clouds over the desert—and land.

There is even less civility for deplaning. The passengers held back in Frankfurt. Now they are home, and they are free. Once we're off the Jetway, the collective pace gets even more frantic. It's as if their life depends on their getting to baggage claim ASAFP. I have to get on step to avoid getting rear-ended. We all reach the baggage carousel, but—no bags. It's like we sped to hit a red light, a habit I'll never understand.

After fifteen minutes, a cherry-red light over the carousel goes off. A buzzer sounds three times. The bags begin to appear. After several minutes, I spot my black North Face duffel and skip through the crowd like a double-Dutch champion. Out of the corner of my eye, I see someone else angling toward it. Not Egyptian. All three objects come together at the same moment—me, bag, other guy—and we both grab the bag and haul it onto the ground.

"Hey, mate. You mind letting go of my sports bag?" Aussie or Brit, white, fit, roughly my age. Probably in my line of work.

"Pretty sure it's mine, bro." He grabs the name tag, tilts it toward me. The handwriting isn't mine. "Sorry, man. My bad," I say.

"All good. Cheers!" He takes the bag and disappears.

A short while later, my bag appears. I grab it and head toward customs.

There are four agents checking passports. I pick the second line from the right. The agent is middle-aged with a blank stare. He looks professional, which I appreciate.

While I wait, a young man comes up to me. Early twenties, black polyester slacks, white Chicago Bulls T-shirt. Mousy features—small nose, eyes too close together. "Sir, sir! Visa? Visa! Only twenty-five, twenty-five." A bead of sweat rolls down his temple. He looks high.

What the fuck? This is customs, in an airport, in one of the largest cities in the world. This is a government-controlled space, and here is a common tout in UNICEF hand-me-downs trying to sell me something I would never buy from someone like him.

"No thanks, kid." He scurries off.

Two steps later and another man glides up. I have to give him credit. Not a lot of people can sneak up on me, but he does.

"Visa," he says melodiously, like he's trying to sell me molly outside a nightclub bathroom.

I turn. This guy is late forties, black Members Only jacket, tan slacks, wicked comb-over. I don't answer, he keeps gliding. He has his technique down. Like any good dealer.

Seriously, what the fuck?

A few minutes later another guy sidles next to me. Only two other people are between me and the agent. This tout is early thirties, brown button-down shirt, tan slacks, loafers. He sports a big smile and a bigger midsection. Like a skinny fat dude. Or a fat skinny dude.

"My friend, my friend!" he calls. "You must buy visa before customs!"

I look around. No one else seems to be buying "visas," which I'm sure are just useless pieces of paper.

"No thanks, my friend. I'll try my luck with the agent."

"OK, sir! I will be here when you need me. I am Asim, by the way!"

Not "if"—"when."

I thank Asim. Finally I reach the agent.

I step up to the plexiglass. The agent slips his hand through a small slot between the glass divider and the countertop. I slide my passport to him.

He flips through its pages. I think he's looking for a blank spot, but he passes a bunch of these. Then he looks at me with a tired, questioning look that directly translates to: "Stupid American."

"Visa?" he asks.

"Don't I get that from you?"

He tilts his head to the side slightly. Then his eyes dart over my shoulder. I turn—there's Asim, smiling and waving.

"Got it. I'll be back," I say.

I turn to Asim.

"My friend, you need visa!" he says. It's a statement, not a question.

"Indeed I do, Asim. Thanks for waiting."

"Of course, my friend."

"Weird system you got here." I briefly wonder how difficult it must be to secure this hustle. I've been to plenty of places where the tourist touts hit you as soon as you leave customs or the airport—like in Rome or Bangkok—but never right in customs. This must be a coveted gig. Clean, air conditioned, and you're selling something people need, not something you have to convince them they want. Asim looks as jolly as an Egyptian Norman Rockwell, but he must have some elbows on him.

I ask, "How much for the visa?"

"For you? Only twenty-five dollars!"

I tilt my head toward a random foreign traveler. "And how much for him?"

"For him? Also twenty-five dollars!"

We both laugh. I hand Asim two twenties and my passport. He reaches into his pocket and produces a roll of stickers, peels one off, and attaches it to a page. He hands it back, along with my change. I hand him back the five. "Thanks for waiting."

"No problem, my friend! You are a good man. Next time you come to Cairo, find Asim! I am always here, Mr. Corbett."

Friendly, smart, good customer service. "I'll do that. See you around."

As I walk back to the agent, Asim calls out, "Welcome to Cairo!"

I'm standing outside a few minutes later. Like I said, I've never been to Egypt, but the sights and smells are familiar. Diesel, cigarettes, open sewers. Hot as fuck. Men everywhere, all yelling and jostling. Not many women. Children darting here and there.

It's a hell of a lot like Iraq.

8

THE *MAERSK KENTUCKY*

I take a cab to the Radisson Blu in Heliopolis, only ten minutes from the airport. I'm not interested in going to Cairo proper, not on this trip. I have to avoid trouble. Trouble is exhausting. Thankfully, airport hotels are good for avoiding it.

The hotel is nicer than expected. The lobby has dimmed lighting and a moody vibe. I check in, swipe my room key, throw my duffel on the purple couch. Grab a shower to wash off all the travel, put on clean clothes. The room isn't a suite, but it's borderline elegant. I email the Trident rep to let him know I'm in-country. He responds that we'll meet in the lobby at 0900 but that I need to allow an hour to check out.

I doubt that. I'm up early the next morning, I hit the gym for a thirty-minute workout, get a light breakfast. The food is generic European continental. The only Egyptian touch is the tea, which I skip. I'm in the lobby by 0820. There are three other American-looking guys. One of them approaches me. White dude, a little over six feet, five o'clock shadow, full head of brown hair. By the look of it, he hits the gym on the regular.

"You Dan?" he asks, sticking out his hand.

"Guilty." We shake.

He gives off a gentle "I'm the senior guy here" kind of vibe. Fine by me. "Name's Allen. We're already checked out, so we'll meet you in the van."

"Roger."

As promised, it takes way longer to check out than it should. So long that I eventually just give up, figuring I can take care of it on the back end when I swing through Cairo before hopping a plane back home.

I head out to the van. Barely 0900 and it's already in the high eighties. I jump in and sit next to Allen. The driver hits a button and the door slides shut. He cranks the AC. Allen gives me a nod.

Two other men are seated behind us. I turn to them. "I'm Dan. Sorry about the holdup."

One of them shrugs. He's fiftyish, scrawny, clean shave, blond comb-over doing a poor job of hiding his male-pattern baldness. Bifocals, which are unheard of in the Teams. He gives off "professor" more than "former SEAL." But if there's one thing I've learned, it's never to assume anything about who can make the SEAL Teams or thrive in them. Maybe this guy was stone cold in his day.

He says, "Don't sweat it. We all did the same thing on our first trip. The Egyptians are not the picture of capitalist efficiency. I'm Jim, by the way." He offers his hand and I take it.

The last guy blurts, "Greg!" He shoves his hand toward me like he's going to shake my face.

"Whoa there, big guy," I say, slipping to the side to prevent his fingers from touching my nose. Greg reminds me of Bill Nye the Science Guy. I take his hand at an awkward angle and we shake.

"Hey," Jim says in a conspiratorial whisper as we pull onto a four-lane highway, "if anything goes down, you and Allen take care of the driver. Got it?"

Roger that, Jimbo.

We don't talk much after that. The van motors out of Cairo's orbit and into the desert, which even this close to Cairo appears endless. We pass one military checkpoint, where the driver doesn't do much more than slow down, flashing a laminated placard at the young soldier in the heat outside.

After a couple of hours, the desert gives way to infrastructure—depots, warehouses, machine shops, roadside cafés, gas stations. Even with the windows closed and the AC blasting, I smell the sea. Within fifteen minutes or so, we see the canal. Or not exactly the canal, which is to the north, but the bay that forms the northern end of the Gulf of Suez. From ground level, it doesn't look like anything other than a large body of water full of ships. There's no hint of the engineering marvel—a 120-mile-long series of canals and byways dating back to ancient Egypt—that lies just over the horizon.

We reach our drop point at the end of a narrow road on the water's edge. Outside is a low, nondescript building surrounded by chain-link fencing.

I get out, hauling my North Face bag from between my feet. The port below is a fucking zoo. Men everywhere, countless small boats—all with eclectic color schemes, all spewing diesel exhaust—plying the water's surface.

Allen walks up to four soldiers huddled in a slash of shade on the east side of the building. The rest of us wait in the van's meager shadow.

Allen hands one of the soldiers a stack of papers. The man flicks through them without studying them. He shakes his head and stuffs the papers back into Allen's hand.

Allen stalks back to the van rolling his eyes. "Typical," he says under his breath. He digs through his bag, producing a carton of Marlboro Reds. He keeps his back to the Egyptians, making sure the soldiers can't see that he has two full cartons hiding in his bag. He removes four packs of cigarettes and returns to the men.

This time he hands over the papers and a pack of cigarettes to the soldier in charge. The soldier nods. He doesn't even check the paperwork. He disappears inside the building.

Allen steps into the shade and hands each of the other soldiers a pack. They smile and tuck them away.

The first soldier reappears carrying two locked Pelican cases, which he places next to Allen. Our guns. The soldier disappears again and then returns with an ammo can and a clipboard. Allen signs for everything and waves at one of us to give him a hand.

"On it," I say. I sling my duffel on like a backpack and jog over to grab one of the cases and the ammo can. While we're walking to the dock, Allen says, "Every fucking time. I don't even smoke. But if I hadn't brought those Reds, there's no telling how long we'd be waiting here for our weaps."

Greg is already at the dock with his bag, and Allen goes back to get his. But Jim—he struggles to unload all his shit: a large roller suitcase, two backpacks, a medium-size duffel—and a high-end camera with a massive telephoto lens. Jim asks Allen for a hand. I'm too far away to hear Allen's response, but judging by body language it's something like, "You bring it, you carry it." Which is precisely how I feel.

Jim looks pissed, but what can he do? It takes him three trips to get everything to the end of the dock.

Allen pays a boat captain for our passage to the cargo ship. Although "captain" and "boat" are generous terms. The "captain," who looks all of seventeen, is a scrawny guy in white jeans and a thin long-sleeved shirt, and the "boat" is a twenty-foot, bright-blue-and-orange wooden vessel that has about half a foot of dark water sloshing over the deck. The captain accepts some cigarettes and signs some papers for Allen.

"Load her up, boys!" Allen shouts over the sound of a tugboat out on the water.

Easy day for all besides Jim. Greg eventually tires of waiting and helps Jim out. Then we head into the channel.

As we motor to the southern end of the Canal Zone, the ships come into full view. All I can think is, *Jesus, those things are big.* The boy captain guns the engine. It chokes and spews black smoke, but we go from an easygoing trawl to a turbulent sprint. The bow plunges over waves every three seconds or so.

Our target is a massive supertanker named *Maersk Kentucky*. Her hull is painted teal, with a Rust-Oleum-colored red band just above the waterline. Her bridge is beige. She's loaded with stacks of containers like Legos. She's already underway.

At two hundred meters, it looks like we're going to drive right into the side of the *Kentucky*. She's moving at a healthy clip. It still looks like we're going to collide at fifty meters, but our young captain, a wet cigarette dangling from his mouth, is in the zone. He's probably been piloting boats since he was in diapers. At the perfect moment, he turns his boat to starboard and we pull smoothly alongside the *Kentucky*. A short ladder made of thick rope and orange plastic rungs dangles from her side three-quarters of the way forward. That's our target.

For a fleeting moment I'm reminded of the closest to death I've ever been. A nighttime training mission in the Atlantic boarding a container ship during a storm. Fifteen-foot swells, the constant spray of water like needles on any exposed skin. Our night vision was so wet that it was like wearing blindfolds. It was my job to hook the ship with a telescoping pole that had one end of a Jacob's ladder attached to it, but conditions were so awful that two poles broke. Our only remaining option was the craft's pneumatic pole, but my first go with that was a complete misfire. Finally, my legs cramping and my kit covered in my and my teammates' vomit, we got it in place. We tried to pull the ladder tight, but that was impossible because of the rough seas. Still, I started climbing, but before I got anywhere the boat's radar dome hit my helmet, scraped the side of my face, and caught my shoulder. If our small boat had dropped over another swell at that moment, my arm would have gotten torn off. At one point, I lost my footing and had to climb a few rungs, which are only about eight inches long, using just my arms. When I finally reached the top, I was hauled aboard by two of my teammates. I was dry-heaving and knew I wouldn't have been of much use in a firefight if it had been for real, but I took a knee and hoisted my rifle anyway. The takeaway: hit the pull-up bar *hard*.

This boarding is going to be *much* easier. Allen and Greg move to the port side to get ready to ascend while Jim attempts to somehow grab all his bags at once. He couldn't do it on land, so I don't know what makes him think he's going to be able to do it now.

As soon as we hit the ladder, the captain slows down to match the giant ship's speed. He's an expert pilot, that's for sure. We bob up and down on the ripples of her wake. Allen immediately grabs the rope ladder and scurries up. It's only about five feet to a metal gangway. Easy enough. Greg passes him the Pelican cases and ammo can, then goes up himself. I go behind Greg. When I get to the gangway, Allen says, "Dan, let's go on up. Can you take the gun cases?"

"No problem."

The other two meet us at the top five minutes later. Allen gets our berthing figured out, and we hit our staterooms, one for each of us. The room is much nicer than expected. I put my shit away, and twenty minutes later, we gather in Allen's room.

"All right, here are the watch assignments. Dan, you're the new guy, so naturally you're taking balls to oh-six-hundred."

"Roger that." I'm totally fine going full vampire.

"Jim, you have oh-six-hundred to twelve hundred." Jim looks pissed but doesn't say anything. "I'm on from twelve hundred to eighteen hundred, and Greg, you've got eighteen hundred to balls."

"Got it!" Greg chirps.

Jim mumbles something. "What's that, Jim?" asks Allen.

"Well, on my last rotation we did two three-hour shifts instead of one six—"

"That was last rotation," Allen interrupts.

Thank God, I think. I have no desire to break up my day like that. Jim doesn't push back.

"I've been on this ship before," Allen continues. "Galley is on the fourth deck and the gym is on the sixth. Both are open twenty-four-seven. I forget the hours for meals, but it's all posted on the galley door. Now." He turns to the Pelican cases.

He lays both on the floor, dials the combination locks, and pops them open. Inside each case are two M4 rifles, eight magazines, and a small piece of folded paper. We each take a rifle and four mags. Allen writes our names next to the serial numbers on the pieces of paper. After that we go to the armory to store the weapons. "Well, that's it. We sail for two days before we start the watch. And it looks like we have plenty of ammo to get dialed in once we hit open waters. Until then, gentlemen. It's been an honor." I can't tell if he's being sincere or making light of the whole situation, but in either case he pushes past us and disappears down the hall.

Welcome to the *Maersk Kentucky*.

9

PIRATES?

For the next two days it's stateroom, deck, galley. The galley is spare but strangely comforting. One long table wrapped in a red-and-white-checkered plastic tablecloth. Three sets of salt and pepper shakers. Five metal chairs on either side of the table. Two massive coffeepots, cranking twenty-four hours a day. One woven basket, full of apples. A perpetually busy cook in the kitchen whom I never feel like interrupting. My job is potentially difficult, but his is downright *hard*. I would not want to trade places. The place gives off a school cafeteria/diner vibe, and I happen to like both.

If the gym were any good, I probably would live there during these two days and any subsequent off time. But it's not any good. The room is no larger than my stateroom, and if it is, only just. There's an old bench wrapped in duct tape trying to hold in wayward bulges of orange foam, a single barbell, and a set of dumbbells ranging from five to fifty pounds. Worst of all, the smell reminds me of the beginning of football season during double days. No thanks.

I scout the ship. Find a place to do pull-ups and some free space on the deck to do burpees and sit-ups in the sun. I binge watch a sci-fi show called *Fringe* on my laptop. I run into the other guys now and then, but they don't talk much.

Except for Greg.

"This is my ninth trip," he says one day over a third cup of coffee and two triangles of wheat toast. "Allen acts like he's the old hand, but I'm the real top dog around here. I just don't care enough to outclass him. What's the point, you know? You think the pay is good now, you should have seen it prerecession. This gig was bumping. My second trip, I made seventy large, for twenty days at sea! We were only in bad water for three, maybe four days. Easiest money I ever made. Of course, most of it goes to the ex. You know what they say—happy wife, happy life. And for ex-wives that goes triple. At least I don't have to go back to Jacksonville every time I finish a job. Ko Samui, that's the place for me! And at least I don't have a family in the States *and* a family in Saigon or wherever the fuck like Jim and some of these other guys. That's why he brings all that shit with him, to distract himself from all of his obligations. And that's why I don't mind helping the guy carry all that shit. You got to distribute the burden of living, you know? I tell you, Dan, he's looking for something out here and it isn't money. Not that there's anything wrong with that. Nothing at all. One time out here I saw a whale hit—"

And so on and so on and so on. If I didn't cut Greg off, he would go off like that for hours, shifting from favorite foods to the Miami Dolphins to pop psychology.

At lunch the next day I ask Greg about pirates. He looks serious, pantomimes looking down sights, and then laughs. No words, just a full hearty laugh. I ask about his time in the Teams, but he doesn't take the bait. He never speaks about the military, not once. I'm not even 100 percent positive he served, although he must have, because it's a Trident prerequisite.

After lunch we meet the others in the armory and gear up. Shockingly, neither Jim nor Greg looks like he's ever worn body armor. Both of their kits hang low. I let it slide initially, but it bothers me. I teach them how to adjust it. Allen's got his shit together, but he doesn't seem to care about the other two, which I consider odd since these are the guys we'll be fighting alongside if we have to engage any pirates. I hope I don't have to teach them how to fire their guns too.

We sight in along the stern, shooting across the width of the *Kentucky*. We can't see land on either side, so the bullets won't hit anything except water. Allen and I are good to go, but, as I feared, Greg and Jim leave much to be desired. Their shots are all over the target, and each has a litany of excuses for why he's not better. At least we have two good shots out of four. If shit goes down, Jim and Greg can lay down suppressing fire.

That night I start my first watch. I'm on high alert but feel powerless. It's a moonless night and all I can do is stare into pitch-black darkness. The stars are insane. I stand on the starboard bridge wing for an hour, then cross to the port bridge wing and stand there. After the third rotation, a young mate pops open the bridge door. "Hey, you want to take a look at the radar?"

"Yes! I thought you'd never ask. If there are pirates out here, I'd never see them coming."

He shows me a screen on the console. "This yellow triangle is us. If anything is close to us, it will show up here. Come look at it whenever you want."

I thank him and check it throughout my shift, but never see anything other than that yellow triangle.

Same goes for nights two and three.

On night four, I bring my earbuds. I play *The Odyssey* on Audible and listen to Homer six hours a night. When I finish that, I listen to *The Iliad*. I chat with Greg at every changeover. The ship makes all the usual stops, off-loading and loading. Somalia, Oman, Pakistan, Bahrain, Saudi Arabia, and Sri Lanka. Then back to Suez.

Throughout all of it, we don't see one fucking pirate or pirate ship. No Somali raiders. No parrots, peg legs, or Jolly Rogers. It doesn't take long for me to understand that we aren't there to fight pirates, we're there to deter them, pure and simple. Allen even once points out some Omani spotters on shore when we leave Salalah. "Those guys tell the pirate network which ships are guarded and which aren't. See them over there? Give them a wave." He waves and then turns to me, jostling his carbine. "I've never fired this thing once for any reason except practice or boredom."

And that's the job. I feel like I've finally settled in when we steam back into Suez twenty-four days later. I've adapted to my vampire schedule and my ship workouts and am deep into season three of *Fringe*. But this acclimation doesn't count for anything—the contract is over. I get paid—and the pay is good—and go home.

Over the next year I do two more trips with Trident. I'm never on a ship that comes under attack, and the most exciting thing I experience is searching for a stowaway who doesn't exist. I also report some Omani spotters who end up getting arrested. Just like Allen, I never once fire my weapon except to make sure it works.

Back in the States, I conclude that Trident isn't for me. This is not the mercenary life I imagined. Not only does it grossly underutilize my skills, but it's also populated by men who don't know body armor from a fishing vest, who bring too much shit on jobs, who have too many wives in too many second- and third-tier countries. I do not want to end up like these guys.

But the main upshot of working for Trident is something I don't expect. I realize I miss the Teams in a bad way.

I can't believe it, but I think I might call up the US Navy.

10
SNIPER, SHOOTER, LINGUIST

One day in early 2014, a friend takes me out to Naval Amphibious Base Coronado to meet with the master chief of SEAL Team 17. His name is Griffin. Old school, wiry, aggressively not politically correct, always has a mouthful of Copenhagen. The place feels a couple decades old (no AC!), but the energy is great. Most important, Master Chief Griffin assures me that I have an open path to retirement and I'll have the freedom to take side jobs. They use "flex-drill," which means that if I miss any drill weekends, I just make them up later. Win-win.

A week later, a navy recruiter welcomes me back as an active reservist with orders to SEAL Team 17, one of two reserve SEAL Teams. Within weeks, I'm offered a deployment to South Korea to be part of a training mission for Republic of Korea SEALs. I'm in. Only problem is, we don't deploy for another eight months. And here I run up against a strange wrinkle of being a reservist: if I'm not on active deployment, I have to figure out what to do in order to collect a check. So I go to school.

First stop, a three-month sniper course. The first part of the course consists of sketching range cards—drawing bird's-eye pictures of the surrounding area—and learning how to take photographs with a digital SLR camera. This part of the course takes place in Coronado. The second part is in Bloomington, Indiana, covering stalking and shooting, which I'm all about. The rifles are bolt-action .300 Win Mags and semiauto MK 20s. The terrain is rolling hills with little ponds here and there and thick vegetation. It's winter and it's *cold*. Most of the younger guys were once my students at CQC, and they stalk and shoot great. I'm proud of them—but they might not be so proud of me. The techniques I use when shooting for speed at closer engagements—resetting the trigger as fast as possible, using a "good-enough" sight picture—turn out to be all wrong for shooting for accuracy at distance. A good-enough sight picture is not remotely good enough for sniping. And instead of releasing the trigger quickly—aka "resetting the sear"—you hold it down to get as much follow-through as possible. The reasons are straightforward. The bullet has to travel a long distance to hit its target, and the smallest movements on the part of the shooter result in large discrepancies when extrapolated across the entire length of the flight path. But even though it's different from what I'm used to, it's still fun.

Except for one thing. My spotter, Nick, is a raging drunk. The spotter's job is arguably more important than the shooter's. He lies on the ground behind the shooter, peering through a tripod-mounted scope. He ranges the target and calls out distances, which the shooter dials into the rifle's scope. Then the spotter blurs the target slightly in order to "see" the wind. When you blur the picture like this, heat rises from the ground, revealing itself in hazy waves. This gives you an idea of the speed and direction of the wind. You blur the picture ever so slightly to see what the wind is doing at different distances—maybe it's blowing three knots right to left at one hundred meters but blowing six knots left to right at seven hundred meters. And your target is at nine hundred meters. So you do a little math and call something like, "Hold three left." If everything is perfect, and the shooter breaks the trigger clean, then both spotter and shooter watch the bullet's tight arc as it makes little circular ripples through barely visible thermals. If everything is on, you hit. If it's off, you try again. Sniping is a science, but a lot of it is throwing chicken bones. It's voodoo.

Point being, Nick is not good, and I'm convinced it's due to drinking. Every day when we're in the van going back to base, he jumps out at a stop sign to undertake some crazy personal escape and evasion mission, jumping fences through backyards, zigzagging across the road like some imaginary sniper is shooting *him*. At first we try to stop him, but we quickly give up. Nick's committed. He was a marine before transferring to the navy, so at first we chalk it up to some United States Marine Corps thing. Only it turns out he has real issues. I'm concerned for him, but also pissed. I *just* pass the final test, and only because I convince the cadre to have an instructor spot for me. Nick also barely passes, and somehow avoids getting kicked out for drinking. (A few years later, I'll learn that Nick has taken his own life. A fate that is all too common for vets. More can be done for veterans to help them find a way. Much more.)

After graduation, I go back to San Diego, catch up on three months of administrative paperwork, get right with medical and dental, and bide my time in San Diego working out and hitting the usual watering holes.

Then the Korea group assembles—a mix of older, seasoned operators and a platoon of young guns. We do one month of land warfare, a training block that covers a wide range of tactics. Following this, we go to another training block, which consists of force-on-force exercises. Essentially, we split into groups and engage each other with nonlethal ammunition. Those of us on SEAL Team 17 do things differently, and I'm told more than once to let the young guys make their own mistakes so they can learn from them. I do, but it's not fun getting lit up by paintballs when you know the wrong calls are getting made over and over. We get through it, though. We have a good team. We head out. First stop, Oahu. Like clockwork, whenever there's a stop in Hawaii, there seems to be a "problem" with the aircraft that will take three days to fix. We take advantage. Next stop, Guam. We spend a week there getting paperwork squared away. Finally we fly COMAIR to Incheon International Airport in Seoul. As soon as the door opens, everyone stands and pushes to get off. No one waits. Then, in the airport, everyone runs—and I mean *runs*—to wherever it is they're going. Me and my guys have to cross the place like we're soldiers sprinting across no-man's-land from trench to trench. We make it out of there onto a bullet train and get to our base that night. Korea is fun, and we do six months without incident—meaning none of the guys knock anyone up, no one gets too drunk, and the Korean SEALs learn what we're there to teach them. While there, I enroll in an online bachelor's program in organizational leadership with the University of Charleston, West Virginia. (A couple of years later, after a lot of intensive study, I graduate.)

After Korea, I get attached to the training command on the West Coast and teach more CQC, this time in Walls, Mississippi, which is about half an hour from Memphis, Tennessee. Every weekend is a new adventure on Beale Street. When that's over, in the fall of 2016, I enroll in a Russian-language course. I must admit that the appeal mostly has to do with Russian women—I don't really have a type, but Russian/eastern European is damn close. Like every other foreign-language course I've taken—Korean, Spanish, French—this one is taught by a woman. This just means that I end up talking like a woman in whatever language I'm learning. When I speak Korean,

I sound like a twenty-three-year-old from Seoul. This time I'm going to talk like a fifty-two-year-old from Kyiv, Ukraine. Her name is Svitlana. She gives off a heavy Soviet vibe—stern, reticent, judgmental. Usually language labs look like elementary school classrooms with pictures of food and cultural stuff, colorful books, calendars, and other silly shit. Not Svitlana's classroom. It's a twelve-foot-by-twenty-foot white room with a desk and two chairs and that's it. With the buzzing white fluorescent lights on high, it feels more like an interrogation room than a place of learning. Every day for six weeks we drill from 0700 to 1400 with a one-hour break for lunch. Despite many attempts on my part, she never engages in small talk. This isn't easy. I like bullshitting. Finally, in week three, I break through. "What brought you to the States?" I ask in English. "Why do you ask, Daniel?" "Just curious." "Well, I was here on a student visa." "OK, then what?" "Then I stayed." "Obviously, but how were you able to stay?" "I married an American." Now we're getting somewhere. "How did you two meet?" "We were neighbors." I can't resist. "So you got married for citizenship? I saw a documentary about American men who fly to Kyiv to meet women and then propose in like three days." She doesn't like the implication. "People can fall in love fast, Daniel!" "Three-days fast?" "Yes, and even faster!" She shuts down the small talk after that. Flash cards, lessons, no more English. From then on it's teacher teach, student learn. Repeat. Repeat. Repeat.

The only other personal thing I manage to get out of her over the following weeks is that she loves caviar. Just before Christmas, I bring her a present—a set of mother-of-pearl caviar spoons (silver spoons interact with caviar, tainting the delicate taste). I'm not trying to suck up, I just want to give her something. "What's this?" she asks when I hand her the small box. "A present." "Oh, I can't take this! I don't have anything for you." I smile. "Don't sweat it! You're a fantastic teacher and I wanted to get you something. Please, just take it." "OK. Well, thank you, Daniel." She pats my arm. It's the most intimate gesture she ever makes toward me. "Thank you, Ms. Svitlana. Merry Christmas." She never says anything about the spoons, but after break we get along better. At the end of the course, I have to have a conversation with another Russian speaker over the phone in order to pass. I score a two, which doesn't sound high to me, but which Svitlana says is the highest mark any of her students has received for such a short course. When I finally graduate, I can tell she's proud of me, which feels great.

And then, after all that, my phone rings.

11

"WE NEED DIRTY"

THE GUY CALLING IS NAMED ISAIAH.

I'd never worked with Isaiah. I'd seen him around town when we were both in the Teams, and he seemed like a good enough guy. The last I'd heard was that he'd had some drama go down on his way out of the navy. Since I wasn't involved, I wasn't going to ask.

Regardless, I heard through a mutual friend that Isaiah was doing some "big things" somewhere in the Middle East. And now Isaiah wants to know if I'd be interested. I'm circumspect, but he flatters me. "The consensus is 'We need Dirty.'" The flattery works enough for me to agree to sit down over drinks.

We meet at a German restaurant called Gordon Biersch just outside of Mission Valley mall in San Diego. I spot Isaiah quickly. He's got on a blazer over a black T-shirt, dark-washed jeans, and I think Gucci sneakers. A bit much for a meeting with me, but he wears it well. He's tall, in shape, and dark skinned. I think he's mixed race, but I never asked and don't care. (I'm a quarter Mexican on my dad's side—which has helped me chameleon all over the world. "Is he white? Is he Central American? Is he Israeli? Is he Serbian? Is he Arab?" No! Yes! Whatever you need!)

Isaiah flashes a big smile as soon as he sees me. I hold out my hand as I get close, but he ignores that and pulls me into a backslapping bro hug. We take our seats at a round high-top near the bar.

"Thanks for coming, Dirty."

"No worries, brother."

A short and extremely cute blond waitress comes up. "Can I interest you in some drinks?"

"Another pilsner," Isaiah says.

"Just water, thanks," I say.

Isaiah eyes me. "Really? Come on, bro. Have at least one."

"All right. Herradura Silver, neat, please." Twist my arm.

"Coming right up," the waitress says.

As soon as she's out of earshot, I say, "So, what's this about?"

"No foreplay. Always liked that about you, Dirty." I shrug. "All right. I'm talking big money, big contract with some real fucking pipe hitters. The real deal Holyfield."

"So we're boxing, that it?"

"Fuck no, Dirty! I'm talking real shit with an elite outfit of high-end contractors. I already did a job with this crew—me and Steven did one—and it got pretty hairy. It was…well, fuck, man. It was fun."

"Did one what? What exactly are you talking about?"

The waitress reappears, sets down our drinks. Isaiah takes a long pull off his pilsner while I just sniff the Herradura a little. Earthy, herb tones, a hint of the agave plant itself. I like tequila.

"Sorry, man. Let me back up. A while ago, I met this guy—Malachi. Older, ex–French Foreign Legion and Israeli special forces, or Israeli something." So far this sounds pretty suspect. "Anyway, he offered me a position on a team of his out of Yemen. Training and advising some Emiratis to go after targets."

"Legionnaire, huh? I've heard mixed reviews about those guys."

Isaiah takes another big sip of his beer, uses the sleeve of his nice blazer to wipe his mouth. I keep sniffing. One great thing about tequila is that from smell alone, it can take you places. Simultaneously you're sitting in some German mall restaurant in San Diego and in a dusty roadside cantina in the Sierra Madre Occidental.

"Yeah, there were a couple of them on this last job. They were OK, but they do operate a little differently than the rest of us."

"And the 'rest of us' is…?"

"Besides the Legion guys it was me, Malachi, Steven, and another guy named François. He was French too, but French military, not Foreign Legion."

"Steven. Our Steven? Your old chief?"

"One and the same."

"All right. Go on."

"That's about it. We're hoping to convince you to join us. Like I said the other day, we need you."

"Why exactly?"

"Ah, you know. Just to have someone who's fresh from the Teams. Some of the guys are—"

I cut him off. "Lost a step?"

"No, no. Nothing like that. We just need you, or someone like you, is all."

"Ain't no one like me but me, brother."

"That's what I'm saying!" He finishes his beer in two more gulps.

"Uh-huh. I got some questions."

"Shoot."

"First and foremost—this aboveboard?" What I'm asking, which Isaiah understands perfectly, is whether this is effectively sanctioned by the US government. Of course, officially it never can be, but unofficially...the world works in mysterious ways.

"Oh, totally. Hundred percent."

"Pay?"

"Pay is goooood," he says, drawing it out. He signals the waitress and twirls his finger in the air for another round, even though I still haven't sipped my drink.

"What is 'goooood'?"

"Twenty to thirty thousand a month, but all expenses paid. So you clear that shit."

"All right. So—training and advising. What's that?"

"You know. Training, the usual stuff. And 'advising.'" He holds up his hands and air-quotes this last word.

The waitress returns with a beer in a frosted glass and sets it on the table. "Did you want another too?" she asks me. She's an excellent waitress.

"I'm good, thanks." She smiles and spins away.

"Tell me more about advising, Isaiah."

"You know. Use your imagination."

I shake my head. "Pretend I have a shitty imagination."

He shifts in his seat. "I'm sorry, Dirty. I can't."

I shoot my tequila and stand. The feet of my stool make a terrible sound on the floor, wood scraping tile. I slide a twenty-dollar bill out of my wallet for the waitress. "Tell her to keep the change. Nice seeing you, Isaiah."

I take half a step. Isaiah reaches out and grabs my arm. He's smiling like a used car salesman. "Wait, wait. Just think about it. Malachi is in town and he wants to meet. Just think about it. He'll tell you more. You have my number."

"Will do, brother." I offer my hand and he takes it. "Best of luck." And with that, I leave.

12

LEVEL THREE

THE FOLLOWING WEEK I'M IN AND OUT OF SEAL TEAM 17, TRYING TO FIND something to do. Any school, any course, any way to get put on orders and get that paycheck. But I keep coming up short.

One Friday after I leave the base, Isaiah calls again. I'm on the Coronado Bridge, which has notoriously shitty cell reception. I use that as an excuse not to answer—I hate taking calls that I know are going to drop—but I'm at least a little tempted. I didn't like Isaiah's demeanor or his pitch, but I need to pay the bills. If the navy isn't going to work hard to set me up, why shouldn't I take him up on his offer?

The weekend goes by slowly. Too slowly. A hard dawn run along the marina, a night out with an on-again, off-again girlfriend, a long telephone visit with Mom, another hard workout session. On Monday I hit up my operations officer, Rivera. Nothing is popping. Same thing on Tuesday. But on Wednesday he calls and asks me to come in.

I'm on base before noon. When I reach his office, his door is open.

I knock on the doorjamb. He turns from his work, shooting me an incredulous look that says, "Why are you knocking?" I like Rivera.

"Come on in, Dirty," he says.

"Thank you, sir." I take one small step into his office.

"Please, sit!" Rivera is what's known as a mustang, an officer who rose from the enlisted ranks. For obvious reasons, mustangs are some of the most respected officers in the entire military.

Rivera's stature is that of a cube. He's my height, but is about forty pounds heavier, and although he is a bit older than I, he's in solid shape. He looks like he could push over a building. He has short, black hair, green eyes, and olive skin. If his last name weren't Rivera, I'd peg him for Greek.

I sit in a blue upholstered chair across from his desk.

"How you doing, Dirty?"

"OK. Trying to get these orders, as you know."

"Exactly why I called you in today. There's a spot open at █████████ level three. You did so well at █████████ level two, getting honor man and all, that Master Chief Polton thinks you'd be the perfect fit." He was referring to a course I once took involving ███████████████████████████████ I had really enjoyed the earlier course, so I'm sure I'd like this one too.

"Sounds great to me!"

"And not just that! Master Chief Polton thinks that if you do well there, we could stand up our own █████████ program here. If you can get honor man again, or close to it, you could run it."

"Are you serious?"

"As cancer, Dirty."

"That would be phenomenal, sir!"

"C'mon, Dirty," he says.

"That would be phenomenal, Riv!"

He smiles. "That's better. Anyway, the program doesn't start for another month, but I've got a good feeling."

"If there's anything I can do to make it happen, let me know."

"Will do. I'll run it up to Master Chief Polton and we should know ASAP. I'll shoot you a message as soon as we get the word."

"Roger that, sir. Thank you."

"Dismissed, Petty Officer Corbett!" he says, ribbing me for using "sir" again.

I stand. As I leave the office, he calls out, "Later, Dirty!"

"Later, Riv!"

I hang around the base for a while, feeling good. I clean out my cage and do some reps on the pull-up bar. The whole time, I'm imagining what it would be like to have a long-term, semipermanent gig in one location. It would be unlike anything I've had in my life to this point. Truly. Even when I was active duty, things were always changing, we were always here and then there, doing this and then that. It was exhilarating, but this new opportunity sounds perfect.

And it would be a hell of a lot better than whatever Isaiah is selling. Sure, navy pay isn't close to the same as mercenary money, but it would be stable. Isaiah is hustling, and there's no hustle involved in running a ███████ program. Most of all, it would be fun.

On the ride back across the Coronado Bridge, my phone rings again. This time it's Rivera. I risk having to talk through a choppy call and answer.

"Riv! What's up?"

"Hey, Dirty," he says, sounding less than enthusiastic. "I'm sorry, son, but I spoke too soon. Master Chief Polton says the course is full. Some guy on Eighteen grabbed the last spot just yesterday. I really apologize, Dirty. I didn't mean to get your hopes up. We'll get you in the next one, but that won't be for a while."

I'm disappointed, but I can't fault Rivera. The navy makes its own decisions, regardless of what guys like us want or would like to do. "No worries, Riv. I'll find something."

"Way to keep the faith, Dirty."

I hang up and grab my tin of Copenhagen from the center console and throw in a fat lipper. Finally I figure, *Fuck it.* Might as well hear what this Malachi dude has to say for himself. As soon as I get home, I text Isaiah.

> **Hey brother. If Malachi is still in town, let's set something up.**

The reply comes as fast as any.

> **Fuck yeah. 7pm tomorrow night. Pony Room, Rancho Santa Fe. See you there, Dirt.**

13

THE PONY ROOM

IT'S RAINING WHEN I LEAVE FOR THE PONY ROOM. RAIN IS A RARITY IN SAN Diego, and it causes amnesia on a massive scale. Everyone forgets how to drive. This means the thirty-five-minute trip to Rancho Santa Fe will take at least forty-five minutes, maybe an hour. I leave early.

I've never been to the Pony Room, but I know it's upscale. Whatever. I'm rolling in a hoodie, jeans, and Chuck Taylors. They're the ones who "need" me, so why bother selling myself? I am who I am.

During the drive I play an audiobook of Alexandre Dumas's *The Man in the Iron Mask*. I listen as Aramis and Porthos flee the wrath of King Louis XIV's impostor, his twin brother Philippe. They gallop across France, changing horses when needed. There are no fresh horses at the final way station, but they remember that the third musketeer, Athos, now retired, lives nearby. They meet with their old friend, who lives in the countryside with his son, Raoul. They are sure that their brother-in-arms will provide horses or whatever it is they need.

I love Dumas's stories. The adventure, the intrigue, the brotherhood. You don't have to squint too hard to see why I love them—it's a romantic version of my own life and the men I've known over the years.

And here I am, fleeing over the California freeways, a deluge in pursuit, to meet some possible new brothers. Even if I have my doubts.

Over an hour later, I reach the closed gate to Rancho Santa Fe. There's a guard shack off to one side. I had no idea this place was behind a wall. You know, because San Diego and Southern California are *so* dangerous. It would have been nice of Isaiah to mention it. I can't help but think, *We're off to a great start.*

The door to the guard shack opens and a black umbrella unfolds from it. A rent-a-cop is underneath. It's pouring hard. He sloshes to my car.

As soon as I roll down the window, rain lashes inside, filling the well of the door handle.

"Name?" the guard asks.

"Daniel Corbett."

He says nothing and goes back to his shack. I wait. One minute, two, three. Fuck this. I'm just about to put my car in reverse and head home when a light goes off at the top of the gate. It slowly swings inward. All right, here we go.

I wind up the hill, passing multimillion-dollar homes, following signs for the Pony Room. Parking is valet only, except for the four VIP spots near the entrance, each occupied by a $200,000 sports car. I pull to a stop at the valet booth. The twentysomething attendant shoots my car a confused look. I doubt there are many 2001 Lexus ES300s coming through here. I can't wait to see the look on his face when he sees how I'm dressed.

I leave the keys and step out. He hands me a ticket. "Thanks, bud," I say.

"Yes, sir!" he squeaks. Sure enough, he's confused. He can't tell if I'm lost or just a super-rich guy who's frugal and doesn't give a fuck.

The restaurant is midcentury farmhouse with south-of-the-border accents. It's well lit, and as soon as I tell the hostess I'm there to meet someone, I spot Isaiah in a corner booth. He's sitting with a man who must be Malachi. Both stand as I approach. Isaiah still has his used car salesman smile. Malachi scans me, head to toe. He's clearly not down with my fashion choices.

First impressions: Malachi is late forties, five-ten and about 140 pounds. He's lean and strong, with beef jerky muscles—obviously his forty-odd years have not been easy. He wears his salt-and-pepper hair long with a beard to match. His demeanor is nonchalant. Still, he's cordial and professional. I can't pinpoint his accent, but, as Isaiah mentioned, he sounds like he's from the French Foreign Legion by way of Israel.

Also, Isaiah is dressed nearly identically to Malachi: nice blazer over a black T-shirt, dark jeans, designer sneakers. I briefly wonder what Malachi thinks of that. They say imitation is the sincerest form of flattery, but do you really want to be flattered if you're the leader of a group of high-end mercenaries? Not so sure. Maybe I'll ask him someday, but by the way things are looking, I doubt it.

We shake hands and sit.

"Daniel, will you please take some food?" Malachi asks. The table is strewn with leftovers, including a slice of Margherita pizza on a metal serving platter. Even though he has a non-English-speaking way of phrasing it, I know he's not asking if I want the last slice, but if I want to order something for myself.

"No thanks. I had something before coming over." There is no way I'm going to sit there and eat while they watch me, sipping their after-dinner drinks.

"As you will," Malachi says, but he looks a little disappointed. Not because he wants to watch me eat, but because refusing the offer of food is always a little touchy, especially if he has Middle Eastern roots.

"So tell me about this outfit of yours and the work you do," I say to Malachi.

"See?" Isaiah says. "I told you he doesn't beat around the bush."

"Hmm," Malachi hums. "Maybe you tell me a little about yourself first."

So this is how it's going to go. A full sizing up before I get any information. Fine by me. "All right. Fire away."

He asks everything he's supposed to: where I'm from, what I can do, where I've been, what I've done, how long I was active duty, and why I left. I give him satisfactory answers, not exhaustive ones. When he's done, I ask him questions, this time about him, not the job. Like me, he's a little cagey with his answers, but he comes into relief a bit more.

He was born Hungarian, he's an Ashkenazi Jew, he joined the French Foreign Legion at nineteen, eventually he got Israeli citizenship. In Israel he "did things." I can't tell if he was Mossad or military or both, but it doesn't matter. Eventually he broke off on his own and for the last decade has been conducting sanctioned but off-the-books operations in the Middle East, Africa, and Central America. He's even undertaken some intelligence-gathering missions in "regular places," which I take to mean first-world countries.

Then I ask about money.

"The compensation is very good, Daniel."

"How good?"

"For someone like you? At least twenty-five thousand a month. Once you are established, more."

"And who provides this money?"

"Me, Daniel. My company."

"No. Who provides this money to *you*?"

The corner of his mouth turns down the slightest bit. Isaiah shifts in the booth. Honestly, I'd almost forgotten he was there.

"This is of no concern, Daniel," Malachi says.

I move to stand, ready to fire the "No thank you" I've had locked and loaded all night. But I only get halfway out of my seat before Malachi raises his hand. "OK. Please, sit." His voice remains strong, but there is a tinge of defensiveness.

Now we're getting somewhere. I sit.

"I will show you." He pulls a Montblanc pen from the inside of his jacket. Using a cocktail napkin, he sketches out a flow chart, labeling it with handwriting I can't understand. The whole time he's talking a mile a minute, even dipping into French and what I can only assume is Hungarian here and there. When he's finished, he slams the pen on the table and shoves the napkin flow chart to me.

"There, super clear. Does that answer your question?"

I lean forward and look at it. No, it does not answer my question. I decide to try a different tack. "Where would we be working?"

"The mission is in Yemen. We will be working with the Emiratis, advising and assisting them on their tactics, mission planning, and operations."

This is what Isaiah said, which is encouraging. It also answers my money question. Either the Emiratis are backing or the Saudis. Both are engaged in a proxy war against Iranian-backed insurgents in the bloody and protracted civil war that's been taking place in Yemen since 2014.

I know from experience that the politics of war are always sticky, and the politics of this war are probably stickier than usual. So this revelation leads to my next question: "Is it legal?"

Malachi laces his fingers together. Amazingly, like he's some kind of mirror self, Isaiah does the same. Dude has no sense.

Malachi says, "Yes, it is all super kosher."

"Good. When it comes to this kind of thing, I'm as orthodox as Jerusalem on Saturday."

"I share your devotion, Daniel." Malachi leans back in the booth. Isaiah does too.

I consider all of this for a moment. I've got a good read on Malachi—unless he's bullshitting, which is always possible. But if he isn't, then I've learned that we're kind of alike. Malachi is tough, old school, and doesn't take no for an answer. When guys like us come together for the first time, there's sure to be tension. But after sitting and talking for more than an hour, we both went from *Who the fuck is this guy?* to *OK, I respect this dude and understand where he's coming from.* Most important, I now feel like we can work together. Or at least give it a shot.

Finally I ask, "If I were to join you, when would we leave?"

"Two weeks."

"Two weeks."

"Yes. Listen, Daniel, I tell you this. Only you can decide what you want to do. You have sat here, and we have spoken. For years you have done things for very little. But your time is valuable. I know this. If you are in, I will wire twenty thousand dollars tonight as a signing bonus. It will be in your account by midnight. This I promise."

I mull it over for about ten seconds. Then I say, "OK, Malachi. I'm in."

14

LAX>>>AUH

As promised, at the stroke of midnight I receive a notification from my bank that $20,000 has just been deposited to my account.

Well, now I really *am* in.

Two weeks later, Steven shoots me a text at 0600. **Yo Dirt. I'm downstairs.** I throw on a black Arc'teryx ball cap, grab my generic roller bag (no more conspicuous black North Face duffel for me), and head out. Steven stands next to a double-parked Chevy Tahoe. He gives me a nod, I head over.

"Nice ride," I say. "You got like ten kids now or something?"

He smiles. "Nah. Still just the one. It's a rental. Didn't want to leave my car in long-term parking for a month or more."

Or more. The words hang in the air. This could be a long trip.

I've always liked Steven, a quiet, humble Team guy. Which is odd since he looks like a cross between a Ken doll and a G.I. Joe: six-four, blond, single-digit body fat. You'd think it would be "Me, me, me" all the time.

I throw my bag in the back and hop in the passenger seat. "Got you a coffee," he says. Two gas station cups are in the center console, steam piping out of their lids, sugar and creamers bunched in a little nest of napkins.

Did I forget to mention Steven is nice too?

We take off, heading for the northbound I-5. We have to pick up another guy near Mission Viejo, just south of LA. Some guy named Brian.

Steven and I don't talk much, but once we get going on the interstate, I say, "Tell me about this Brian guy."

"Never met him. But Malachi says he's all right."

"Team guy?"

"No, some MMA dude. Malachi wants him to be our personal trainer or something."

"Huh. OK."

"Yeah."

After more than an hour of driving, Steven pulls off the interstate and follows the GPS through a maze of roads and cul-de-sacs until we pull up in front of a two-story house in the middle of a huge development. All the houses are clones of each other, and the only thing differentiating Brian's home from all the others is, well—Brian.

There on the sidewalk is a five-six redhead covered in tattoos. He's 150 pounds of pure muscle but looks more like he's going to a Guns N' Roses reunion concert than like he's about to hop a plane to Abu Dhabi as a mercenary. He's wearing a bandanna over a tangle of wild hair, a Megadeth T-shirt, skinny jeans, Chuck Taylors. A military backpack is slung over his shoulder and he's holding the handle of a huge roller bag. All-black everything, even the Chuck T's.

Steven pushes a button to open the lift gate, but Brian bounds up to the passenger side of the vehicle. He looks like he sprinkled his granola with cocaine.

I roll down my window, but before it's even halfway open, Brian shoves his hand into the Tahoe. I lean back to keep some personal distance.

"What's up, brothers!" Brian blurts. Between his rocker aesthetic and his super-enthusiastic "brothers," I can only conclude he has no idea what he's getting into.

Either that, or I have no idea what I'm getting into.

"Hello, Brian," I say, shaking his hand. "I'm Dirty."

"OK, OK," he says awkwardly. "Nice!"

Steven raises his right hand off the steering wheel. "Steven."

"Fucking awesome! Yeah, you and I spoke!"

"Yup," Steven says, grabbing the steering wheel again. Brian just stands there, kind of hopping up and down, nodding a little, beaming. Maybe he's always like this. Maybe he's just super jazzed on living. "You getting in?" Steven asks.

"Oh, yeah! Fuck yeah, man. Let's go!"

Finally he moves around the back of the Tahoe and throws his stuff inside.

"What the fuck?" I say under my breath to Steven.

"No idea, man."

Brian hops in the back seat and we get on the road. It's like riding with a Labrador puppy. He shifts around for a while and then gets right between us, damn near making a middle seat out of the center console. "So you guys are SEALs, right? I mean, like, ex-SEALs?"

"Uh-huh," Steven groans.

"I guess so?" I say.

I turn over my shoulder and catch Brian with a confused look.

"I was joking, Brian. Yes, we are."

"OK! Cool, cool." He glances out the window. "For a second there I thought maybe I got in the wrong car!"

"Nope. You're in the right car," I say.

"How do you know Malachi?" Brian asks.

"I don't," I reply.

It's too early for this shit and I can tell Steven feels the same. Brian takes the hint and is silent the rest of the way, except for the sound of two Monster Energy drinks being cracked open and guzzled down within ten minutes of each other. Why the hell Brian is drinking concentrated caffeine, I do not know. He does not need it.

Blessedly, we're spared LA traffic and make great time. We drop the Tahoe at Hertz, get to the terminal, check in. Somehow I'm the only one with TSA Pre—but whatever. All roads lead to Rome, or in this case Abu Dhabi.

Hudson News, browse the bestsellers, pick up a sugar-free Red Bull, two protein bars, a pack of gum, a bottle of water. Since I don't like eating airplane food, this is likely my sustenance for the next sixteen hours. The checkout lady is a Filipina. When I was in the Philippines with the Teams I got fairly good at Tagalog. As she gives me my change, I say, "Salamat po!"

Her eyes go big and her smile goes bigger. "Walang anuman!" I've always thought that working in an airport Hudson News must be one of the world's worst jobs, so it feels good to bring a little light into someone's day.

From there I wander through the duty-free. I'm not tempted to buy perfume, chocolate, or booze, but I do buy two cartons of Marlboro Reds. I have Trident Group America to thank for that. You never know when American cigarettes will come in handy.

I mill around the gate, my group gets called. Check-in, Jetway, plane. It's nearly full—mostly Indian-looking passengers. This isn't that surprising, since most people who live in the United Arab Emirates are not Emirati but Indian, Bangladeshi, and Filipino.

I get to my seat—a window, thank goodness. The aisle and middle are taken by a seventyish Indian couple, already strapped in and ready to go. She wears a bright blue-and-green sari and he's got on khakis, a white button-down shirt, loafers, and Coke-bottle glasses. They're holding hands. Neither acknowledges me as I hoist my carry-on into the overhead bin. When I'm ready to sit, they don't move. I might as well be invisible.

"Sorry, but that's my seat," I say, pointing past them.

The woman looks at me blankly. The man is locked in a death stare with the back of the seat in front of him.

"Excuse me, sir? Can I get by you?"

Still nothing, and now I'm engaged in an awkward staring contest with the wife. I have no idea why they're ignoring me. Maybe they're hoping I'll move on and take another seat. Maybe they don't have assigned seating in India. Maybe this is only their second flight ever, and they're returning home after visiting their daughter, who's finishing up at UCLA med school.

Like when I first flew to Egypt from Frankfurt, I've fallen into one of those odd cultural space-time folds that only happen on long-haul international flights. Physically, we're still in Los Angeles, but here on this Etihad flight sur-rounded by non-Westerners, we're already on the other side of the world.

Finally I tap his shoulder. He looks up and gets it. Says something to his wife in what I assume is Hindi, she releases me from her gaze. I thank them and slide into my seat. They don't say a single word to me during the entire flight.

Get settled, eat a protein bar. I catch sight of Steven, give him a two-finger salute. No sign of Brian, but he probably boarded when I was in the standoff with the Indian parents. Takeoff. While the plane climbs, I scroll through the movies on the in-flight entertainment system. Another quirk of these kinds of flights is they have stuff to watch that Americans are *never* exposed to. I fall into the Bollywood section. I'm actually led there by the wife sitting next to me, who's watching a ridiculous-looking cop melodrama complete with lav-ish singing-and-dancing numbers. Fuck it, looks fun. I put it on. The main character, a detective, has a bushy mustache and aviator sunglasses that he literally never takes off. He beats up rooms of thugs, *Oldboy* style (if you know, you know). He never loses a fight, and the laws of physics don't apply to him or anyone he touches. It's a blast.

When it's over, I drift off to sleep. And when I wake, we're descending into Doha, Qatar. Two-hour layover. Burgers with Steven. No sign of Brian. Whatever, he's lurking around somewhere. Cruise the Rolex store, don't buy anything. Prayer rooms, signs here and there showing the direction to Mecca. New flight, takeoff, enjoy my last protein bar.

Two hours later, we land in Abu Dhabi.

15

RESERVOIR DOGS

No problems with bags or finding a taxi, but still no sign of Brian. Maybe he missed the connection in Doha, or maybe he got turned around at UAE customs because they didn't like the look of him. Wouldn't be shocked. Neither Steven nor I cares enough to figure it out.

We take a cab to the Jumeirah Emirates Towers Hotel. It's dusk. I've never been here, and my first impression is that we're driving toward a set for *The Truman Show*. I've never seen so many cranes or construction sites. They must finish a building every other day. Most of the buildings are tall, and none of them look like any of the others. Curved steel, structural glass, ribbons of poured concrete defying gravity. It must be an architect's dream working here.

Steven calls Isaiah. We're the last to arrive, we'll meet everyone as soon as we get to the hotel. We pull up and grab our bags. The hotel is one of the science-fiction towers I saw from the cab. Mirrored glass twisting skyward. We walk in, Steven leads us to the bag check. "We'll get our rooms figured out after the meet."

"Got it."

I follow Steven through the lobby. Without a doubt, I have never been in a nicer hotel. When I was in the navy, we'd get an average of $125 per diem for lodging, which with military rates would land you in the Virginia Beach Courtyard by Marriott or Holiday Inn Express. You know what those are like—they're nice.

This hotel was *N-I-C-E*.

Marble floors, otherworldly lighting, plush couches, bursting flower arrangements. Space, light, scents. The whole thing adds up to *wealth*, like you could touch it. Like you could walk through it and be transformed without any effort.

I'm glad I'm not paying for this.

We wind down a wide hallway and come to a sitting area. I see Isaiah lounging in a low round chair. Malachi is next to him, and nearby are three others.

As soon as Malachi sees us, he rises and greets us with hugs. Isaiah also hugs us. Before introducing everyone, Malachi looks around. "But where is Brian?"

"Don't know, boss," Steven says.

"Was he not on your flight?"

"Yeah. We picked him up. But none of us sat together. Honestly, I haven't seen him since LA."

"Me either," I say.

Malachi makes a little *tsk-tsk* sound. He gives Isaiah a nod. Isaiah disappears to make some calls.

Malachi then introduces us to the other three guys, all of whom have been dressed by Mercenary Central Casting. To a man, they have either a black ball cap or a "team" hat featuring their last unit's insignia; an Under Armour T-shirt; matching tactical pants; a G-Shock or Suunto watch; and of course all-black Salomon Speedcross shoes. Each reminds me of the cookie-cutter mercs I saw in Iraq back in the day. Mind you, we all wear this type of clothing when working, but apparently these guys dress like this all the time.

Malachi, Isaiah, and I are the only ones who've bothered to dress more like businessmen. I'm wearing a gray Paul Smith blazer, regular white cotton T-shirt, fitted jeans, suede chukkas, and my go-to black-dial Rolex Submariner. Isaiah is a less expensive version of Malachi (surprise, surprise), who is by far the sharpest of the bunch. Kiton blazer. Tom Ford jeans and shirt. Hermès belt. Berluti shoes with a custom patina. Cutler and Gross glasses tucked in his breast pocket. His watch is an Audemars Piguet Royal Oak Offshore Diver with a sharkskin band, but I soon learn he has a whole collection, many of them Rolexes.

It may seem trivial, but knowing designer fashion is an essential skill for mercenaries. Isaiah and Malachi are perfect examples of this. To the uninitiated, they look identical. But if you know your shit, you know that Malachi's clothing costs four times Isaiah's. That's not counting the watch, which by itself costs more than everything on Isaiah's body and in his suitcase. Being able to recognize these differences quickly at a club, a restaurant, or any kind of sit-down meeting enables you to recognize who is number one, who is number two, and who knocks heads for both.

After this, we head to the front desk to check in, Malachi leading the pack. We must look like something out of *Reservoir Dogs*. Adding to our mercenary mystique, when we retrieve our bags, I see that everyone but me and Steven is traveling with one of the giant rolling duffels colloquially known as "dead hooker bags." Because, you know, they could hold a dead hooker.

The others have already checked in, so they head upstairs. Malachi tells me and Steven to get settled and meet in the lobby in half an hour for a team dinner. "Until then, I will go to find Isaiah," Malachi says.

We get in line, wait, step to the counter. Then, while I'm talking to the Filipino check-in clerk, Bruce appears.

I don't know his name yet, but he sure looks like a Bruce. He emerges from a nearby bathroom and makes a beeline for me and Steven. He's practically got a soundtrack, which would be some twangy country power ballad, or maybe some old-school Tom Jones. He's a hulking six-three with a push-broom mustache, custom snakeskin cowboy boots, a Canadian tuxedo (blue jeans, blue jean jacket, blue denim shirt), a saucer-size Lone Star belt buckle, all topped off with a straw cowboy hat. On one arm of his jean jacket are three military patches: airborne, ranger, and special forces, an arrangement known as the Triple Canopy. This is a dead giveaway that he's ex–Delta Force. Under one of his arms is a stack of books—all the same. *His* book.

Fucking incoming.

"Hey, brother!" he growls at Steven. Close your eyes and he sounds just like Macho Man Randy Savage.

"Hey, Bruce," Steven says.

He turns to me. "Hey, brother!" he repeats. "Bruce Bridgewater." He holds out his hand.

I shake it. He's strong. "Dirty."

"Nice to meet you, brother," his voice is somehow raspier, like he just inhaled a fistful of cigarettes.

"How've you been, Bruce?" Steven asks.

"You know me, Steve-O, never better! Ready for our next adventure. I'll see you brothers at chow!" His soundtrack resumes and he marches toward the elevators, disappearing around a corner. I half expect him to be wearing spurs. Thank goodness he isn't.

I turn to Steven. "What the fuck, man?"

Steven just smiles. "Don't let the package fool you. Bruce is a good dude."

"Okaaay."

After getting our room keys, we ride upstairs in one of the elevators. Steven's on twenty-one, I'm on twenty-three. He's got a double—if Brian ever shows up, they'll bunk together—and I have a single. The room is small but immaculate with plenty of luxurious touches. I put my bag in the closet and lock my passport in the safe. I'll unpack later. I stand at the floor-to-ceiling windows, taking it in. The view is to the Persian Gulf in one direction and the desert in the other. It's dark outside now. The brand-new city twinkles below. The gulf is a black expanse to the northeast, dotted here and there by the lights of ships. If you peer toward the desert, at one point every sign of human presence just stops. There's no gradual progression from one to the other. It's a hard and thin line.

I head back to the lobby, everyone's there. Malachi tells Isaiah that he needs to make some calls but that we should start dinner without him. Isaiah takes point and we follow. He leads us through what feels like half the hotel, then outside, down a set of stairs, then back up another set of stairs, then back inside. Finally we arrive at Tori No Su. Japanese. Fine by me.

A young Russian hostess takes us to a private dining room with a large circular table. As we sit, I can't help but think of the Knights of the Round Table. We order drinks, but otherwise food just starts to appear. Gyoza, tempura, fried tofu, spinach balls, sushi, sashimi, slices of perfectly cooked wagyu, sides of pickled vegetables. As you can imagine, the seven of us eat a *lot*. Probably the equivalent of what a dozen normal people would eat.

The mood lightens. Midway through the meal, Malachi joins us. The team consists of Jan, Polish, late thirties, bald, a little out of shape—he was in the French Foreign Legion; François, mid-thirties, bearded, also bald and slightly out of shape—a former French Commando Marine; Tep, American, huge at six-five, short hair, massive beard, tattoos on his hands and fingers—a former army medic; Bruce, who as expected is a former Delta Force operator; and us former SEALs: myself, Isaiah, Steven.

Throughout the evening, Isaiah takes each of us aside to give what he must think of as a pep talk. The one he has for me goes something like this: "Hey, Dirt. Malachi and I are really glad you decided to make the trip. We're looking forward to working with you. We know you're the most current operator on this team, but the rest of us have a lot of collective experience. Obviously Malachi is top dog. But I need you to know that when he's not around, you bring your shit to me. I'm number two. In fact, if you have any concerns or ideas, shoot them my way first. It'll help keep things moving in the right direction and everyone will be happy."

I tell him not a problem. But I think to myself, *Whatever, dude. I'll play along. But if things go sideways, I need you to know that I'll make my own decisions, no matter what fake rank you're giving yourself.*

16

BRIAN BOURNE

ROOM, TEETH, BED. I'VE BEEN TIRED FOR HOURS, AND NOW I'M FULL TOO. I fall asleep fast.

The next morning I wake with a searing pain in my eyes. Sunlight, and a lot of it. I was too wiped to figure out which button lowered the blackout shades. Now the sunlight streams in.

I roll over and find the controls. I hit a button, the shades slowly descend to the floor. I grab my phone from the bedside table. It was on do not disturb, but Isaiah texted only minutes ago.

> **Morning, brother. Team dinner tonight, 1800, SOLE Ristorante. Otherwise, day off.**

Roger, I respond.

There's no going back to sleep. I turn on the TV and scroll through the channels. I pass some European soccer match, BBC World News, CNN International, and Al Jazeera. Finally I land on a local channel.

A man in a traditional dishdasha and a red-and-white ghutra headdress stands under a pop-up shade structure in the middle of the desert. His left forearm is wrapped in a tube of green Astroturf. Perched on this is a stunning white falcon speckled with black. The falcon is hooded. It lifts one foot, then the next. It ruffles its feathers.

An announcer speaks quickly in Arabic. The man lifts the hood from the bird and raises his arm. The bird takes off.

The announcer starts barking. Arabic is a strange language, like English in its cadence, but completely foreign. I don't understand a word, but it sounds like he's calling the Kentucky Derby.

The camera follows the bird, then cuts to another angle. Now I see tripod-mounted radar guns, digital clocks, tall markers along the sidelines. The course is four hundred meters in a straight line. This is a sprint. The bird flaps its huge wings, its body and head lined up like a missile. Relative to the ground, the head and body stay still while the wings flap and the tail feathers move this way and that to stabilize the bird. It's mesmerizing.

Another man comes into view. He's dancing around, twirling something on the end of a rope that's about ten feet long. Maybe there's a frozen rat there, or some other bird treat. The falcon hits it, the announcer's excitement ebbs, the race is over. A clock at the finish line reads 16.097. These things are timed to the thousandth of a second. Not even the hundred-meter dash is timed to the thousandth of a second.

Also, the world's fastest man, Usain Bolt, can cover one hundred meters in a shade under ten seconds. These birds can cover *four times* that distance in sixteen seconds.

I spend the next three hours googling "how to be a falconer." It amounts to "Buy a bird, quit your job." Some of these birds in the Middle East are worth millions of dollars. The crest of the UAE features a golden falcon. Peregrine falcons can reach two hundred miles per hour in a dive. Females are faster than males and are more coveted. Humans may have been using raptors for hunting for eight thousand years. Fascinating.

Around noon I conclude that I probably won't drop everything to become a falconer. I call Mom, we talk for about an hour. She updates me on her and Dad, extended family, friends. Some real estate scandal between cousins. Always good to hear the latest gossip from Mom. I end the conversation by telling her that I'll be traveling for a while and not to expect to hear from me. She gets it, but I know she's bummed. So am I. We both enjoy our conversations.

Then I drag my ass out of bed and look for the gym. When I get there, Jan and François are leaving, we exchange nods. I hate hotel gyms. They always feel like they're designed by people who never exercise. As great as this hotel is, the gym is ho-hum. Three treadmills, a set of dumbbells, a quiver of yoga mats, one of those sit-down bikes. No one else is in there. I play my "Run" mix on Spotify and grab a treadmill. It takes all my concentration to peel off three miles, mostly because I'm nursing some plantar fasciitis in my right foot. My pace is a pathetic 8:30. I do some push-ups and planks and leave. At least I did something.

Room, shower, more exotic sports. This time it's cricket. Looks a little like baseball, but if you think baseball doesn't make sense, then you'll be hopelessly lost with cricket. I wish the falcons were still doing their thing, but that show is over.

At 1750 I head downstairs. It takes me a while to navigate to SOLE Ristorante. At first the hostess thinks I'm dining alone, but then she realizes whom I'm with. "Right this way, sir. Your friends are outside." I take it as a small compliment that she didn't lump me with them right off the bat. I'm pretty sure Bruce didn't get that treatment.

We come out onto a gorgeous patio overlooking a pool. She holds out her hand, I spot the crew. And I can't believe it.

There's Brian.

He's with Malachi, they're engaged in a serious conversation. The smoke from Malachi's cigarette is clearly bothering Brian, but he's in no position to protest. I'm sure Malachi is smoking for that exact purpose. I have to do a double take, but it looks like Brian is wearing the same clothing, except for the T-shirt. It's not Megadeth anymore, it's Iron Maiden. And the bandanna isn't tied around his head, it's wrapped around his wrist.

Everyone besides Jan and François is here. I exchange quick hellos, and after a couple of minutes, Malachi leans across Isaiah and says, "Dirty, I don't greet you properly only because I have serious business with our friend Brian here. I do not want you to think I am being rude."

"Thought never crossed my mind, Malachi."

"Good."

"Hey, Dirty!" Brian yelps. Whatever, dude.

Malachi then turns his sights back on our redheaded rocker.

Jan and François show up, the waiter appears, we order. Malachi and Brian finish their mano a mano. "OK. Now we are alllll here," Malachi says. He places his hand on Brian's back. It almost looks like he squeezes his neck a little. Brian gives a small wave as he looks around the table, his head slightly bowed. Malachi has been giving Brian a paternal lecture, but the whole scene also has a gangster vibe. If this were a movie, it'd be obvious that Brian just punched a one-way ticket to the afterlife, except lucky for him, he's going to get one more good meal out of the bargain.

The first course arrives. Caprese salad, roasted figs, beef carpaccio. Four bottles of Super Tuscan. The mood is light, except for Brian, who hasn't left Malachi's side and has barely touched his food. When I'm done with my appetizers, I think, *Fuck it.*

"Yo, Brian. What happened?"

Brian looks at Malachi as if he's asking for permission to speak. Malachi gives him a nod.

"Well," Brian says, "a security agent at LAX wouldn't give me back my passport because apparently it was damaged or something, I don't know, and, well, I got spooked. So I snatched it from him, turned around, and made for the exit, which was dumb, but no one chased me, I guess because I hadn't really done anything wrong, and I got in a cab and got the hell out of there. I went home and tried to chill and then you called me, Isaiah, and told me that Malachi told you to tell me to turn around and get back to LAX, which I did, boss was nice enough to get me rebooked, and my bags were already here or on their way or something. I got to LAX stat, you know how it is, I had to like, you know, sleep in the airport and eat Starbucks and shit until the next flight, which was today. I think. Maybe not. What day is it? Anyway, I just got in like seriously an hour or two ago. Been a real ride, you know? Fucking Arabia, amirite?"

The rest of us sit there, our jaws on the table. Is this guy high on blow? If he brought drugs into this country, he is in for a potential life sentence.

François breaks the silence. "Who are you?" he asks in a thick French accent. "Some kind of Brian Bourne, running from everyone?"

"Goddamn *Bourne Stupidity*," Bruce says, laughing.

"OK, OK," Malachi says, putting a stop to the jokes. Like him or not, Brian's had a long day.

"Well, Brian," I add, "just make sure to take care of that passport so it doesn't get any more nicks."

"No problem, Dirty! I got it right here!" At this, he stands a little and pulls the passport out of his back pocket.

We all stare at him. He sits back down, immediately unsure of whether he's done another boneheaded thing. Malachi twists in his chair and stares at him too. "Brian. Go and put that in your safe like the rest of us." He says it quietly, but he might as well be yelling.

Brian stands. "O-OK, boss." He puts his passport in his pocket and then pats himself down. "Hey, uh, Steven? Can I get the room key? I left mine upstairs."

"Sure," Steven says in a monotone.

As Brian bumbles around the table, I lean over to Isaiah and Malachi. "We need to get rid of this guy," I say.

"Hmm," Isaiah says, then looks to Malachi.

Malachi's eyes narrow. "I think Dirty is right." Pause. "No, he is one hundred percent right." He shifts his focus to me. "Please take care of it, Dirty."

"No problem, boss."

Brian leaves, we eat some more, he returns thirty minutes later. The main course arrives, we all dig in. Except for Brian, who stares directly through his veal chop. Halfway through the meal, he says, "Uh, may I be excused?"

"Of course," Malachi says. "You are not prisoner."

Brian stands so fast he nearly knocks his chair over, then spins and hustles away. We're glad he's gone.

The group begins to break up over coffee and dessert. Steven, Jan, and François turn in first, followed by everyone else but Isaiah, Malachi, and me. Malachi pays, and we make our way back through the hotel to our rooms. It's still early, which is good. Need a good night's sleep. The job starts for real in the morning.

Near the elevator, Isaiah says, "Dirty, mind taking care of Brian?"

"Easy day." I shoot Steven a text.

What's your room number again?

2110.

I head up, ride with a young Middle Eastern couple who are headed to the top floor. Maybe they're on their honeymoon. I get to room 2110, rap the door three times. Steven opens it. "Hey, Dirt."

"Hey."

This room is a double, but it's the same exact size as mine. Between the two queen beds, the huge bags, and a pair of men, it is *cramped*. Steven sits on his bed and resumes working on his laptop. Brian sits on the side of his bed, elbows on knees, head hung low.

I sit perpendicular to Steven, he scoots over to give me a little room. I'm directly opposite Brian. The beds are so close that our knees almost touch.

I grab my tin of Copenhagen and pack it three times. I pop it open and take a decent pinch. I say, "Brian—"

He cuts me off. "Dirty, please, j-just let me call my son first. I've been trying all night but it's like morning there or whatever and he isn't answering." He lifts his head, our eyes lock. He's on the verge of tears.

"Yeah, man. Do your thing."

He half turns, fumbles with his phone, dials. His right knee begins to bounce spasmodically. "C'mon, Luke, c'mon," he whispers under his breath. "Fuck." He hangs up and looks at his phone like it's the most useless thing in the world.

I no longer think he's high, I just think he's a nervous, insecure wreck. It's impossible not to feel a little sorry for the guy.

"Hey, brother, just try him later," I say.

His head whips around. "Later?!"

"Yeah, later."

"B-but…w-what about…?" He trails off.

For some reason Steven stifles a laugh. I ignore him.

I lean forward and change the subject. "Listen, man. I need you to do me a favor. I know it's a pain in the ass, but I need you to get your shit together and head to the airport. Malachi is going to take care of you. You're going home."

Brian stares at me, then his eyes widen, then he smiles. "I'm what?"

"You're going home."

He actually reaches across the small gulf between the beds and throws his arms over me in what has to be one of history's most awkward man hugs. Realizing this instantly, he pulls back. His hands are shaking. "Oh, Dirty, thank you, brother! Thank you!"

Steven can't hold it in any longer. He bursts out laughing. His computer nearly slides from his lap, but he catches it. With his other hand he reaches over and grabs my shoulder to steady himself. "Oh man," he manages between belly laughs. "I'm sorry, Brian."

Brian doesn't care, but I'm still totally confused.

"What the fuck?" I ask.

Steven settles down. Brian stands and practically starts dancing. Steven says, "Brian thought you were coming up here to kill him, Dirty."

"*What?*"

"I heard you downstairs," Brian explains, already stuffing what few things he'd unpacked into the top of his bag. "You know, how you wanted to 'get rid' of me."

"I just meant send you home, dude. What are you, a fucking idiot?" I'm not trying to needle him, it just comes out.

He says nothing. Feeling a little bad, I accompany him downstairs and put him in a cab for the airport. He wasn't even in-country for five hours.

And with that, Brian Bourne has completed his first, and only, mission as a mercenary.

17

GOING IN BLACK

I WAKE ON MY SECOND FULL DAY IN ABU DHABI ON THE FENCE ABOUT THIS whole mission. I trust Steven and Isaiah, but the other guys, in particular Bruce, leave me wondering. Do we *really* need this guy? Will there be language barriers with the French and Polish guys? How good is Tep, who's barely said a word?

This is putting aside the whole Brian fiasco, which Malachi could easily have avoided by not hiring him in the first place. Why the hell would we need an MMA personal trainer? We're going to be on a firebase in Yemen, not on a self-improvement retreat in Santa Fe. It makes no sense.

The way I see it, these are two blatant red flags. And I know from experience that bad things come in threes. As I sort my things that morning, separating what I'm taking to the desert from what I'm leaving behind with the hotel luggage check, I promise myself that if number three does pop, then I'm headed home on the next transport out.

I hit the lobby early. I spot Malachi on one of the many overstuffed club chairs, sipping an espresso and reading something on his tablet.

Check out, get a little yellow ticket for my left luggage, and walk over to him. He's finally ditched his high-end clothing for his work clothes—climbing pants, desert boots, a black T-shirt. He still wears a blazer, but it isn't as expensive as his other jackets. I'm sure it'll get folded up and stowed the minute we hop on our first plane or helicopter ride.

"Good morning, Dirty," he says as I step up to him. He doesn't look up from his tablet. "Un moment," he says in French.

"No problem, boss," I say, taking a seat.

He wraps up whatever article he's reading and places his tablet on a small circular table between us. "I am happy you are here, Dirty." I like the French inflection he gives to my nickname: "dir-TEE."

"Happy to be here, boss. Hey, can I ask a question?"

"Of course."

I lean forward. "I had no problem telling Brian to pack his bags and get lost, but I'm curious why he was even on this trip to begin with. He's not like the rest of us."

Malachi raises an eyebrow. "Well, Dirty, optics are very important. The Emiratis say they have good intel for us and we will hit the ground running once we are in-country, but as you know, intel is almost never as good as anybody says it is."

I nod. This is true.

He continues, "Even if it is 'good,' we still need to vet. Which, as you also know, this takes time. And if there is *no* intel, and I worry this is the case, then it takes longer."

"I'm with you, boss, but Brian wasn't going to help with any of that."

He scoffs. "Mon Dieu. No, no. But while this vetting happens, we cannot be just sitting. It is good for the client to see us train, fight, drill while we do more invisible work of getting intel. They may not understand how long this takes. Or perhaps they do. We will find out. But this way or that, we have to be busy. Look serious, because we are serious. As I say, optics."

"All right, fair enough." This makes sense, but I'm still not sold. Why an eccentric wannabe rocker like Brian who's never been to a place like Yemen? Why not get someone more like one of us? I almost press Malachi on this, but just then Isaiah and Steven show up. Until I get a fuller explanation, Brian remains a red flag.

The rest of the team trickles in, deals with the front desk, drops off bags. Malachi goes outside to finalize transportation. I spot Tep at one point, nose buried in a book. Since he's basically only said "Hello" and "See you later" since we met, I ask what he's reading.

He glances up and tilts the book so I can see its title: *Division and Brigade Surgeon's Handbook*, FM 4-02.21.

"Fun," I say. He smirks and goes back to reading. I guess it's a good thing that our medic is reading an army field manual on surgery—or maybe not? Hopefully we won't find out the hard way.

A few minutes after that, we go outside and climb into a tinted-out Mercedes Sprinter. No one talks as we drive to the edge of the city. Just as I saw from my room on the twenty-third floor, we eventually cross one street and are thrust into one of the driest, most desolate deserts I've ever seen. It's just sand and rock and heat distortions, power lines snaking here and there, as far as the eye can see.

After twenty minutes we come to the edge of a bare-bones Emirati air base. We unload and board a twin-engine turboprop. As soon as we take off, we disappear. Where we're headed—Yemen—we're going in black. No government agency, politician, or military official will know we're there.

I have no idea what the itinerary is, and from the looks of it neither does anyone besides Malachi and maybe Isaiah. After a couple of hours, we land at a desert airstrip to refuel. Saudi Arabia. I can tell by the flags snapping in the wind lining the airstrip. While we're taxiing, Malachi zigzags across the cabin, stooping to peer out the windows. "You all right, boss?" I ask when he comes near me.

"Yes, Dirty." He winks at me. "Just small stress being a Jew in Saudi."

I bet.

We stay on the plane and the refueling goes off without a hitch. Then we take off again and rise into the sky. I catch myself gazing out the window at the endless desert below. Orange, yellow, brown, ocher, rust. A surreal landscape, an ocean of sand.

The plane is loud. We don't talk, most of us have in earbuds. Tep, with his six-five frame, is squeezed into the seat across the aisle. At one point he takes a break from reading. I lean over. "Hey, Tep!" I yell over the engines' din. "You just brushing up? You're making me a little nervous reading that field manual."

He laughs. "You still go to the range, Dirty?" His voice is as big as he is.

"Hell yeah."

"Is it because you don't know what you're doing, or is it because you like to be ready when it's time to rock and roll?"

"Good point!"

That's about as much conversation as we need or can deal with. Any more than that would leave us mute tomorrow.

After another couple of hours, we begin our descent. Malachi stands in the center of the plane, bracing himself against some light chop. "First we are stopping in Eritrea on Emirati base! From here we will helicopter to Yemen!"

Eritrea. OK. The last time I was anywhere near this country was on one of those container ships with Trident.

We hit a rough patch of turbulence at around five thousand feet that feels like a hurricane. I peer into the cockpit. The pilots act like it's just another day in the office, which it probably is. We pass through it at around two thousand feet, smooth sailing. I look out the window. Teal water meets massive mangroves and blinding white sand, as well as hundreds of rose-pink flamingos. Not bad.

Land, taxi, finally cut the engines. Malachi stands in the aisle three-quarters of the way forward. "OK, everyone," he announces. "We are here to meet with Major General Khalil of UAE. I know you are all professional, and you know I respect you, but we need to look the part. When we get off, we line up shoulder to shoulder. Isaiah will be to my left, then I don't care the rest of the order."

Malachi yields to Isaiah, who takes over. "After boss and me, it's Bruce, Steven, Dirty, Tep, François, Jan. Got it?" Yeses sound off through the cabin. François says "Oui!" I just give a thumbs-up.

Deplane, line up. The heavy odor of JP-8 aviation fuel hangs in the air. There are several other planes, as well as a few helicopters coming and going, down the field. Major General Khalil watches us get organized. He's about six-two, decent build, but difficult to tell if he's hard or soft since he's not in fatigues but a traditional dishdasha and ghutra. My bet is on the soft side. Hawkish nose, trim black beard.

Once we're lined up, he gives us a curt nod. It's not so much "Hello" as "So this is what our money has purchased?" He then pulls Malachi aside to talk out of earshot.

As soon as Khalil leaves, we quit with the military posturing and migrate to a stack of wooden pallets just off the runway. In our line of work, the thing we kill most often is time. We're all well practiced. We mill around for several hours, waiting for the CH-47 Chinook to Yemen. Malachi and Isaiah pow-wow. Tep reads his book. Bruce finds some AC in a nearby building. I like the heat, so I stay outside. Everyone else does too. François plays some game on his phone—he looks focused—maybe chess. Steven has his headphones in and sunglasses on, probably sleeping.

At one point I'm next to Jan. We're leaning against some pallets in the shade. Jan tosses a pebble up and down, staring into the distance. "Hey, Jan," I say.

He quits tossing the pebble, looks at me. "What." He's annoyed.

"You ever do any big missions when you were with the Legion?"

"That was past. I only focused on present now." His thick Polish accent amplifies his annoyance.

"Did you like the Legion?"

"If I liked the Legion, would I be here?" He turns away from me slightly. End of conversation.

"Good point," I say anyway, mostly to his back.

Bruce comes back bearing an armful of water bottles. "Gotta stay hydrated, brother!" he says as he hands me two bottles.

"Thank you, sir!"

"Never call me that. I work for a living." A tired joke that's been around as long as there have been soldiers. I bet the Sumerians, Greeks, and Romans told the same joke thousands of years ago. We share a laugh anyway.

Malachi passes out some snacks, most everyone but me smokes, we nap here and there. At 0300, our bird is finally ready to go.

We're led across the pitch-black tarmac, the unmistakable sound of a CH-47's rotor whomping in the darkness. We walk up the rear ramp, the hot exhaust dousing us. Khalil is already on board. I sit on a foldout seat made of red cargo straps. The sounds, the smells, the feeling of boarding a CH-47 all are very familiar. This is more like it. Sure beats riding some container ship with nothing to do.

Then we take off and fly back east across the Red Sea.

18

RULE OF THREE

We arrive at 0400.

Khalil, Malachi, and Isaiah lead us off the back of the helo. No moon, total darkness. I can barely see my hand in front of my face. It's so dark that we have to walk "caver style" with one hand on the shoulder of the man in front, all of us following Khalil's faint red headlamp. After a hundred meters we come to a stop.

Malachi, Isaiah, and Khalil launch into a muted argument. The gist seems to be that Malachi wants something but Khalil is pushing back.

At one point I'm close enough to hear Khalil hiss, "Tomorrow, tomorrow. Everything is safe."

"No. Tonight, not tomorrow!" Malachi says loudly.

Khalil replies, "Inshallah, inshallah." *God willing, God willing.*

"No inshallah. God has nothing to do with it. Make it happen or we go back to helo right now," Malachi retorts.

Pause. "OK, OK," Khalil says. "Do not worry, brother. I will bring them now."

Khalil spins, his red headlamp illuminating a metal panel. He reaches out and a door opens. At first I'm confused. Blinding white lights flash on as the sound of an engine comes to life. The whole time we've been standing next to at least one car, invisible in the darkness.

Khalil gets behind the wheel. The headlights reveal seven-foot-by-seven-foot HESCO barriers made of sand and metal wire. We're in a courtyard, roughly square, forty meters along one side. Khalil's car—looks to be a Toyota Land Cruiser—drives through a break in the barriers. I risk turning on my own headlamp and look around. I spot three folded cots against one of the walls. I flag Isaiah, we grab them and set them up in a little triangle.

Just as we sit, Khalil's vehicle returns. He stops near Malachi and kills the engine.

"You will be happy!" Khalil proclaims. He leads Malachi and Isaiah to the rear of the Land Cruiser. Isaiah calls us over, we assemble around the car, we peer inside. A large metal box with the lid open. Rifles. Brand-new ones.

Malachi and Isaiah turn toward us. Each holds an M4 in one hand and a single magazine in the other. Khalil passes out the other rifles, making sure to note serial numbers as he does so.

When he passes me mine, I thank him, but my expression says, "Are you fucking kidding?" Good thing it's dark. This is a bare-bones M4 with nothing on it besides factory iron sights. I'm good, but I can only do so much with one mag and no optics. I flash Isaiah a look. He knows I'm disappointed but shows no intention of doing anything about it. I head over to a cot and take a seat. The rest do too, except for Malachi and Isaiah, who disappear into the darkness.

We spend what's left of the night there on those cots, holding those less-than-adequate rifles. Most everyone drifts off, but not me and François. Just as the sky begins to lighten, I whisper, "François?"

"Oui?"

"How long have you known Malachi?"

"Oh, I don't know, maybe ten years." I don't respond. "Dirty, I trust Malachi. He is smart. I've worked with him all over the world."

"Uh-huh. François, have you ever heard about how bad things happen in threes?"

"Trees?"

"No. Un, deux, trois…" I count with my fingers.

"Ah, oui! D'accord. But what things are bad?"

"Well, for one, we have Bruce."

François shrugs. "What is bad with him besides his fashion?" He laughs.

I laugh a little too, but still. "I don't know. I think it says something about someone, walking around dressed like that."

"Oui, peut-être. But maybe he thinks you are dressed like a klune."

"A klune?"

"Yes. A klune, like in le cirque."

"Oh, *clown*!"

"Oui! Klune!" OK. Fair point. "What is deux, Dirty?"

"Brian."

"Mais Brian Bourne is gone. So who cares?"

"I don't know. I mean, can you imagine what he'd be like if he were here right now? People like us, we're used to this. But him?"

"Oui," François says slowly, appearing to take my point. "But maybe he would steal the helicopter and crash into the sea!" We laugh again.

"I don't know," I say. "Maybe I'm just superstitious."

Almost reading my mind, François jostles his gun. "Maybe you are upset about these?"

"For sure."

"Dirty, it is OK. This cannot be three, because there is no one or two. Trust François, OK? We will get better guns soon. Trust François," he repeats.

"OK, François. I'll try."

"You will see."

I hope so. But if we don't get real guns soon, then I'm thinking this has been fun and all, but I'm out.

19

THE RANGE

I ATTEMPT TO SLEEP. I INSIST FRANÇOIS TAKE THE LONE REMAINING COT, SO I get comfy against a HESCO barrier, using a balled-up shirt for a pillow and my cap for an eye mask. I've been awake for close to twenty-four hours, so it isn't hard to drift off.

I don't sleep for long.

By 0730 the sun is up and shining down on the Emirati base. It stirs to life, the sounds of heavy things waking up. A Chinook coming in to land. Trucks coming and going. A generator in the distance. The Chinook creates a massive red plume as it sets down. The air takes on a reddish tint as it fills with fine powder. It tastes like an old penny. For a moment I'm reminded of the melange spice in *Dune*. Good book.

I stand and stretch. My vertebrae pop. Bruce and Steven are awake, the others are still asleep. François is curled up like a baby. Malachi and Isaiah are nowhere in sight.

I take a better look around. We are on a base within a base. Our new home is a courtyard of Martian dust. Besides a small cement structure against the northern HESCO barriers, it's empty. I wonder if we're supposed to just sleep outside. No port-a-potties or obvious latrines. Are we going to have to dig a shit ditch? Where are we going to get food? If this is where we're staying, they are not ready for us. Feels a lot like strike three.

Parked at the edge of our new home are two white Toyota Hilux pickup trucks—the ubiquitous auto de guerre for the Middle East and Afghanistan—as well as two up-armored Toyota Sequoias. I figure these are for us. Hopefully, we won't have to take turns sleeping in them.

Malachi and Isaiah appear, walking in from the larger Emirati section of the base. Both smoke. Malachi occasionally holds his cigarette from the bottom. So very French. They approach us. Isaiah flicks his butt into the dust, Malachi drops his and mashes it with the ball of his foot. "Messieurs!" Malachi announces. "Good morning." Those of us who aren't awake begin to stir.

Isaiah says, "Get up and take a piss or shit. Splash some water on your face. First order of business is to sight in our M4s."

Good, I think. I raise my hand. "Where?"

"There's a range not far from here," Isaiah says.

"No, where are the bathrooms?"

"Oh. They're just outside our camp, that way and left."

"We will have our own facilities soon, gentlemen," Malachi assures us.

We better.

A few of us use the bathrooms—which are pretty nice as far as firebase bathrooms go—and we reassemble. Malachi asks Jan and François to stay behind to keep watch on our gear. It's obvious that Malachi and François are friends, but François respects Malachi's authority and takes orders like a true professional. I doubt anyone is going to come into our desolate courtyard to steal our bags or vehicles, but this is standard operating procedure and it sits well with me.

Isaiah takes point and leads the rest of us out of our section of the base. While we're walking, he produces a bag of individually wrapped orange-and-yellow foam earplugs from his backpack. He passes these out.

The range is only fifty meters away. Like everything here, it's defined by more HESCO barriers. We line up off to one side in the shade.

"All right," Isaiah says with authority. "The western wall is the impact area. This is the firing line." He drags his bootheel through the sand to create a ten-foot line. "We don't have any targets, so just find a spot on the ground near the impact area. And of course, keep your rifles pointed in a safe direction." As range briefs go, this is about as lax as they come. But we aren't in the military anymore and we're all big boys, so it works for me.

"Can we keep the range cold for a sec?" I ask, raising a half-filled water bottle.

"Go for it," Isaiah says. I make my way downrange to set up my target. "Nobody shoot Dirty!" Isaiah yelps. Everyone laughs. I start creeping backward with my rifle at the low ready, the barrel pointed at the ground. They laugh harder. I'm happy to help with a joke, or even be the butt of one if it'll bring us together.

"Lock and load!" Isaiah calls out jokingly.

Haha, dude. I spin and jog back to the firing line, eyeing Isaiah, who's smiling from ear to ear. No one locks or loads before I make it back to the firing line.

We're going to take turns. Isaiah announces that I'm first.

I jostle my M4, seat the mag in the magwell, give the mag a quick tug, and send the bolt home. I've been handling M4s my entire adult life. I can tell by sound and feel when the bolt has chambered a round and when it hasn't. I can also tell if a rifle has ever been fired. This one has not—or if it has, only by a machine during a round of factory testing.

"Range is hot!" Isaiah calls.

I drop to the ground and go prone, driving my hips into the sand. I set my legs wide, point my toes out. Tep stands next to me, all six-five of him. With me in this position, he feels unnaturally tall, like a storybook giant.

I fully extend the buttstock to minimize the gaps on either side of the front sight post in the rear aperture. I prop myself up on my elbows, shoulder my rifle, and put the tip of my front sight post halfway up the water bottle. "First one to hit the water bottle for a pack of Reds!" Isaiah says as he also drops into a prone position to my right.

I couldn't care less about the cigarettes—I'm still sitting on nearly two cartons, and I barely ever smoke—but I'm competitive by nature. "OK, you're on," I say, without removing my eyes from the sights.

"Good," Isaiah says, getting adjusted. "Alternating shots. You first. Go for it!"

I take a deep breath and slowly let it out, squeezing the trigger as I exhale. At the bottom of my breath, the trigger breaks. The bottle shakes, the ground around it darkens with water.

"Lucky fucker!" Isaiah says.

He's not wrong. No matter how good you are, out-of-the-box rifles are rarely on for any shooter. It has as much to do with the weapon as with the person. Every shooter sees differently, and not everyone uses the exact same technique. You can sometimes anticipate these differences by aiming with the "lollipop" or "pumpkin-on-a-stick" method, where you put the tip of the front sight under the intended target. This is usually a circle on a paper target, hence the phrasing. I prefer a technique simply called "center mass," where you put the tip of the front sight post directly in the center of your target. For whatever reason, this has worked for me over the years.

Isaiah takes his shot, sending his round just to the left of the bottle. A cloud of dust snaps into the air and quickly dissipates.

"Dirty wins," Tep says.

"Hundred bucks he can't do it again," Bruce calls out.

"Keep your money," I say, beginning to stand.

"Dirty, do you mind?" Malachi asks from the back. "If you miss, I will pay for Bruce." Malachi isn't interested in the wager, he wants to see if I can make the shot again. "If you hit, Bruce will pay…and I will double it."

I can't say no to that. "All right. You better be good for it, Bruce." I know Malachi is good for it.

"Don't worry, brother," Bruce rasps.

I get prone again and line up my shot. I hold just at the base of the bottle cap, which I can barely make out from this distance. Inhale. Slowly exhale. Squeeze. Break.

Bang!

The bottle shakes, the white bottle cap shoots straight up in the air.

"Hell yeah, Dirt!" Tep exclaims. As I stand, I catch Steven grinning.

"Good shooting, brother!" Bruce says, clapping me on the shoulder. "That's a fair hundred I owe you. Glad you're not pointing that thing at me."

Isaiah says nothing.

Malachi tells Isaiah to man the range while he and I go back to relieve François and Jan, who still need to sight in. "You got it, boss," Isaiah says unenthusiastically.

As we cross to our section of the base, Malachi says, "Dirty, you are very good. And humble, which I like. The men respect you."

"Thanks, boss."

"Listen, we have structure here. You know this. Isaiah is number two. But keep doing what you are doing."

"Roger that. It's the only way I know."

We take a few more steps in the dust and sand. "I like this answer, Dirty." He holds out a pack of Reds, the flip top open and three or four cigarettes poking above the foil. "Smoke?"

I take one and he lights it with a worn Zippo.

Maybe number three isn't headed our way after all.

20

ACCOMMODATIONS

When I get back to our section, I find François and Jan milling around. Just like when we were in Eritrea, François is playing something on his phone, a look of stern concentration on his face.

I can't help but wonder. "Hey, François, what's that you're playing? Chess?" I hope so. So far I like François the most, and chess is a great way to pass time when you're at the ass end of nowhere like we are.

He shakes his head and turns his phone toward me. On it is a brightly colored grid of little cartoon shapes. I've never seen it before. "*Candy Crush*!" He pronounces that last word "croosh."

I've never heard of it. "A *kid's* game?"

"Non, non, non. C'est pour tout. For everyone! Come, I will show you."

He hands me his phone and walks me through an early level. "It's pretty easy," I say. It's certainly not chess.

"They get much more difficult. Download it and you will see!"

Just then Malachi appears and tells François and Jan to get to the range and sight in their weapons. Both march off into the heat. I can't believe it—but I download *Candy Crush* and play it until everyone returns from the range. François is right, of course. It gets difficult fast.

Later that morning, Malachi assigns Isaiah and me a task: go to Major General Khalil and get us better accommodations. We jump in one of our Hiluxes and make our way across the base to the area our Emirati partner force calls home.

A single soldier in full body armor mans the Emirati checkpoint. As we pull up, he doesn't even bother to rise from his plastic chair under the dappled shade of camo netting. He looks confused. Isaiah's skin tone and dark hair make him look local, except that he's six inches taller than anyone else in the country, which shows even from behind the wheel of the pickup. And then there's me, who could feasibly pass for local, but only after I spend a couple of weeks in the desert. Not to mention Isaiah's uniform is all black and mine is MultiCam. The guard must wonder what kind of outfit we're with.

After an awkward pause—the two of us eyeing him, him watching us—he slowly rises from his chair. He sticks a cigarette in his mouth but doesn't light it as he saunters up to the driver's side of the Hilux, stooping slightly to pass under the red horizontal post acting as a barricade. He is in no rush.

The guard says something in Arabic, which I don't understand. I don't think Isaiah does either. He says, "I'm here to see Major General Khalil."

The guard makes the smallest of nods, his gaze shifting to me. The cigarette flicks between his lips.

"He's with me," Isaiah says, stating the obvious. "We're both here to see Khalil."

The guard squints, then shrugs. His confusion lifts. He turns away from the truck and pushes down on a cement-filled red ammo can attached to one end of the barricade, which rises just high enough for us to pass. Isaiah gives him a wave along with a loud "Shukran."

We drive twenty feet, hang a left, and park next to Khalil's Land Cruiser. "Better off leaving these in here," Isaiah says, pointing at my M4.

"Good call."

The Emirati camp is twice the size of ours, a dusty quad roughly eighty meters to a side. Four clamshell tents and a trailer with toilets and showers. It reminds me of a VIP section at a music festival, like Isaiah and I have just pulled into a small-scale Middle Eastern Coachella. Isaiah goes to the second clamshell on the right and knocks on the composite door. A young, slender Emirati in traditional clothing opens it. Cool air wafts out. Another man appears—older, bigger—who recognizes Isaiah. He forces out a "Hello" in English and motions for us to enter. As we begin to cross the threshold, he holds out his left arm like a fullback. He points at our feet. Stupid us—we forgot to remove our shoes.

I reach down and loosen my Speedcrosses' distinctive quick-release laces and slide off my shoes. Isaiah does the same. We stow our shoes and enter, quickly closing the door behind us to keep as much cool air inside as possible.

About a dozen Emiratis sit on red-and-black carpets on the wooden floor, eating and talking quietly. They appear mostly fit and range from twenty to thirty-five years old. We haven't eaten a proper meal since Abu Dhabi, and I can't help but stare at their food. Baked chicken, rice, hummus, pita bread, all of it smells fantastic. Isaiah and I are each handed a plate and invited to sit in a pair of folding chairs.

No one in the tent seems to mind that we're here, to the extent that it almost feels like they're going out of their way to act like we aren't. Every now and then I catch one or two of them eyeing us peripherally. They are certainly talking about us as they murmur to each other in hushed Arabic. Whatever. Isaiah and I don't mind. We dig in.

As we finish eating, Major General Khalil enters the tent. The Emiratis scramble to stand at attention. I can tell by the way the men act that he's no tyrant, nor does he abuse his rank. He's respected. He immediately gives a command in Arabic, which must be something akin to "Carry on." The troops relax, sit back down, and continue eating and socializing.

Khalil walks across the tent toward us. We stand, awkwardly holding our dirty paper plates and plastic utensils in our hands. Just as Khalil reaches us, a young Emirati takes the trash from our hands and throws it into a black bag.

I wipe my hands on the sides of my pants for a handshake, but there is none. "Where is Malachi?" Khalil asks with a confused, almost offended look.

Isaiah says, "I am second in command, and Mala—"

Khalil cuts him off. "Ah, it's OK, it's OK." Khalil smiles. Maybe he was just having some fun with us. "So, gentlemen, how can I help?" He's addressing me.

I start to reply but catch myself. I take a half step back, deferring to Isaiah.

"Major General Khalil, thank you for your hospitality," Isaiah says. "We sighted in the rifles this morning and the guys couldn't be happier. They are fine weapons. But we need things for the camp, and urgently." I have to hand it to Isaiah, he's good at this.

Khalil holds out a hand, palm up. "Please, whatever you need."

Isaiah clears his throat, opening a weatherproof notepad to a page covered in illegible scrawl. "Please, sir, if you will. We need two clamshell tents, two AC units, twelve cots, electricity, water to run the toilet, shower, and a washing machine. We need food set aside for us at each meal, the same as your men eat."

It sounds like a lot to me, but Khalil doesn't miss a beat. He brings his other hand on top of his open palm, like he's making a sandwich. "No problem, Isaiah. It will be done by tonight."

I'm extremely skeptical, Isaiah too. This must be obvious, because Khalil reaches out and puts a hand on Isaiah's shoulder. "It will be done by tonight," he repeats. "Now, come with me."

He leads us outside, pausing so all three of us can slip our shoes back on. As soon as we're in the heat and dust, we're greeted by two more Emiratis, each holding two Mermite hot food cases. Khalil pops the lid off one—it contains more of the same food we just ate inside, along with plates, napkins, and utensils. "For your men," he says. I'm still skeptical about him making sure we get everything by tonight, but I like the guy.

We thank him, load up the Mermites, and go out the way we came in.

As we drive under the barricade, Isaiah says, "Thanks for letting me run that, Dirty."

"No problem, man. That's your job." When we pull into our camp, the guys are all sweating from an impromptu workout session led by Malachi. And as soon as I see this, I understand that it looks a lot better than a bunch of dudes hanging out, smoking, playing *Candy Crush.*

Isaiah jumps out of the Hilux yelling, "You guys hungry?"

We all chow down. Isaiah and I have seconds. The overall mood of our camp gets lighter. As we eat, Isaiah tells everyone what Khalil said, but they just laugh. There's no way all that gets put up by nightfall.

But not two hours later, three flatbed trucks roll into our camp manned by a couple dozen Yemenis. They know zero English and we know only basic Arabic. Isaiah takes charge, using body language to guide the workers. They're an efficient crew. Eight men set up the clamshell tents, and eight others work to hook up power and water. By nightfall, we have everything we requested and more.

At one point while the Yemenis work, I take Malachi aside and remark that it's odd the Emirati military isn't doing the construction. He laughs. "Daniel, UAE is a young but rich country. Nobody joins the army to be in construction. Their military—other than pilots, tank drivers, and some specialists—it is completely outsourced. You see those watchtowers?" I nod. "Those are manned by Colombians. In this country there are many Brits, many Americans, many French. The Emiratis hire us as instructors and fighters. Look at us. They never have had a team capable like we are. But now we are here, and we can bring them with us to show them."

"'Train and advise,'" I say.

"Yes, Dirty." He winks.

"And what does that mean exactly?"

He claps his hands. "We will talk about this soon, with everyone. OK?"

"OK, boss."

"Now, let us get settled into our new home."

As Malachi walks away, I stand there for a minute or two watching the Yemenis pack up. For some reason, I'm transported back to the *Maersk Kentucky*, where I spent hours listening to Homer and all those stories about ancient Greece. I can't help but think of the myth of Theseus's ship. This was a vessel that, over thirty years of continuous service, had been completely rebuilt from bow to stern, from keel to mast. The Greek philosophers wondered: given all this work, was Theseus's boat the same ship that had originally set sail, or was it something else?

And I wondered: Was an Emirati military made up of so many non-Emiratis still an Emirati military? The whole arrangement was so different from that of the US military and the SEAL Teams. There we came together and fought for a set of ideals. Here we've been brought together to fight for money.

Whether this is an improvement, I can't yet say.

21

TIME TO HUNT

It takes two days to fully set up camp.

The small building against the northern wall now has running water to the shower and toilet, as well as a tiny washing machine that can take one change of clothes at a time. The two clamshells have AC, and each structure has its own function.

The northernmost one is our barracks, with six cots on either side and a wide corridor down the center. Malachi, Isaiah, Bruce, and I grab the extra cots and use them for personal shelving.

The second clamshell is our common room. It has chairs, a flat-screen TV, a coffee machine, and a four-foot-by-eight-foot table that François and I built from a sheet of plywood and other salvaged materials. Isaiah finds a metal pipe, which he secures between two HESCO barriers—our pull-up bar. This, plus a heavy metal wheel we use for Russian twists, makes up our gym.

Over the next several days, each of us accepts or gravitates toward certain roles. Malachi is obviously the officer in charge (OIC); Isaiah is his second. Every morning they exercise together, running around the interior perimeter of the entire Emirati base, which all told is about a mile long. I assume they talk about Khalil, the rest of us, the mission.

Despite Isaiah's status, more guys come to me than him for answers. If Bruce, our demolitions guy, needs detonators, he asks me (even though I have no idea where to get any). If François needs playing cards, he asks me (I get two decks from the Emiratis). If Tep wants a new notebook for surgical notes, he asks me (also from the Emiratis). More than one of the guys asks me for fine-tuned shooting advice on the range. I happily give it. Steven doesn't need anything. He's so twisted by some family drama back home that we decide to leave him be. My money is on an early departure, but we'll see. And then there's Jan. One morning, I notice that two of the trucks' gas tanks are half-empty. (Or half-full, depending on your perspective. I'm an optimist, so in civilian life, I'd call them half-full. But out here, where resources are always limited, and those limitations can be fatal, half-filled gas tanks are always half-empty.) Jan is our vehicles guy, and one of his jobs is to fill them whenever they drop below three-quarters of a tank. "Hey, Jan," I say, "make sure to fill those two up."

"Hmph," he says, barely looking up from his phone. "They have reserve tanks. And besides, the gauges are off. They have more than half a tank."

"Don't care. Please go top them off."

"No! Fuck that. They are fine!"

I'm shocked. I don't mind confrontation, but really?

Just as I'm about to respond, Malachi sweeps in from nowhere. "What did you say, Jan?"

"I said they're fine," Jan answers quietly.

Malachi raises his voice. "If Dirty tells you to do something, you fucking do it. D'accord?"

Jan stiffens to a half-assed attention. Malachi immediately launches into a profanity-laden ass-chewing, all in French. I only catch a few choice words. Jan takes it all silently, biting his lower lip like a child getting reprimanded.

When Malachi is finished, Jan scurries off and hops into one of the trucks. Yeah. Must be a Foreign Legion thing.

After that, whenever I need Jan to do something, I just yell at him and sprinkle in a few "fuck"s and he does it. Fine by me!

On the morning of day nine in-country, while Malachi and I sip coffee in the common room, Malachi says, "Dirty, let's go for a run."

I'm still getting over my plantar fasciitis, but I'm not going to say no. "All right. I'll find Isaiah."

Malachi waves his hand through the air. "No. Only you and me."

Just as we're about to take off, Isaiah trots up, ready to go. "Hold up, guys, I'll come with."

"No, brother," Malachi says with a kind smile. "It will be me and Dirty today."

Isaiah stops in his tracks, clearly offended, but it only lasts a moment. He smiles back and continues walking toward the common room, mumbling something about how he should probably take a day off anyway.

Malachi launches forward at a decent but not fast pace. I'm concerned for my foot, but after a few steps I can tell it'll be fine. I match his pace without much effort. He speeds up, I match. This continues for the first half mile. I kind of want to drop the hammer, but that would be poor manners, so I refrain.

He ups his pace once more, and this time my competitiveness overtakes me—and him. I get up on my toes, lean forward, and go. Malachi tries to hold pace, but then he waves the white flag. "OK, Dirty, OK! You can run," he says between heavy breaths. "I am old, let us go easy from here."

We slow to a jog. Now I get it. Just like when we sighted in, this is a test.

"Dirty, you are doing super good. You for sure are getting a bonus this month."

"Thanks, boss," I say.

We get back to camp just as François departs to pick up breakfast. Malachi heads straight for the shower, I head for the common room to grab another coffee. Isaiah asks how the run went. "Good," I say. He clearly wants to know more, but I say nothing.

That night as dinner wraps up, Malachi quietly tells Isaiah that I will be joining them on their morning runs. To Isaiah's credit, he doesn't protest. The runs quickly become competitive, and Isaiah and I engage in some camaraderie-building feats of strength. Isaiah can be annoying, but he's a good athlete, and we post our accomplishments on a whiteboard in the common room. Fastest lap around the base, quickest hundred burpees, max pull-ups before failure, and so on. One day I'll post a record, two days later he'll beat it. We work on the honor system, but I don't get the sense he's cheating. I'm certainly not. We both have fun with it.

One evening toward the end of week two, we gather in the common room and take seats in plastic chairs around the table. I don't know if the chairs are just cheap or are not designed to hold more than 150 pounds, but we've already broken four of them. François passes out dinner. Tonight it's rice, stewed vegetables, diced lamb in oil and herbs, pita bread. As far as military food goes, it's five star.

We eat in relative silence. Malachi and Isaiah finish first, and each lights a cigarette. I mop up a final mouthful of the vegetables with a wedge of pita. Malachi leans back in his chair. He only weighs a buck forty, so he's not going to come tumbling to the ground. I know by now that Malachi is rarely in a rush and is very respectful of personal space and time. Just this morning he was worried that I hadn't had my morning coffee. When I showed him the cup, which was hiding behind my cot, he said, "Ah, good. I am glad you have it. You have forty-one million minutes in life, Dirty, you should try to enjoy each one."

When he's satisfied that we're done eating, he stands. "Great job settling into camp, gentlemen. We are coming together. But as you know, we are not here for some sort of desert survival competition. We have come here to work." Everyone leans in. "As you have noticed, Major General Khalil has been meeting with me every day. I tell you nothing so far because there is nothing to tell. But today I have news. Khalil has identified the Emirati unit we will be training and going out with. He tells me these men are very eager now that they have the green light."

Isaiah interjects, "Khalil still needs to determine the ten *best* men, though."

Malachi nods. "Yes. But more important than our Emirati friends, we now have two targets on deck. One is an AQAP commander who lives super close to this base, and the other is a bomb maker." As we all know, AQAP stands for al-Qaeda in the Arabian Peninsula. "Forget about bomb maker for now, I just share with you because you deserve to know. First, we look at this AQAP man. So—all good?" Malachi asks, looking around the table.

"All good, boss," we say in unison.

Bruce raises his hand, Malachi nods in his direction. Bruce says, "We still getting better stuff than these M4s? Because we're not going after either of these guys with just those rifles."

This is not the first time this question has been asked, and until better rifles arrive, it won't be the last. And Bruce has his reasons to be concerned. One night over a game of cribbage, François told me how on their last job they got "supplied" with some rusty Chinese AK-47s, a couple of magazines each, a thousand rounds of ammunition, and a small block of C-4 explosives—and nothing else. The rumor was that their real shipment of higher-end stuff had been intercepted by another mercenary group in a bid to submarine the contract. They had to conduct a real mission with those weapons, and they just barely made it out. François even told me that this was the incident that had prompted Isaiah to tell Malachi, "We need Dirty."

"Tomorrow," Malachi says to Bruce. Then to all of us, "The next day at the latest. This time it is for real." Everyone's face says, "We'll believe it when we see it."

But what do you know, the next day we do see it. Right after our morning run, a twenty-foot shipping container arrives. Major General Khalil is there when Malachi opens its bay doors and hops inside. Crate after crate, military manna from heaven. There are MP7s, M4s with quad rails, EOTECHs, AN/PEQ-2s, night vision, bolt-action sniper rifles, spotting scopes and tripods, 40 mm grenade launchers, belt-fed machine guns, better armor, bricks of C-4, spools of detonation cord, blasting caps, initiators, suppressors—and enough ammo for all these systems to sustain multiple missions.

It's on.

It's time to hunt.

22

CAMEL CRUSHING IT!

THE NEXT MORNING, MALACHI ASKS ME TO STICK AROUND THE COMMON ROOM for the daily briefing with Isaiah and Major General Khalil. Seems I really am moving up the command structure.

Major General Khalil is accompanied by Faisal, an Emirati intelligence officer who's been hanging around our camp for the past couple of days. About my height, slightly thinner, strong looking. Unlike many of the other Emiratis, he chooses desert camouflage instead of the dishdasha. He rocks a permanent five o'clock shadow and has close-cropped jet-black hair. He leads the brief.

"Good morning, gentlemen," he says in perfect English. Sounds like he went to school in the UK. "We have determined the target's pattern of life. Every morning, after the first prayer, he sits outside with one of the two other inhabitants of his dwelling. Another inhabitant remains inside baking. Possibly his mother. At around ten in the morning he leaves by foot, spending most of his day at the mosque located three hundred meters southeast of his home. For as long as we have been observing him, he returns just after sundown."

"Thank you, Faisal," Malachi says. "We will discuss with the others. Major General, we will come up with an action plan and report it back to you ASAP."

Khalil dips his chin and stands. He approves. All the other men stand as well.

I remain seated and raise my hand.

"Yes, Dirty?" Malachi says. "Do you have some confusion?"

"Just a question, if I may?"

"Yes, of course," Malachi says.

"Faisal, thanks for the intel. But I'm curious about your sources?"

"Of course," Faisal says. "The main source is human intelligence."

"Main source?" I ask.

"The only source," he says. "We trust him thoroughly." Faisal is blunt, but he's not defensive. I appreciate that.

Every one of us knows that single-source intel is always suspect and, if acted on, can be very dangerous. "With respect," I say, "I'm sure your source is good, but for the type of intervention you're expecting—and thank you for the equipment, Major General—I would prefer dual source at least. And those two sources should not know each other."

Faisal sits and tents his fingers. I can't be sure, but I get the sense he agrees with me and brought up the same issue with Khalil. "We have been working to recruit another man near the target, but he has not been fully vetted. Regardless, we have also been watching the target."

"With the helicopter drone we see taking off now and then?" I ask.

"Correct, Mr. Dirty."

"Just Dirty."

Faisal smirks almost imperceptibly. "Correct, Dirty. The pilots operate out of this base. Their control room is next to the helipad."

Strange. On our daily runs, I haven't noticed any building of any kind near the helipad.

Malachi turns to Khalil. "Major General, is it possible for Dirty to look at the drone operation?"

Malachi, you're reading my mind.

Khalil and Faisal chat in hushed Arabic for a few moments, then Faisal says, "Yes, of course. Dirty, meet me at the helipad tonight at eight."

"Roger that. Thank you both," I say.

"Yes, thank you, gentlemen," Malachi says.

The meeting ends, the Emiratis leave. Malachi and Isaiah are both glad I asked these questions. "We don't want to roll into any bullshit like that last job," Isaiah says. "Good job, Dirt."

"Thanks, Isaiah."

I depart our camp for the helipad that night at 1945. It's already dark, and the base doesn't have much outdoor lighting. There's a full moon, slung low over the horizon, so I can see all right, but I don't want to get hit by some knucklehead driver. I click on the red light of my headlamp and sling it loosely around my neck.

The helipad is only a hundred meters to the south, so I reach it quickly. No one's there. I'm early, but I can't help thinking that maybe Khalil and Faisal were just giving lip service to my request in front of Malachi. But then, at 2000 sharp, a Hilux pulls up next to a rusted and abandoned shipping container propped on cement blocks. Faisal jumps from the driver's seat and waves his arm. "Over here, Dirty!"

I jog over.

"You ready?"

"Yep." I grab the pickup's door handle to hop in.

"No, Dirty. We're here already." He holds his hand out, indicating the old shipping container.

"Oh," I say. "I thought this thing was empty."

"No, no. Come. Follow me."

We walk around the far side to three wooden steps I had never noticed before.

"Shoes and light," Faisal says.

I remove my Speedcross shoes and turn off the headlamp. We step inside.

Like all drone control rooms, it's dark except for the cool glow of monitors and the tiny flickering lights of CPUs. It's also damn cold—a lot of AC for all the equipment as well as the three men hunched in front of screens.

The silhouette of one of these men twists toward Faisal. They speak in Arabic, then Faisal says, "Dirty, this is Nishad. He is our finest drone operator."

"Hello, Mr. Dirty." A thin hand hidden in shadow reaches toward me. I take it and we shake. He's not strong. He has the soft hands of a full-time computer nerd. "Nice to meet you, Nishad," I say.

"Dirty, Nishad is in charge of his three-man team," Faisal explains. "At the other stations there are Ibrahim and Oumar." I nod at two other men only a few feet away. "Nishad, please," Faisal says.

Nishad clears his throat. "Yes, Mr. Dirty. Come and look." He scoots his chair to the side. "This is our live picture," he says, indicating his screen. The main image shows a black-and-white infrared video feed. I can't make out any specific details, and no telltale heat signatures of people, dogs, vehicles, or anything else. Nishad points at Ibrahim and Oumar. "There is where we watch saved clips and log and compare data." One of the other men—maybe Oumar—is poring over an Excel spreadsheet. He grunts in our direction.

"Very impressive," I say. Of course, by US military standards it's not impressive at all. What is impressive is that this bare-bones drone operation has been here all along, hiding in plain sight.

We stand there awkwardly. Faisal breaks the silence. "OK, Dirty. Shall we go back to your base?" He thinks I'm satisfied and that's that.

"Actually, if it's all right with Nishad and his guys, could I hang around for a little while?"

Faisal and Nishad share a look. "Sure. Stay as long as you like," Faisal says.

"Thank you, Faisal," I say holding out my hand. Faisal shakes it and leaves. Nishad says something to the others and one of them hands me his plastic chair. "Shukran," I say, easing into it.

"You are welcome, Mr. Dirty," he replies.

Nishad says, "Mr. Dirty—"

I cut him off. "Guys, just call me Dirty. Mr. Dirty is my father."

All three men laugh, and Nishad continues. "All right, Dirty. So you know, we all speak English."

"Cool." I pull my chair closer to Nishad's monitor. "So it's just you three running the drones?"

"Drone. One drone," Nishad corrects. "We are one team. Night shift. The other team operates during the day. We live in the tent on the other side of the helipad."

"One drone? How do you manage twenty-four hours in the air?"

"We don't, unfortunately. Every day, it is grounded for refueling and repairs for about eight hours."

Not ideal. I can tell by the tone of his voice that he shares this opinion. "Got it. Why don't you live at the bigger camp on the other side of the base?"

"Ah, well. They have a better living condition, yes, but we prefer it here. Look at how we dress!" I hadn't noticed, but all three wear basketball shorts, T-shirts, and their indoor-only flip-flops. "No uniforms or dishdashas for us, Dirty! Yes, we prefer it here."

"I can relate. I don't like being near the flagpole either."

"A good way of putting it," Nishad says. "Come, let me show you what we have."

Nishad walks me through the image on his screen, pointing out a man I can barely see as he lights a cigarette. "He smokes quickly, and always smokes three cigarettes. Watch." Sure enough, over the next fifteen minutes or so, I make out

two more little flashes of a lighter or match as the man lights two more cigarettes. I'm tempted to ask if this is the AQAP commander, but I don't want to
step on anyone's toes—least of all Faisal's, who gives these guys orders—so for
now I just observe. After half an hour or so, Nishad asks if I want to go outside
to have a cigarette. I say yes. Drone work can be intensely boring, and cigarettes
certainly help break the monotony.

In the light of the moon, I'm a little shocked to see that Nishad looks like
he can't be more than fifteen or sixteen, but I don't say anything. I smoke one
of my Reds, and Nishad smokes some kind of Camel he calls "Camel Crush."

"It's a regular cigarette, but it has two flavors you can pick from," he explains,
since I'm obviously curious. "You push the blue button for blue, and the purple
one for purple. Then you light the cigarette like normal, and it tastes different.
That's how you Camel Crush it!"

"Weird. Can you crush both?"

"Yes, if you are crazy!"

We share a laugh. After a few minutes, I say, "Nishad, I have to ask. How old
are you?"

"Twenty-one."

"Really? You look so young."

He laughs again. "How old are you, Dirty?"

"Thirty-two."

"Really? You look so old!"

It's true. I look forty at least. "Too much time in the sun."

"I will stay young," Nishad says. "I will stay in the dark, with the drones."

"Good call." I drop my butt to the ground and mash it with my foot.
"Hey—is it all right if I come back tomorrow night?"

"Of course, Dirty. We look forward to it!"

"Thanks, Nishad."

I return to the incognito control room the next evening. Malachi has given
me a map showing the location of the AQAP commander's house according to
Faisal's source, and he's tasked me with asking Nishad if he can put eyes on this
location, to see if we can corroborate any of this man's movements and habits.

I knock on the control room door at 2000 sharp. Nishad opens it and invites
me in. They've already prepared a seat for me. I take it. The image Nishad has
from the live feed looks different from the one from the night before.

I point at the screen. "Same guy?"

"No. This morning we were asked to monitor a house very near to the base." He points to a low building that backs up to what looks like an orchard of some kind, maybe olive or lemon.

"Do you have a map in here where you can show me where this house is?" I could show him my map, but I don't know what Faisal told him about me and don't want to mess anything up by revealing something I shouldn't.

"Of course," Nishad says with no hint of secrecy. He pulls a piece of paper across his desk and shines a pen flashlight on it, his index finger pressing into the location.

It's a perfect match for the circle on my map. "Cool," I say.

"Mr. Faisal told me you are very interested in this area," he says.

Loud and clear. They know.

"Yes, we are."

"Good. Let us watch together."

And so we do. For the next two weeks, I sit with Nishad and his crew from 2000 to 0400, sleep for a few hours, run with Malachi and Isaiah, hang around camp, take an afternoon siesta, eat dinner, repeat. Nishad and I take smoke breaks—Nishad likes my American Marlboro Reds, I like the "blue" flavor of Camel Crush—and watch Mr. AQAP. He leads a boring-ass life. Smoke, eat, pray, sleep; smoke, eat, pray, sleep—but that's good. Boring is predictable. And predictable is deadly, or at least it will be for Mr. AQAP.

Faisal also pops by from time to time, relaying whatever news his humint source has gathered. With only a couple incidental discrepancies, our intel lines up. I report this to Malachi, he reports it to Khalil, it goes up the client's chain of command. We're satisfied. We now have our second source of intel.

All we're waiting on now is the green light.

23

TECH GUY

"Dirty! Wake up, man." It's Isaiah. He's standing over my cot, drenched in sweat. A new best lap is posted on the whiteboard nearby. Six minutes and nine seconds. Shit.

"What's up?" I ask groggily. The late nights with Nishad and his boys are sapping me.

"Malachi wants to see you in the common room."

"Roger that." I spring to my feet, slip on my shoes, throw on a shirt. I don't bother to brush my teeth or anything.

When I get to the common room, Malachi is pacing, arms crossed.

Fuck. Did I mess something up? "Hey, boss. You wanted to see me?"

He stops and spins on his heel. "Dirty, sorry to disturb you, brother. I know you have not gotten enough sleep."

"Just part of the job," I say.

Malachi waves his hand. "I just had a very upsetting conversation with the client in Abu Dhabi."

I stand there, rubbing the sleep out of my eyes. "About what?"

"You."

Double fuck.

"What about me?"

"He calls and says he received a call from Major General Khalil complaining that we have a tech guy on payroll, but that we never said we would bring a tech guy."

"But we don't have a tech guy. Just operators."

"This is what I tell him! But he insists. 'No. Khalil says you have a tech guy in the drone room. He is there every night. We never agreed for a tech guy.'"

"Oh, *that* tech guy." I'm embarrassed that it takes me a minute to catch on. Clearly I *do* need more sleep.

"Yes. Now you see."

"Yeah."

"I think Khalil, he does not understand. I tell him he is totally super crazy and he doesn't know what the fuck he is talking about, but he insists that you are not operator but some kind of sneaky nerd."

I laugh at that. "I'll stop going. Nishad and his guys are good. We can trust them."

"No, no. I like you being there. It is important. But still, we have to deal with this. I have an idea, but it is a favor I ask."

"No problem, boss. Name it."

He explains what he wants me to do. When he's finished, I give him a big smile. It's a clever idea.

"Let me go splash some water on my face and freshen up. I won't let you down, Malachi."

"I know. Thank you, Dirty."

Thirty minutes later, I grab my rifle and meet our team on the shooting range. It's everyone except for Malachi. Khalil and Faisal are already there, along with some of the Emirati soldiers we've begun training. All of them stand off to the side in the shade.

I look downrange. Tep is finishing setting up the targets, three postcard-size steel plates, against the HESCO barriers. Isaiah has already drawn the firing line in the dirt at about twenty-five meters. As Tep walks back, Isaiah gives a range brief. "Gentlemen. Today's drill is speed shooting from a standing position. Two rounds on each target, left to right, as fast as you can. Most points go to whoever can land all six rounds the quickest. Since Dirty is our resident shooting guru, he goes first. Dirty, I know you're short on sleep from the drone work, but you ready?"

I toe the line and plant my feet. "Yep."

"Tep, range ready?"

"The range is prepped and it is hot!" Tep booms.

I lock and load.

"Shooter ready?" Tep says.

"Yup!" I shout, my rifle at the high ready position. Deep breath. Hold it. Slow exhale…

"Standby. Three…two…one…BUST 'EM!"

I present to the first steel plate, obtain a sight picture, and squeeze off two rounds in immediate succession.

PING! PING!

I don't fight the recoil of the second round, but instead direct the energy to help swing my gun to the next target. Sight picture. Squeeze, break, squeeze.

PING! PING!

Again, using the second shot's recoil to guide my gun to the third target.

PING! PING!

The whole thing takes three seconds.

I step back, draw an even breath, and clear and safe my rifle. No one says a word. I'd love to look at Khalil, but that would be rude. I turn to Isaiah. "We good?"

"We're good, Dirt. Thanks for your time. See you at lunch."

"Let me know how you guys do," I say to the others. One thing good soldiers learn early is how not to laugh, even when laughing is the only thing you want to do.

"Will do, Dirt," Bruce growls. "We'll tell you who comes in second."

"Roger that."

I turn and walk back to our camp, smiling the whole way. When I get to the common room, Malachi is there smoking. "How did it go?"

I head to the coffee machine with a thumbs up. Malachi lets out a cackly belly laugh.

We don't hear anything else about our "tech guy" problem.

24

PARTNER FORCE

And just like that, we get the green light for Mr. AQAP.

But first we've got to bring our partner force up to speed.

We've been training a group of ten men off and on for a couple of weeks. "Training" is an extremely relative term, however. They were so far below our standards that rather than drill them on tactics or give them shooting instruction, Malachi started with basics: physical training. For about a week, he led them through a raft of exercises—a gauntlet of pull-ups, sprints, burpees, and low crawls—but most of them were so uncommitted that they low crawled right out of there. It was too difficult. It's been a source of tension for Malachi, and Khalil has been in his ear about it. This is not what Malachi expected of the Emiratis.

Malachi maintains that the upcoming raid is an opportunity for everyone to start over and get on the same page. Khalil fully expects his men to accompany us, and we fully expect to take them. As far as I'm concerned, it's bullshit—are we here to do a job or hold hands?—but it's nonnegotiable. It's part of the contract, in writing and everything.

Before we take the Emiratis outside the base for a real operation, though, Malachi is adamant that we put them through a hasty crawl-walk-run program. We will do a daytime run-through inside the base, then do a nighttime run-through inside the base, and then do a daytime dummy run off-base at a location nowhere near Mr. AQAP. If these go smoothly, we will conduct the real raid at night within the week. Khalil agrees to this approach.

Before we can initiate these exercises, we need to brief Khalil and our Emirati partner force's commander, a newly arrived twenty-four-year-old named Walid. Malachi starts the meeting, Khalil whispers quietly to Walid in Arabic.

Isaiah raises a hand. "Wait—Walid. Can you not speak English?"

Khalil says, "It's all right. All good. I'll translate."

"But you're not coming with us, right?" Isaiah asks Khalil.

"No, of course not. I am not an operator."

Tep makes a muffled sound on the other side of the room. He coughs right afterward, attempting to pass it off.

"It is all right, Isaiah," Malachi says. "It will work."

"OK," Isaiah says, obviously unconvinced.

Bruce, who's sitting next to me, whispers, "Fuck me, man."

"No thanks, brother," I say quietly. Luckily, no one hears us.

Malachi continues the brief. The dry run will be straightforward. We're the assault team, the Emiratis are support. If all goes as planned, they won't even need to leave their vehicles. The movement will go like this. Two mine-resistant ambush protected vehicles (MRAPs) driven by the Emiratis. Followed by two up-armored Land Cruisers, one with Tep, Bruce, Jan, and Steven, the other with me, François, Isaiah, and Malachi. Followed by a single MRAP, also Emirati. We bat around the idea of putting Jan in one MRAP and François in another as drivers, but Khalil and Walid demur. "Our guys are good drivers," Walid insists through Khalil. Both of our guys are also resistant—they don't want to get in a jam with a bunch of men they can't communicate with—so we scrap that idea.

During each exercise, we pretend we're doing the real job. That will go like this: At 0100, we will drive in formation to the "vehicle set point" and establish a cordon at a nearby intersection one kilometer from Mr. AQAP's house. MRAP One will block the eastern side of the intersection, while the Land Cruisers follow MRAP Two to the set point just north of the intersection. When we reach the set point, MRAP Two will stop while our Land Cruisers turn west down a narrow alleyway. MRAP Three will stay back at the intersection and block the western and southern roads. Doing all this will ensure that no other vehicles can sneak up on us.

We'll signal using procedure words, aka pro words. Through Khalil, Walid assures us he and his men will have no problems with this, despite the language barrier. Pro word "Alpha" signals the mission has begun. Isaiah will be on comms. He'll say the word and wait for each of the other vehicles to confirm by repeating it back. The MRAPs are not to move unless they hear pro word "Echo," meaning the mission is complete, or pro word "Break," meaning abort.

Once "Alpha" is confirmed, our two Land Cruisers will proceed down the alleyway. We'll drive two hundred meters and stop near the orchard that abuts Mr. AQAP's home. Pro word "Bravo," passed back and forth in the same way as before, confirms our position. The assault team—me, Malachi, Isaiah, Steven, Tep, and Bruce—will exit the vehicles. Jan and François will turn the Land Cruisers around and wait for us to get back. Once we're ready, pro word "Charlie" will be conveyed.

Hustle through the olive trees, enter the house quietly, do the job—one suppressed headshot on a slumbering Mr. AQAP—and leave. (Hopefully there's no wife or wives like with Osama bin Laden, hopefully Mom has her own room.) We confirm that we're back in our vehicles with pro word "Delta." Then we roll back down the alleyway and hang a right to the intersection, MRAP Two following us. Once we have visuals on the other MRAPs in the intersection, we give them the pro word "Echo" and convoy up and roll home.

Once this is all solid with the Emiratis, we go over a loss-of-comms plan and a few other contingencies. Mostly these contingencies rely on the pro word "Break." If the pro word can't be passed due to radio failure, a signal using both hands to break an imaginary stick will fill in, carrying the same meaning. If it's too dark, a rapid succession of three flashes from our infrared flashlights will also carry the same meaning.

If an abort is called for any reason, Walid is responsible for getting his guys back to base safely while we take care of ourselves. This is not the best contingency—in the SEAL Teams we could get bailed out by air support or helos putting down door-gunner cover fire—but it's what you get when you're an outfit like ours and in a country like Yemen. For myself, if I have to run home, I will. Mr. AQAP's house is only three kilometers away—I could do that in about fourteen minutes, even with a rifle and twenty-five pounds of gear.

The meeting ends. Walid and his men will return at 1600 for our on-base daytime rehearsal, then again at 0100 for the nighttime run-through. We'll do a dry run in town off-base the following day at 1015. Then, if all goes well, we'll roll out for real at 0100 the following night.

At 1600, Walid and his men come into our camp. No Khalil this time. Using hand signals, Walid's limited English, and Malachi's limited Arabic, we go over everything and load into our vehicles. It goes surprisingly well. We establish a few additional signals in case the radios fail. We break for dinner, get a little rack time, and they return at 0100. The nighttime practice maneuver also goes well, no one has any issues with night vision or comms. We break again, get some more sleep, and are all up by 0800.

Walid and his men roll into our camp at 0945 in their three MRAPs. We do last-minute radio checks and map studies and review the pro words with everyone, especially the Emirati drivers. At 1000, we roll out of the base for our final mock run.

Everything looks good as we move down the road. The convoy spacing is perfect, and the Emiratis are driving the massive MRAPs better than they were the day before. Twelve minutes later, we reach the dummy vehicle set point. Again, this is nowhere near Mr. AQAP, but it's still risky. We are in town, in military vehicles, obviously doing something. A few civilian lookie-loos here and there. One man in a tan suit sips tea half a block away, a cigarette in his mouth. A child runs down another street, away from the MRAPs.

MRAP One and MRAP Three take their positions. Jan, driving Land Cruiser One, and François, driving Land Cruiser Two, follow MRAP Two to the set point. Jan turns left down a narrow side street—the stand-in for the alleyway—and after a short distance comes to a stop. We do too.

Isaiah picks up the radio handset. "Alpha," he says into it.

No response.

"Alpha," he repeats.

Apparently the radios have shit the bed. Just like that, we've lost comms.

Isaiah spins to Malachi and me. "Boss?"

"It's OK. François, continue."

François flashes his high beams at Land Cruiser One. Steven and Tep crane their necks in the back seat of their vehicle, looking at us. Isaiah gives a thumbs up. Charlie Mike—continue mission. Jan starts down the street, a dirt path flanked on either side by squat cement buildings. We follow. After only fifty meters or so it passes another side street and then curves to the south. Still, we continue, going at a pretty good clip for such a narrow road.

Steven remains turned around in Land Cruiser One while he and Isaiah have a full-on discussion using SEAL Team charades. The gist is this: "Radios not working." "Roger that, we will complete the run-through." "What about the Emiratis?" "They are in position." "We need radios. Should we abort?"

That last question comes from Steven.

"They're wondering if we should abort, boss," Isaiah says. "They're nervous. I bet Bruce is having flashbacks to the last mission."

Just then, Land Cruiser One's taillights go cherry red. François mashes the brakes to avoid rear-ending it. A man has suddenly appeared in the alleyway about a hundred meters in front of Land Cruiser One. We can just make him out from our obstructed position. He's not a lookie-loo civilian. He's a soldier, an AK-47 slung across his chest. He's not in the high ready, he's just standing there, waiting.

Steven signs to Isaiah. "No go."

"OK, Isaiah," Malachi says. "Finished for today." He's calm, but clearly annoyed.

Isaiah nods at Steven, drawing an index finger across his throat. He then raises it and twirls it around, the universal sign for "Let's wrap it up and go home." This is not the "Break" signal—that would indicate a precarious situation in which all bets were off and we would just plow home without worrying about the Emiratis.

The upshot is the same, though: the practice run is off.

At the same moment, Jan and François put their respective Land Cruisers in reverse. This road is too narrow for a three-point turn of any kind. We'll just head back around the bend to the last street and turn there.

I'm farthest back in Land Cruiser Two, so I can see where we're going before anyone else. As soon as we clear the bend, I'm the first to see the intersection with the main road.

"Fuck me," I say. "Stop the car, François."

François slows to a stop.

"What is it, Dirty?" Malachi asks, turning in his seat. But now we all see it.

MRAP Two broke protocol and followed us. Its side-view mirrors are bent flush to the vehicle and its passenger side is scraping along the nearest building. The MRAP is too wide.

"MRAP Two is fucking stuck," I say.

"Mon Dieu," François says.

I twist all the way around and get on my knees in the back seat. I squint. "Wait," I say. "Jesus. The other two MRAPs are there too. I think they're all fucking stuck!"

Malachi lets out a drawn-out *pfffffft*, a very French expression that translates to equal parts "Fuck me," "Is this really happening?" and "Of course this is happening, this is the world." Disbelieving but indignant acceptance. God bless the French.

"What should we do, boss?" François asks.

Before he's even finished asking the question, I spot two men outside, both armed. One is in a second-floor window. Another in a street-level doorway.

"Boss," I say.

"I see them," Malachi says.

"We have three more in front of Jan's vehicle," François says calmly.

"Now we break," Malachi says.

"Roger that, boss," Isaiah says.

I pass the break signal to the MRAP behind us, but no one inside acknowledges. I pass it again, still no response.

While I'm doing this, Isaiah passes the signal to Steven, who's still spun around in his seat, watching intently for instructions. As soon as Isaiah makes the signal, Steven yells it out. Jan puts the lead vehicle in gear and takes off. The Emiratis are going to have to unfuck their vehicles and get back to base on their own.

François follows Jan in tight formation, riding fewer than five feet from his rear bumper. The armed man in the doorway jumps back as we pass him, then he runs into the street in our dusty wake, yelling something. Jan passes the point where we first stopped. After another twenty-five meters or so he brakes hard and yanks the Land Cruiser to the right, into an even narrower side street. Bruce must be giving Jan rock-star directions, because after just a few more quick turns, we're back on the main road.

We make it back to base safely. About forty-five minutes later, the Emiratis show up in their damaged MRAPs. Everyone is in one piece, but no one is happy.

25

ROLLING SOLO

WE TRY A DEBRIEF IN THE EMIRATI COMMON ROOM, BUT IT GOES OFF THE rails fast. Isaiah is livid that the radios broke. Malachi is livid that the MRAPs followed us. The Emiratis are livid that we didn't sufficiently explain what was going on. All of us are livid that they didn't follow the hand signals we agreed on and drilled at least half a dozen times. François and Jan are livid that they had to drive forward through a potential shooting gallery. Walid is livid that his MRAPs got stuck. Khalil is livid that this contract is not working out. I'm livid that this mission is patently less professional than it should be, not because of us but because of our "partner force."

Everyone leaves the debrief angry. Malachi hangs back to talk with Khalil. I'm sure he's trying to stroke his ego and do whatever he can to keep the contract going. While we're walking back to our base, I pull Isaiah aside. "If we're going to work with these guys, we need to train them. For real."

"I hear you, Dirty," he says. "We can put together some stuff tonight, come up with a schedule and get started tomorrow."

"I'm sorry, brother, you're not listening. We need real training with real facilities. A straight up six-month workup like in the Teams. These one-hour classes here and there on this little base aren't cutting it."

"Cool idea," he says dismissively as we walk into our compound.

"It's the only way this works," I say. Isaiah shrugs and heads to our common room. I head to my cot to think things over.

Malachi is back with us thirty minutes later. He calls us to the common room and says, "We still do the job. But now it is just us."

Bruce says, "Good." François says, "Bon." I say, "For the better." We all speak at once.

"For the most part, just us," Malachi clarifies. "We need to bring some Emiratis—two men, three at most—for observation and, how do you say? In case things go bad?"

"Plausible deniability," Isaiah says.

Malachi snaps his fingers. "Yes! This. Also, they need to see that we are doing what we have come here to do."

We agree.

So, how to go about it?

We go around the room, pitching ideas, and settle on two approaches. These are Bruce's way and my way.

Bruce's way is to go in at night, set off a loud explosion to breach Mr. AQAP's front door, but also to let everyone know we're there and that we are not to be fucked with. Bruce is a demolitions expert. It's what he knows and loves. While the compound burns, three of us move quickly inside, do the job, and then we all leave.

My way is diametrically opposite. "I was a lead breacher too," I say. "I can open any door between here and Damascus with a flathead screwdriver and a can of WD-40. No one will wake up. We hit AQAP while he's asleep, then we leave. No one will fuck with us because they won't even know we're there." To me, this was the main fault of Bruce's plan. Yes, local people would be scared, but they would also know something was going on. They could make calls. Men with guns could materialize out of nowhere. But most importantly, Bruce's explosion would wake our target, and he could run.

Sleeping targets don't run.

We have it out. In the end Malachi says, "We will do it Dirty's way."

"You're the boss," Bruce says. He stands and walks out of the common room, clearly frustrated. The meeting ends.

In fact, Bruce is so frustrated that the next morning he helos out of Yemen. A few days later, he'll be back in Texas or wherever he lives, ironing his Canadian tuxedo or writing his next memoir. Like the rest of us, he's been here over two months. Aside from the blowup last night, he's been a good teammate. He'll still get paid. Probably $50,000, maybe more. Not bad. Let him count his money.

With Bruce gone, we are now seven.

Later that morning, after our daily run, we block out the mission. We'll load into the Land Cruisers at 0130 that night and drive to our set point, two kilometers from base. The lead car will have François, Tep, Steven, and one Emirati. The other will have Malachi, Jan, Isaiah, me, and Walid. We will approach the house through the orchard on foot. Mr. AQAP's house is surrounded by an eight-foot wall, which we'll scale with a telescoping ladder. We'll drop the ladder to the other side so we can use it to get out. We'll move silently through the courtyard, take care of Mr. AQAP, and leave.

Easy day.

I take a nap that afternoon, but as soon as it's dark I don't bother sleeping. I visit Nishad and the guys at drone HQ to put some eyes on Mr. AQAP. There he is, plain as day. He goes to bed around 2230. I can see his heat signature. He doesn't move—he's sleeping. He's alone. No wife, no girlfriend, not even a dog. I say good night to Nishad, leave him an unopened pack of Reds, and head back to our little barracks. I throw new batteries in my helmet-mounted night vision and my rifle's EOTECH optic. I place my helmet just outside the tent at 0000 so the night vision can acclimatize. It always takes a little while for its internal components to transition from the cold of air-conditioning to the nighttime heat of the Arabian Peninsula.

Everyone's dressed in whatever he's comfortable with. I'm in my black Crye Precision pants and a black long-sleeved Lululemon Metal Vent Tech shirt. I tape up my Salomons using a roll of rigger's tape. François asks what I'm doing. "A SEAL buddy in Iraq taught me to tape my shoelaces so I don't trip over them and get killed."

"But those don't have shoelaces."

"Doesn't matter to me. Shit breaks sometimes, and single points of failure are a no go as far as I'm concerned."

I don't think François fully gets "single points of failure," but he still asks for the tape to cover his own laces.

At 0100 we do a comms check and line up near the Land Cruisers. Khalil arrives with Walid and the other Emirati who will be accompanying us.

As Malachi is doing a head count, his phone rings. He pulls it out and looks at the screen. He frowns a little and holds up his index finger. He swipes the phone and walks away. "Hello?" we hear him say. Then he moves out of earshot around a nearby HESCO barrier.

We wait in silence. We hear his raised voice every now and then but can't make out any words.

Except for a very loud "Merde!" about five minutes later. He emerges from the other side of the HESCO. He walks toward us, spins, paces ten feet or so, spins again, paces toward us, repeats. His hands are balled into fists, which he holds at his sides. I can't remember the last time I saw someone literally pace in anger.

He approaches the nearest Land Cruiser and plants his hands on its hood. Everyone presses closer, including the Emiratis. "Guys," Malachi says, not looking at any of us, "the man I just spoke to, he is very important." He shares a quick, knowing glance with Khalil. "I am sorry. I fight for us. But the op is off tonight and for the near future. I don't know why. Stand down. Go to sleep. Tomorrow we will move on to target two."

He draws a deep breath.

"The bomb maker."

26

CAMP YEMEN

NOT JUST ANY BOMB MAKER, IT TURNS OUT.

During our meeting the following morning, Isaiah announces, "Our target is none other than the bomb maker behind the USS *Cole* attack!"

This was the infamous 2012 suicide bombing of a US Navy destroyer that killed twelve sailors and wounded thirty-seven others. Apparently Isaiah is stoked to be going after this guy, but we've been here for two months, and at this point, none of the rest of us really care. We just want to work. A target is a target is a target.

Isaiah sets his enthusiasm aside and brings us up to speed. "According to Emirati intelligence, the bomb maker is in a village four hundred kilometers to the north, near the Saudi border. Since we're not officially in Yemen, gentlemen, moving this far from our current home would put us in a tricky spot. Thankfully, there's a ragtag air base about twenty-five kilometers from the bomb maker's village. Currently this base is manned by a small detachment of Emiratis and some Senegalese commandos. That's where we're headed."

"When?" Tep asks.

Malachi answers. "Next week. First, I would like for Dirty to see if he can get his drone friends to look at our bomb maker."

"You got it, Malachi," I say.

That evening I rejoin Nishad, Ibrahim, and Oumar in the drone room. For the next week, we watch the bomb maker. I answer questions about the United States, they tell me about living in the UAE. I ask Nishad where he learned English. "Some in school, but mostly playing PlayStation." Of course. I go through a carton of Reds, handed out not as bribes but as tokens of appreciation.

By day eight, a picture emerges. The bomb maker sleeps in a two-story compound just west of the main highway. He shares the compound with five other men. No women, no kids. Every morning he leaves, walks about eight hundred meters south, stops at his welding shop. There he stays until 1500, when he crosses the main highway to find a spot in front of a favorite restaurant. He has dinner, drinks tea or coffee, and smokes. At dusk, he returns to the compound. He is asleep in bed most nights by 2300.

The plan is to fly north and stage out of the air base. We'll only stay for two, three nights tops. There is a lot of AQAP activity in the area, so the less time we spend there, the better. As soon as the job is done, we'll hop on a helo back to our current position.

We fly out the next morning. It's all of us, the Emirati helicopter crew, Walid, and Faisal. As with the aborted smaller mission to get Mr. AQAP, it's essential we always have Emirati officers with us. They need to be there as our nominal leaders, even though we're the ones in charge. It also keeps us in the clear with the whole "advise and assist" thing. Most important, though, it gives us some small measure of insurance. Double crosses, political intrigue, and getting used as a pawn in the larger chess game of geopolitics and war are constant concerns in the mercenary trade. The simple fact is that the client is less likely to hang us out during a mission if its own people are also along for the ride.

The flight crew we get this day is exceptionally skilled. The pilot and co-pilot keep our Chinook low, hugging the dunes at high speed. I knock out for forty-five minutes of sleep while we hurtle over the desert.

About ninety minutes later, we land at the air base. It's littered with the carcasses of ancient planes and the husks of derelict buildings. It smells like iron and diesel. Part of the base is being used by the aforementioned mercenary force from Senegal. I don't get a good look at them, but from what I can see, they are all short, lean, and bald.

We hop out and keep our distance. As Isaiah said, we're not officially in Yemen, we don't exist. No reason to contradict that by chumming around with the Senegalese or anyone else.

Faisal guides us to a small outbuilding far from the main gate. It has a working toilet and a sink. Next to the building is an old shipping container whose top has been cut off for some reason. It reminds me of an open can of sardines. We set up shop here. This is where we'll bed down too. No rain in the forecast, just like every day in Yemen.

While we're organizing our gear, a base worker comes around with a push-cart full of water bottles. He looks all of fourteen. I take two large bottles and give him a curt nod. Everyone else takes two or three bottles for himself. Once we're settled, we get out the maps and do a walk-through. The plan is simple. That afternoon, just before dusk, we'll confirm with the drone guys down south that Mr. Bomb is in place. Then we'll head out in two indigenous unarmored vehicles. We'll keep our distance from each other, like we're two cars traveling in the same direction but not together. The trip will take about twenty minutes. We'll park one vehicle on the side of the road while the other continues a little farther on, turns around, and stops. I'll be in the first vehicle.

From here, we'll have eyes on the restaurant, about seventy-five meters away. As soon as Mr. Bomb is confirmed, I'll take the shot from the back seat with my M4. Headshot, an easy target for me at that distance. Then we'll scream back to base, hop on the Chinook, and haul ass back south before AQAP can respond.

At 1715 we load into a Kia Sportage and a Toyota Hilux. I'm in the Kia, François driving. We follow the Hilux to the main gate, pull to a stop. I'm staring at the seat in front of me, visually running through the mission like I always do, and don't realize that it's taking longer than it should to get off-base. I look up.

The Senegalese soldiers manning the gate and the two towers flanking it are yelling and pointing their rifles at something outside the base.

Faisal, Malachi, Isaiah, and I jump out of the Kia and approach the gate on foot. We take turns peering through a crack under one of the hinges. Waiting in the road just outside are twenty-five men and two Toyota Hilux pickups adorned with the black-and-white Islamic State flag. Heavy machine guns are mounted in the bed of each truck, their barrels pointed directly at the base. This is my first time seeing AQAP up close and personal. With their chest rigs over their dishdashas and their traditional headwear, they look a lot like the Taliban in Afghanistan.

We approach the nearest guard tower. Speaking French, which thanks to François I now kind of understand, Malachi asks one of the Senegalese merce-naries to come down. The man is in his fifties, but he slips down the ladder like a twenty-year-old. The rough translation of their conversation goes like this:

Malachi: "Have you ever seen AQAP assemble like this?"

Senegalese: "No, sir, I haven't."

Malachi: "Do you know why they're there?"

Senegalese: "We can't be sure, sir. They come around from time to time. We have an agreement not to shoot at each other unless we are outside the gates."

Malachi: "How'd you manage that arrangement?"

Senegalese: "I don't know, sir. I didn't negotiate the terms. But there is a rumor. I think they are here because they know you are here."

Malachi thanks the man, turns toward us, spits on the ground. "Fuck," he says in English. The Senegalese soldier scampers back up the ladder. "They're here because of us," Malachi says.

Isaiah says, "So no going out tonight?"

"Correct," Faisal says. "We won't leave the base tonight, or any night, as long as they know we're here."

"Do you think they know *why* we're here?" I ask. "Because if they do, Mr. Bomb is going to be long gone right about now."

"Fuck," Malachi repeats.

We load into the vehicles and make our way back to our trailer in silence. As soon as we're there, I get on the satellite phone with Nishad. I tell him to watch Mr. Bomb like a hawk. Any deviation from his pattern, I want to know it, ASAP. Any indication that he might know he is in danger. Anything. Nishad is happy to comply. "Dirty, if he farts, I will call you."

"You do that, Nishad."

That night, while we're having a shitty meal around a paltry fire, we try to figure out how AQAP learned we're here. The only logical explanation is that someone on the base told them. But who? Not any of us. Not Faisal or Walid. Not the Senegalese. Who?

François slaps his forehead. "C'etait le jeune qui nous a filé l'eau!"

"Of course," Malachi says.

"What was that?" Steven asks.

"It was the water guy," I say.

"It must be," Malachi says. "Gentlemen, I am sorry. That is on me. I have to be more careful."

"We all do, boss," François says.

Some of the most dangerous people in these settings are the invisible ones you take for granted. It was true when I was in the Teams, and it's even more true here. The water kid could be an AQAP spy, but the more likely explanation is that he is just a hustler. People in these far corners of the world live desperate, hour-by-hour lives. Often it doesn't take more than an extra twenty dollars per week to convince people not merely to inform, but to switch sides. You'd see it in Afghanistan all the time. One week you might be having tea with a guy, the next week you might be shooting at each other. And the only reason that guy went from one side to the other was a few extra dollars. The rest meant nothing. It was probably no different for our water carrier.

We sit in silence for a little while. Isaiah gets up, wanders to the trailer, returns. He passes out a Mounds candy bar to each of us. "Where did you get these?" I ask.

"Secret stash."

I tear mine open and sink my teeth into it. I know they're not the most popular candy, but I love Mounds. Super sweet, moist on the inside with all that coconut. Maybe that sounds gross, but whatever.

We finish our dessert in silence. I go back to the trailer and check the sat phone. No news from Nishad, which is good news. I look at some offline maps Nishad loaded onto a tablet, scanning the area all around us. I pinch and zoom and scroll. Maybe there's another way. Maybe.

The rest of the guys filter into the trailer and get into their bedrolls. I brush my teeth, spit the white paste in the dirt, and join them. A couple guys say good night.

As we're drifting off, François says, "Guys! We are very lucky."

"Why's that?" Isaiah asks.

"Look at this hotel. It is very nice!" We all crane our heads in his direction. What's he talking about?

He points directly up at the sky. "This hotel has many, many stars. Look!"

We all look to the heavens. Sure enough, it is full of white pinpricks. Extremely full. There is no moon. The base is dark. The Milky Way is a bright slash, diving into one edge of the horizon. It's beautiful.

François starts laughing, and then everyone else laughs too. Even Faisal and Walid crack up.

Camp Yemen. A million stars and counting.

27

FALSE EXTRACT

I WAKE UP EARLY THE NEXT MORNING. I KEPT THE SAT PHONE NEXT TO ME ALL night. I check it. Still nothing. I call Nishad. "No changes, Dirty. He is as before."

"Thank you, Nishad."

"You are most welcome."

I hang up and grab a tablet. I look at the maps again. Maybe. I get out of bed. Tep, Jan, and Steven are still asleep. Keeping the phone and the tablet, I tiptoe around them and head out of the trailer.

I spot Malachi and Isaiah. They're smoking. I walk over to them. "Morning," we say.

Isaiah offers me a cigarette. I take it. Malachi lights it with his Zippo. "You know, I think we can still do this," I say.

"How, Dirty?" Malachi asks.

"False extract. If everyone on the base thinks we're gone, then AQAP thinks we're gone, and the area around the base lightens up."

"Yeah," Isaiah says slowly. "Yeah, that could work."

Malachi takes a long drag and holds it in. "Tell me how you see it, Dirty." Smoke drifts out of his mouth while he speaks. With the beard and the sharp features, he looks like some kind of Israeli dragon.

"So tonight, a few hours after the sun goes down, we load into the helo, headlamps on and everything. Just as it's dusting off, we jump back out, headlamps off, and hop in the two vehicles. Not sure if you noticed it, but there's a small back gate in the southwest corner of the base. And next to that on the inside of the base is a small depression, surrounded on three sides by double and triple HESCO barriers. We should be able to hide there until we roll out the next day to do the hit."

Isaiah raises his hand. "Devil's advocate?"

"Always. Shoot."

"OK. Number one is vehicles. We can keep the headlights off, but the interior lights are trickier to deal with. We can turn off the dome lights, but I think the Kia for sure has footwell lighting."

"We pull the fuses. And we keep them pulled until we're well off-base during the mission. Once we're a few clicks away we can add them back for lights on the road."

"OK," Isaiah says, satisfied. "Number two. I've walked the base and seen that depression. You're right that it's a good hiding place, but there's always one Senegalese guard posted there."

"That's dicier for sure. We're going to have to accept that risk. Maybe Faisal can get him replaced with an Emirati he trusts. Or maybe we can give the guard some of those Mounds. You got any left in that secret stash?"

"Sure do."

"Good. Keep them. Anything else?"

"Don't think so."

"Good. Now, hanging out there all day will suck—there's no shade and no toilets and we won't be able to move—but we're big boys and we can handle that."

"Agreed," Malachi says. "I like this plan, Dirty. But if we do it, and we stage there, how do we get to the set point to do the job?"

"Let me show you." I jam what's left of my cigarette between my teeth Clint Eastwood style and hold out the tablet. They lean over it. "There are small dirt roads here and here"—I indicate them with my finger—"that will take us here." I point to another spot. "And from that point we have an open avenue to hit him at the restaurant. I've checked and double-checked. I can have Nishad proof it too, even look at it from a few different approaches. We'll have to be out there a little longer to do some off-roading—and that's a risk we shouldn't discount—but it's very doable."

"I like it, Dirty," Malachi says.

"Me too, Dirt," Isaiah says. "Good work."

"Thanks." I lower the tablet and remove the cigarette from my mouth, flicking it away. Just then, François, Walid, and Faisal round a corner. Walid has a large pot, and François is carrying a bundle of something. "I found pasta!" he exclaims. "And some sheep butter and milk and a package of salt. I'm going to make us some good food before we leave!"

"Fantastic, François!" Malachi exclaims. The three men continue to the trailer. As soon as they're gone, I say, "So what do you think, boss?"

"I have to pitch it to the Emiratis, but I think we do it."

"Great."

Malachi breaks from us to grab Faisal and Walid. The three of them walk from the trailer a short distance, deep in conversation. Nodding, smiles, a firm handshake. Faisal steps aside to place a call on the sat phone. Walid disappears into the bigger part of the base. Malachi lights another cigarette.

A few moments later, Faisal hangs up and returns to Malachi. More nods, another handshake. Malachi claps his hands in excitement and walks toward the trailer. He shoots me a thumbs up, a big grin on his face.

"Gentlemen! Gentlemen!" he calls. "Come here. I have great news." We gather around. "We are Charlie Mike."

That evening—after we've all packed up, after Jan has pulled the vehicles' fuses, after I've double-checked our target's daily movements with Nishad—François dishes out a delicious camp meal of al dente pasta boiled in milk. It's obvious from his enthusiasm that he loves to cook—and to eat. Like a good Frenchman. He and Walid also scrounged a small block of cheese from somewhere. The guys ask if Isaiah has any more Mounds, but he waves them off. "Saving those," he says.

The helo arrives at 2100. We drive to the landing zone and get out. We keep the engines running. No one will hear them over the din of the Chinook. All our headlamps are on, we trot over to the chopper. We clamber on board. We turn off our headlamps, the pilot turns off all but the most essential lights. The helo lifts a foot or two off the ground. Malachi jumps first. He steps to the side and waves his hand frantically. "Allez, allez, allez!" he calls.

We jump out and run as fast as we can to the vehicles. We tumble inside. It's like they're a couple of clown cars, but in reverse. Jan drives one, François the other. We scoot over to the southwest corner of the base, a short drive, as the Chinook lifts a hundred feet into the sky, turns south, and punches it. So far none of the Senegalese have seen us.

We reach the back gate quickly. We get out and stay low. A white search-light pops on and shines down from the guard tower. Malachi says something quickly in French and the light shuts off. We hear the Senegalese mercenary climb down the ladder. Malachi waits for him at the bottom. They talk quietly in French. The conversation stops, Malachi calls Isaiah.

"Isaiah, give this nice man the candy," Malachi says.

Isaiah reaches into a pocket and pulls out three Mounds bars. The man's pearl-white teeth cut a smile through the dark. More French, sounds good. Our Senegalese friend won't be a problem.

We bed down for the night and don't talk. The stars are even better than the night before.

The next day is extremely uneventful. We continue not to talk, piss in a far corner, smoke. It's hot, and there is no relief from the sun. At one point, I tent a shirt over me with my rifle. The shade is hot too, but not as hot as the sun. I feel like a Bedouin, like Lawrence of Arabia. All that's missing is Omar Sharif and some camels.

While I sit there, I think about the mission over and over again, visualizing it, running it. I check the map on the tablet, check it again. Check it again. I see everything going well and try to anticipate how things could go wrong.

That afternoon, as the sun finally sets, a triangle of shade forms along the wall closest to the back gate. We huddle up. Malachi yields to me for the final walk-through.

I sketch a map in the dirt of the area closest to the target—first we have to get there, which will take close to half an hour, and there's no need to show anyone who isn't driving these directions.

I mark three turns. The first, turning from south to east, I mark with a bottle cap. We'll drive along this road for a short distance, then turn north. I mark this with the pinched butt of a Red. We take this road for a little longer. At one point of interest, I place a live 5.56 round on its end. We continue north on that road for a little while, then turn a third time, at a place marked with an unsmoked Red. Finally, at turn four, which heads back to base, I place a black BIC lighter.

"All right, the markers have meaning. Bottle cap, here—finish your water so your hands are free. Cigarette butt, here—no more smoking. If you've got 'em, put 'em out. François, our car stops at the ammo round, here. Jan, you continue down the road. Don't stop, just slow up a little. Time on target is eight seconds. Anything more than that and we'll draw too much attention. It's a small window, but Mr. Bomb has been there every night at this time for three weeks. If he doesn't show, it's just bad luck and we return to base. If he does show—and he will—I take care of business from the back seat, as originally planned. Once that's done, we take off. When we hit this unsmoked cigarette—congrats, get out a smoke. And then when we get here, to the lighter, smoke up! We're headed home."

"Good job, Dirty," Malachi says. "Everyone, finish getting ready. We leave in five."

Once again I tape up my shoes and put fresh batteries in my night vision and EOTECH optic, and I make sure I have a couple of spare batteries too. I go around and make sure everyone has his passport on him in a plastic bag. On some missions you want to be "nonattributable," but if something goes wrong and we have to boogie, we do not want to get caught in this country. We have to do whatever is necessary to get back to the base down south or to the Saudi border, which is very close. And if you're going to make an emergency cross into Saudi, you'll need your passport.

We're ready.

We load into the vehicles at 1715. The engines are running. Our Senegalese friend up above ignores us, quite happily. It's amazing what a little chocolate can do.

Just before we leave, Malachi takes a call. He steps away for a few minutes. We aren't actively eavesdropping, but everyone suddenly hears him bark, "What the fuck! Are you serious?"

Malachi hangs up, his face contorted by anger and confusion. He comes to my side of the vehicle, props his arms on the door where the window is rolled down, and looks straight at me. "I am sorry. No operation tonight."

A chorus of "What?" and "This is bullshit" and "Merde" bounce around the inside of the car.

"Again?" I ask.

"Oui, Dirty. Again."

28

TERMINATED

THE CONSTANT SPINNING UP AND SPINNING DOWN HAS FINALLY TAKEN ITS
toll. We're so drained that standing watch that night is almost impossible, and
besides that, it doesn't seem very urgent. The Chinook returns the next morning, we get on board. By lunch, we're back at the base down south.

The following week, Isaiah and I accompany Malachi to the helipad. He's
headed to Abu Dhabi to take some meetings and do what he can to keep the
contract alive—and also to try to figure out why both missions got canceled
at the eleventh hour. We all agree—even Khalil agrees—this is not what we
should be getting paid to do.

While we're standing there, Malachi sends Isaiah back to camp. He wants
to speak to me alone. Isaiah isn't happy about it, but there's nothing he can do.

Malachi takes me by the arm and guides me to one side of the helipad.
"Dirty, I know Isaiah is number two, but all the men follow you. It is clear now
that you are the leader after me. Keep up the good work and keep things cool in
the camp while I am away."

"No problem, Malachi."

"I will be gone three, maybe four days. Remember. Cool."

"No problem at all."

Malachi is gone for more than a week.

During this time, we keep doing what we're doing. François and I play a
lot of *Candy Crush* and cribbage. Tep reads his Bible four or five hours a day.
Steven broods. Jan smokes. We take turns shooting on the range. Isaiah and I
work out.

I can tell Isaiah isn't happy about the effective change of command, but to
his credit, he doesn't complain. I didn't do this intentionally, it just happened. If

anything, I feel like he and I have just grown closer over these last few months. That's to his credit too.

While Malachi is away, I also spend a lot of time in the drone room with Nishad and his guys.

We watch Mr. AQAP, who has continued going about his life, happy as a clam. Still follows the same daily pattern, still has the same habits, still lives only a few clicks from base. One evening, while Nishad and I are smoking outside the drone trailer, I say, "You know, we could still get this guy. I could run outside the wire by myself and fucking do it."

"You should, Dirty."

"I'll run it by Isaiah and Malachi."

He pushes the purple side of a Camel Crush and lights another cigarette. "Honestly, I do not know why they have not asked you to do this already."

Neither do I.

That night, I discuss the idea with Isaiah. We both know that SEAL Teams do small operations all the time. A unit of three or four men equals speed, and speed equals security. I ask Isaiah: Why are we playacting like a larger Team? For the benefit of the Emiratis, our client, even Malachi? None of them seem to care. The fact is that we *aren't* a SEAL Team, or any other proper special forces unit. We don't have air support, we barely have a drone crew, we can't fly anywhere on a moment's notice, we don't have medevac, we don't have dogs, we don't have artillery. "Instead of showing Khalil and his guys what a larger Team can do, let's show them what just you and me and Tep can do. It would be a fucking cakewalk."

And, again to his credit, Isaiah agrees. "Let's call Malachi." He grabs his phone and dials. "Hey, boss. Dirt has a notion." He puts the phone on speaker.

"Hey, boss."

"Hello," Malachi says. "What's up?"

"Dirty wants to hit the first target. Three of us, one Emirati for observation and safety, all in one vehicle. In and out."

"And we earn some of this money the client's bleeding," I add.

"Dirty, brother, I know you can do this. I know you want to. But we cannot move. I don't know why it is like this, but it is. I try to change it. This is why I am in Abu Dhabi for so long. I am trying to keep the client happy." The sound of him lighting a cigarette. A long pull, an exhale.

"But this can help keep the client happy, right?" I ask.

"In theory, yes."

"I *want* to do this, Malachi!"

"I hear you, brother. But please, Dirty, listen to me. Do not go and do this. If you do this, we are fucked and the contract will be canceled. They will never hire us again."

"I would never do it without your OK, boss," I say, deflated. "I just think it's crazy. We've been here for months, Mr. AQAP is a stone's throw away, these guys have spent a million bucks on us easy—and for what?"

"I understand. But this is the job too. It is just like in the military, but sometimes worse. The waiting, I mean."

"Thanks for hearing us out, Malachi," Isaiah says. "Dirty will get over it. Won't you, Dirt?"

"Yeah, I'll be fine."

We say goodbye and hang up. Isaiah claps me on the shoulder. "It was worth a try."

I guess.

The next day, I start planning the trip home. I'll spend a night in Abu Dhabi, get my left luggage from the hotel, maybe spend a few days in Amsterdam or Frankfurt or Brussels before flying home. Have some fun before reentry.

We're all together in the common room that evening. It's after dinner. Another feast of hummus, lamb, and rice. Good food, but man I'm tired of it. Tep is reading his Bible in one corner, Isaiah and I are tag-teaming the *New York Times* crossword on a tablet. I'm fantasizing about nachos, french fries, cheeseburgers, a fucking apple.

Zip-snapsnap-zip! The supersonic cracking of bullets flying over us.

Zip-zip-zip. SNAP!

We move outside for better situational awareness. Just as we exit—*BOOM!* It comes from outside the base. The ground shakes.

"Jock up!" Isaiah shouts, immediately taking charge.

We run to our barracks tent and grab our weapons, night vision, and body armor. As soon as we come back outside, our night vision fogs up as it goes from the air-conditioning to the outdoors. Fuck! By now we're aware of this problem. I should have built a little hutch right outside our tent so it was always acclimatized.

Whatever, we have to deal with it.

While I'm fumbling with my night vision, Isaiah steps forward. "François, take your pig and get up on the HESCO barrier to cover west."

The "pig" is François's belt-fed 7.62 machine gun. He hands it to me and climbs up the HESCO wall, then I pass it to him. I climb up and get prone next to him, facing south.

While I'm climbing up, Isaiah orders, "Jan, you do the same on the other side and—" *BOOM!* Another explosion, this time louder—or closer.

Must be closer since my entire body briefly lifts off the top of the HESCO.

"Hold to the north, Jan!" Isaiah barks.

More supersonic snaps overhead.

"François, get fucking low!" I yell. Just as François burrows himself as deep as he can on top of the wall, a symphony of rifles, machine guns, and grenade launchers erupts in the near distance. One of the Colombian guard towers on the southern wall is unloading on something outside the wire to the south.

BOOM! Another explosion, more bullets snapping all around.

"Tep, double up with François. Steven, you're with Jan! Dirty, down here with me."

I hop to the ground while Tep climbs up.

"One sec," Isaiah says before running into the common room. He emerges with two radios, tosses one up to Tep. They do a quick radio check.

BOOM! Another explosion, this time farther away.

"All right, gents, listen up!" Isaiah yells loud enough for everyone to hear. "Dirty, you speak Spanish, we're going to see what the fuck is going on. Tep has comms, he will relay anything we learn. Roger?"

The four men on the HESCO walls sound off: "Roger!"

"Let's roll," he says to me. As we jump in a Hilux, I can't help but be impressed. Isaiah is killing it. His mission planning and day-to-day leadership aren't as good as mine, but his in-the-shit, figure-it-the-fuck-out-right-now game is on point. I'm glad he's running things.

He starts the truck, we peel toward the southern guard tower. As we're driving, he says, "Dirty, what do you think?"

"I think—"

BOOM! Another explosion. The closest so far. A plume of fire rises in the sky to the west, just outside the main gate.

"I think that's fucking close, that's what I think. I also think vehicle-borne IEDs are blowing up the checkpoints leading to the main gate."

"That's what I think too. Let's find out what we can at the guard tower. If worst comes to worst and a VBIED blows open the main gate, we get back to camp and fight with the boys."

Isaiah brings the truck to a stop and we get out. Several Emiratis huddle around the base of the guard tower, including Khalil. We try to talk to him but it's useless. Too much going on.

We look up. The Colombians are four abreast at the top of the tower, unloading a stockpile of munitions. Either there's a massive swarm of fighters attacking the base, or these guys can't aim for shit.

Isaiah taps my shoulder. He points to the guard tower ladder, then points at me, then at himself, and then makes a V with his index and middle finger and points at his eyes.

I nod. We clamber to the top and survey the landscape around us. I can't believe it.

There's nothing.

Just an open field with a couple of bodies in it. Also, there's a lone boulder sitting dead center in the field about eight hundred meters away. The Colombians are pelting it relentlessly.

Isaiah and I are standing on four inches of spent brass at the back of the tower platform. The Colombians have no idea we're there. I lean forward, one of them catches me in his periphery. He spins around.

"Qué tal?" I yell.

"Detrás de la roca!" he explains. "Uno más!" He continues firing.

"Solo uno?"

"Sí, sí, sí!"

"Ahhh," I say. I turn to Isaiah. It's too loud to talk, so we descend, Isaiah leading the way. "What'd he say?" he asks as soon as we hit the ground.

"Dude up there says there's one more behind the rock."

"Jesus. Just one?"

"Just one."

We head back to camp and tell the guys to stay vigilant, but that everything is fine. "They're trying to kill a rock," Isaiah says. I laugh. No one gets it, so I explain.

As we're talking, an Apache attack helicopter crosses overhead from the north, no more than a thousand feet off the deck. It banks hard to the east, then turns back west, gaining altitude along the way. Then the nose pitches downward and its 30 mm cannon roars to life. It continues east, turns, and makes another pass. This time the cannons only let out a short roar. The Apache then turns again and is gone as quickly as it arrived.

After that, things go quiet and we head back to our common room. Isaiah orders us to leave our night vision outside, just in case. Good call.

Not that it matters. The next day, our contract is terminated. After three long, strange months, we're all headed home.

29

HANK AND KERRY

I don't bother with a European vacation. Before leaving Abu Dhabi, I check in with Rivera at SEAL Team 17 to make sure my flex-drill weekends aren't getting too backed up. They're not. I fly to Washington, DC, to spend time with friends there. I'll get back to San Diego soon enough.

I've returned from war zones and far-flung places often enough that I'm used to reentry. Mostly. What gets me more than anything isn't the cleanliness of certain places, or the availability of any kind of food, or being able to get a beer whenever I like, or even consistently hot showers—what gets me is the fact that other people have gone on with their lives. When I'm away for work, my life goes on pause. Shouldn't other people's lives pause too?

I get to DC only to discover that one friend has moved away and another has moved in. We go to a couple Nationals games and hang out with one of their players, who's a friend of mine. I call a few girlfriends, and two of them tell me they're engaged. I call Mom and Dad—actually, nothing has changed with them. Which is nice.

One day in early May, Malachi shoots me a text.

Where are you?

DC.

Aha! I hoped this. I am in Georgetown. Can you meet for lunch?

Yes!

Good! I have news. I will tell you there.

Interesting. Get out of my sweatpants, brush teeth, cab, Georgetown. Malachi sits outside in front of a café on the sunny side of the street. He's in a far corner smoking, the building to his back so that no one can sneak up on him. It's a perfect late-spring day. DC's famous heat and humidity haven't settled in yet.

He stands and we wrap each other in a hug. "Brother, it's good to see you!" I say.

"And it is good to see you, brother. Let us eat." We sit, he waves over the waiter, we tell him what we'd like. I light a cigarette, Malachi has another. I'm not sure if smoking is allowed here, but no one tells us otherwise, so fine by me. We catch up for a while, and then Malachi leans closer and says quietly, "I have a new job. You and me in charge. It will be easy. Are you in?"

"Don't know. What is it?"

"Well, you were right in Yemen. About many things, probably, but super right about the men they wanted us to train. We could not do that in that place."

"Yeah, those guys needed a full workup, six months at least."

"Agreed. And the UAE client agrees also. They want us to train them for real."

"And no direct-action stuff?"

"No. None."

"What about our other guys?"

"We will have a team, but at the top it is you and me."

"What about Isaiah?" I ask.

"Isaiah is busy," he says diplomatically. I don't know if it's true, but it's none of my business. "Dirty, it is you. You are the one. We start June the first."

"That's soon." I think for a moment. "I have one condition."

The waiter arrives, three plates balanced on his left arm. Charred octopus for the table, grilled salmon for Malachi, veal Milanese for me. We pick up our silverware. Malachi cuts a bite and scoops it onto his fork. "What is it?" He takes the bite of food.

"I need to pick the team."

He chews quickly, raising his fork hand in an apologetic way. He swallows. "Dirty, this is what I mean with 'you and me in charge.' I am the client liaison; I am the number one. You are the number two. And like with Isaiah before, you of course pick everyone."

"I'm in."

He gives me the details as we eat. We share a panna cotta and smoke over espressos. Lunch ends just as it started—with a big hug. "See you soon, brother."

As I ride an Uber back to my hotel, I mentally go through the Rolodex of guys I want. As soon as I get to my room, I check my encrypted messages. Malachi has sent me a mission brief and wired a deposit to my bank account. I start making calls. The job will be physical, so everyone on my list is a cardio freak. I call ten guys, go over roles, pay, location, length of contract. Six accept. That's all we'll need.

Three weeks later, we arrive in Abu Dhabi. Five-star hotel, two nights of delicious meals and bullshitting, hitch a helo to the desert. This time we're taken to a military base in the middle of nowhere surrounded by sand, more sand, and a few date trees sucking up water from a tiny underground aquifer. This isn't a black operation like the one before, and we never leave Emirati soil.

The next day, twenty Emirati recruits show up. We immediately launch into a monthlong physical conditioning program. My guys work them hard. We stack on the miles and reps. We shorten the rests. We lengthen the intervals. Some of the guys respond well, most are toasted by week two, a few turn green. We bark "Yallah!" at them until we practically can't speak. *Let's go, let's go, let's go!* We have to tone it down a little when one of them comes down with rhabdomyolysis—a potentially fatal condition where muscle tissue breaks down and enters the bloodstream, which can lead to sudden kidney failure. He gets a few days off but is cleared by medical and returns to the program.

The others get no time off. By week three, a few of them aren't hitting their benchmarks. I pass this to Malachi, and we bring it up with their superiors. They're unsympathetic. We're told—no, ordered—to see to it that every Emirati makes it through training. OK. We'll find a way.

I talk it over with Malachi and the other guys. About half of the Emiratis can physically keep up. They will be the A Team, our assaulter element. They will keep up with the physical training but will also concentrate on close quarters combat (CQC), fast-roping, breaching, marksmanship, and so on. The other half of the guys, who are more average physically but just as smart and driven, will be our support element. They will work on comms, tactics, vehicles, cyber, sniping, demolitions, and basic medical. Together, when we're done, they will be a formidable special forces unit for the UAE.

By week seven we are deep into CQC training. The Emiratis have spared no expense with their kill house, a sprawling compound of buildings with high-end ballistic walls in the middle of nowhere. For days I prowl the rafters, barking orders, correcting mistakes, encouraging the men when they deserve it, skewering them when they fuck up.

One day our top student mentions that there are other Americans on our training base, instructing another group of Emiratis. "Their rifles are not like ours," which are standard-issue Colt M4s.

"What do you mean?"

"They have four-sixteens," he says, referring to the HK416 assault rifle. That's what SEAL Team 6 uses. "They also have some higher-end kit," he adds.

I don't think much of it, and we continue.

A couple of days later, during a night training exercise, I get a better look at the other band of Emiratis and their American trainers: ten men sporting decidedly sexier gear than ours, just as my guy said. I call the range cold to stop any live fire and approach their kill house.

When I get about twenty meters away, I stop.

I *know* these men.

"Hank? Kerry?" I call out. "Is that you?" They turn. It's hard to make out details with the night vision, but it's them. Two guys from my SEAL Team days. Two guys who, as far as I know, are active duty.

"Dirty?! What are *you* doing here?"

I snicker. "What are *you* doing here?"

We catch up quick. Short story: they're here with ███████ and one of the three-letters doing "some things from on high," which means overseeing a special operations crew with drone support. When I tell them I was in Yemen for a while working jobs that kept getting called off, it's their turn to snicker. "Dirty, I think we should sit down with you and your boss."

The next day, Malachi and I make a day trip to Abu Dhabi. We meet Hank and Kerry in the lobby of the Jumeirah. Malachi and I are in mercenary casual, but it looks like Hank and Kerry just jumped out of a helo. They scream operator, but no one in the lobby seems to mind. That's the UAE for you.

I introduce Hank and Kerry to Malachi, they shake hands. My SEAL Team buddies are visibly tense. We order some drinks—espressos for me and Malachi, Diet Cokes for Hank and Kerry—and huddle over our table.

Finally Hank says, "Dirty, you said you guys were, um, *over there*"—he sticks his thumb in a southwesterly direction—"and kept getting waved off last minute before hitting targets. Right?"

"Yeah, that's the gist of it," I respond.

Malachi leans closer.

Hank glances over his shoulder. He whispers, "Bro, we're working with some people to do some kinetic things in the same places, and over the last several months we heard a lot of rumors about nongov Americans on the ground." He points at me. "And it seemed like every time we were going to use the asset to go kinetic, this mysterious group"—again, he points at me—"was near the target we were looking to drop on. These targets weren't as high priority as our other ones, so we didn't force the issue, but we passed the word down the line. More than anything, we didn't want anybody getting hurt who wasn't a turd."

"No shit?" I say.

"No shit," Kerry confirms. "Of course, if we had known exactly who and where these nongovs were, we would have warned them. But everything was so damn sensitive, and you were incognito."

"Completely black," Malachi says.

"I know," Kerry says. "Even some of the Emiratis didn't know you were there. It was sketch."

Well, at least it finally made sense. Malachi's handler was either the same person handling Hank and Kerry's team or was someone close to them, and out of an abundance of caution, the missions got called off on both occasions. Malachi and I shared a quick look of relief—it's one thing to die while trying to get Mr. AQAP or Mr. Bomb, but it's something else to get killed by an American Hellfire missile shot from a drone while actively engaged.

After an awkward pause, I blurt, "Guys, thanks for not blowing us up!"

Hank and Kerry finish their Diet Cokes and leave. We return to the base that afternoon. I see Hank and Kerry here and there, but then, a couple of days later, they disappear. That's how it is in this world.

A few more months pass, we finish training the Emiratis. Malachi and I observe the final exercise. It goes off without a hitch. The men we've taught are so adept at executing and adjusting on the fly to some "surprises" we built into the exercise that I daresay I'm proud of them. Following this success, Malachi and I both expect a six-month extension. Maybe we'll deploy with the Emiratis to Yemen or Afghanistan to function as true advisers. Maybe we'll train another unit.

But the Emirati brass aren't interested. They now have what they want—a special operations team of their own—and feel like they don't need us anymore.

We don't get that extension. So be it. Back to the hustle.

30

THE MODERN MERCENARY

THE HUSTLE WAS GOOD.

Can't get into specifics, so let's talk loosely about how a modern mercenary works on smaller, more direct-action jobs. As I said at the outset, Hollywood it isn't. You can't pull a Jason Bourne with multiple passports and identities in this era of biometrics. You enter countries as yourself, with your legitimate passport. Yes, someone from that country might follow you around to see what you're up to. So for jobs like that, you do touristy, boring shit for a few days. Hang out at bars and clubs, see the sights, chat up people who have nothing to do with the job. Become uninteresting, and your watchers move on. Then you can do whatever it is you're there to do.

Also like I said at the outset, you travel with cash, never more than $10,000. If you need more, you get a trusted source to make a run. Only euros or American dollars, every other currency is trash. Hollywood gets this one right from time to time.

Hollywood never gets weapons and gadgetry right. Often we see our protagonist open a suitcase with enough guns to arm a dozen men, GPS trackers, butterfly knives, lethal doses of poison, C-4, and so on. In the real world, you're responsible for getting what you need. You need a high-end SLR camera? Go buy one. You need a GPS tracker? Make one. You need weapons? Find a way.

Mainly because it makes for interesting storytelling, or maybe because they're obsessed with moving images, Hollywood does a pretty good job of addressing the growing threat of cameras and other kinds of surveillance. Cameras equipped with biometric and AI technology are a game changer and have triggered a classic cat-and-mouse contest between those who value their privacy and companies/states surveilling the public. Several TV shows depict a person wearing certain patterns, say a cream-colored sweater with stripes. These "adversarial patterns" can confuse the software and make you unrecognizable. Does it work? Sometimes. But people, who are not cameras attached to software, know to look out for these things, so sometimes it's better not to wear things that are known to actively disrupt surveillance technology.

A classic Hollywood trope that also works in the real world: a good disguise. Wigs, oversize clothes stuffed with newspapers, larger shoes, even makeup.

What about DNA? Hollywood loves working with this one, and filmmakers can get it right too, but they don't always go far enough. First are preventative measures. Scrubbing dead skin, wearing scrubs and a shower cap, shaving your body, putting Vaseline on your eyebrows and up your nose, and so on. Second is the destruction of DNA: bleach is pretty good, but fire destroys everything. Third is DNA confusion. Litter a scene with enough evidence, and pictures become blurry. Sometimes mercenaries will gather used cigarette butts and drinking glasses, even pubic hairs from the bottoms of urinals, and leave them here and there.

Perhaps the telltale sign of a Hollywood mercenary on a job is a guy pulling on a pair of latex gloves before he breaks into an office or someone's home. Good call! But doubling or tripling up is even better, since fingerprints can still imprint through one layer of latex on certain surfaces.

What about phones? In Hollywood, the ringleader of some crew tells the team to turn off their phones or leave them at home. Sure, that may give you plausible deniability when it comes to location, but having your phone off while something happens is also not a good look. Fortunately, there are apps that create and send messages automatically and can even place calls while you're off doing your thing. Even better, have a trusted source man your phone for a while. Scroll that Insta! Text Mom! Call your accountant! Why not?

Most people think mercenaries do only one thing. Not true. Some jobs require finding kids who have been kidnapped by their father and returning them to their mom. Some jobs involve confronting card-carrying KKK members over debts they owe. Some mean recovering hostages from terrorists, or liberating children from the grip of warlords.

Regardless of the job, certain things never change. Mercenaries always have to be able to defend themselves, they always need cash, and they always, always, always need a plan to get out of whatever country they're working in. Exfiltration is usually the first consideration. As a practical matter, this means no serious jobs ever in Western countries. Law enforcement in these places is just too good. Period and end of story.

31

DOES SERBIA COUNT AS A WESTERN COUNTRY?

ONE DAY IN LATE OCTOBER 2017, MALACHI REACHES OUT. CAN I MEET HIM IN Abu Dhabi ASAP? You bet.

Etihad business class, direct flight, check into a suite at the Four Seasons. After dropping my stuff in my room, I head down to the lobby.

I spot Malachi immediately in a lounge chair, a blue cloud of cigarette smoke hanging over his head. He's engrossed in something on his tablet. Probably some article in the *New York Times* or *Le Monde*.

Before I left the United States, he told me this would be a casual meeting. "Dress dirty, Dirty," he said. I took it to heart and am now sporting the kit an entertainment executive might wear. Blazer, tailored jeans, all-white Onitsuka sneakers. Nothing too expensive. But as I approach Malachi, I see that he's got on one of his Kiton cashmere blazers.

He looks up and smiles as I reach him. Stands, big hug. "Super great to see you, brother," he says.

"And you," I say. We pull apart, grasping each other by the shoulders. I tug at his blazer. "I thought you said dirty?"

"Oh, this? It's nothing."

"Nothing my ass. What's that—ten grand?"

He chuckles, I shake my head. "Did you bring your appetite, Dirty?"

"You know it."

"Good. Let us go and eat."

We head to the Four Seasons Galleria to the famous steak house Nusr-Et.

We meet our client, who must remain anonymous, so let's just call him Al. He's a repeat client and by now we're all friends—or at least very friendly.

Al is very well dressed. I'd give him an A, Malachi a B, and me a D. From the look Al gives me, he agrees.

A hostess leads us to our table—the best in the house, a private seat overlooking a blue inlet leading to the Persian Gulf. Technically, the UAE is dry, but in hotels wine flows like water, especially when an Emirati is entertaining Westerners. We drink a $1,200 bottle of French cabernet. Then we drink another. A short while later, a wooden cutting board overflowing with steak and lamb is placed in the middle of the table. It's tender and bloody and doused with large flakes of white salt. We dig in. It's some of the best meat I've ever tasted, but there's so much of it that eating it is exhausting.

At one point Nusret himself, aka Salt Bae, stops by to ask if we're satisfied. We are. He sends another small course of exceptional fillets. I can't resist, forcing down a few more bites.

At the end of our meal, Al gives us our target: a lead member of a group financing the Houthis in Yemen. For reasons I don't fully grasp, this man currently lives in Belgrade, Serbia.

Our task—really *my* task, since this will be a solo mission with Malachi remaining in the UAE—is to spend a couple of months gathering incriminating intel on the target. Anything Al can use as leverage "to compel him"—Al's phrase—to stop financing the Houthis. The job will not be kinetic—if it were, we wouldn't take it. Also, if it were in France or Germany or the UK, we would reject it outright. But Serbia has a weak and corrupt law enforcement system, making it easier to get out of the place in a pinch. Plus, this job will mainly consist of just hanging out. I can do that, no problem.

At one point Al departs to let Malachi and me chat. Specifically because it's not kinetic, we think it's a good opportunity. "It's straight humint. This will be easy," I say.

"I bet it will be fun for you," Malachi says with a wry smile.

I bet it will.

Malachi waves Al back to the table. We agree to take the job.

After dinner, I head up to my room. I pull out my tablet, throw on a VPN, and do a quick Google search on the target. We'll call him Peter. I check LinkedIn. He has a PR business with nine employees. I browse his social media.

He enjoys museums, fine Italian and Turkish dining, fashion shows, and nightclubs. Not very halal, if you ask me. He lives in a small mansion in an upscale neighborhood called Dedinje. If he's married—and he must be because every Muslim man over the age of twenty is married—his wife is not with him. Ditto kids. He drives—or is driven around in, I won't know until I get there—a late-model Mercedes E-Class sedan. Al claims that Peter likes supporting local female "entrepreneurs," but I won't know for sure until I see him in his element.

That's it. Not a lot, but it's a start.

The job officially begins in five days, meaning we have time to kill. It's not a good idea to fly directly from a client's location to the place you'll be working, so the next afternoon, Malachi and I fly to Cairo. We're not there on business, we're tourists. We hire a guide, visit the Pyramids, take stupid tourist pictures, and have a ton of fun. We even ride camels, and the camels saunter past the Sphinx. It's the first time I've done anything remotely normal in any Middle Eastern country. Or if it's not the first time, it's the first time in a *long* time. It feels good.

Then, on November 3, I say goodbye to Malachi and board a plane for Istanbul. From there it's off to Belgrade.

PART II

32

WELCOME TO BELGRADE

Here I am boarding a plane in Turkey. Here I am in business class sleeping like a baby. Here I am freshening up in the airport. Here I am taking a nice car to the hotel. I've never been to this country and don't know much about it, but it's plain as I cruise through the streets that Serbia is an old and hard place, full of hustlers, criminals, and gangsters.

Here I am checking into Square Nine, one of the nicest hotels in Belgrade. Its sunken lobby looks like an oversize dining car from the Orient Express. Loro Piana sofas, plush high-backed chairs, handmade globes, coffee tables piled with books. A black Steinway grand piano by the bar, which is stocked with the finest spirits and Baccarat crystal. To the right of the lobby is a well-lit dining area. To the left are the elevators. The staff are all uniformed: gray slacks, white shirts, black ties. They constantly move here and there, taking orders, filling glasses, changing ashtrays.

The clientele are among the best dressed and best looking I've seen anywhere. The women all look like models. They're in Balenciaga, Louis Vuitton, Givenchy. The men are split into an older crowd and a younger one. The older guys rock Tom Ford, Hermès, Berluti. The younger cats are in Philipp Plein, Dsquared2, Off-White. Everyone has a watch, and not just any watch. The place is filled with Audemars Piguet, Richard Mille, Patek Philippe. My Submariner feels like a Casio.

I go to my suite. I'm a go-anywhere-and-do-anything mercenary. I unpack my Rimowa suitcase. It's as if Guy Ritchie were unpacking a merc's bag as he arrives for a job, with an assist from Wes Anderson. On one side you have tactical gear. I won't need it on this trip, but better safe than sorry. On the other you have all my nice clothing and accessories. I remove an envelope from the bottom of my bag, inside is €9,000 in cash. If I need more—and I will—Malachi will get it to me. I put the money and my passport in the hotel safe. I take a quick shower, change, and go downstairs.

Downstairs is where I spend the first couple of weeks. My target runs in these upscale circles (and a few downscale ones), so I'll run in them too. I hang in the lobby. I hang at the bar. I befriend the owners. It's a father-and-sons operation. Dad worked his ass off to build the place. The eldest son, Bogdon, presents as a refined connoisseur. Grounded, enjoys expensive wine, which we do together from time to time. The younger son, Nebo, is the smooth-talking ladies' man—or maybe men's man? Whatever his tastes, he's the face of the property.

I take morning coffee and late lunches. I watch people come and go, many of them followed by a trail of whispers. Intrigued, I ask Nebo about these people. "He's a big Albanian businessman." "She runs the largest prostitution ring in the Balkans." "He's a pink panther—a gentleman thief." "Meh, she's just another starleta."

Day turns to night, Nebo takes me to a club down the street. Maison Boho. "Bohemian House." This becomes my home away from home. The first time we go, we're greeted by a massive man at the front door. Black beanie, black jacket, black jeans, black shoes, no smile. A purple scar across his left cheek from nostril to earlobe. An old, deep cut. Nebo has a quick conversation with the giant, the giant opens the door. We enter. The sounds of bongo drums, a saxophone, a trumpet spill from inside. The place is dark. My eyes adjust. A thrumming bar/restaurant/club. In the middle a drummer jams on a small stage. He's surrounded by bongos, cowbells, toms, bass drum, cymbals, tambourine. The saxophone player walks among the crowd, weaving between tables. Nebo pushes through to the back, I follow.

We reach a small bar, Nebo strikes up a conversation with the bartender. She points up, my eyes follow. Above is a loft covering a quarter of the space, more tables, more happy patrons. A handsome, well-dressed man climbs one of the upstairs tables, trumpet in hand. He slips, lands in a patron's lap, they both laugh. The man toting the trumpet brings it to his lips, the trumpet blares out a god-awful sound. More laughter.

The bartender gets the trumpet player's attention and waves him over. Nebo greets him with a big hug, pulls out a wad of euros, points to a large booth at the back of the club occupied by two young couples. The man refuses the money, then saunters over to the booth.

"Who's that?" I ask over the din.

"That's Fratello," Nebo says. "He runs the place."

I watch Fratello chat up the couples. The exchange is short. Fratello must be the most charming guy in the world, because all four people smile and laugh as they're relocated to another table upstairs. Fratello waves us over and we take the best seat in the house. This will be our nightly table for weeks to come.

Nebo introduces me to everyone. There's a lot of overlap with Square Nine's more upscale crowd, but there's a shadier element here too.

I meet Montenegrin heroin dealers, in-their-prime prostitutes, football hooligans, and at least one plachenik ubitza—a contract killer. I meet several Hells Angels. I've known a few Hells Angels over the years and like them. I quickly befriend their president, Branko, who happens to know of Malachi from his days in the Foreign Legion.

Branko points out the top madam in the Balkans, Sonja. My target is reputed to frequent prostitutes, so she would be a logical place to start if I want any of this kind of dirt on the guy. Problem is, Sonja isn't someone I can just walk up to. I need an introduction. Branko tells me that another HA—Zed—is my guy.

Zed makes a few calls, and before I know it, I have a meeting with Sonja in the Square Nine lobby the following afternoon. We're supposed to meet at 1700, I head down to the lobby ten minutes early. No sign of Sonja, but Zed's already there smoking a cigar on one of the low couches. I grab a seat. Next to him is a hot twentysomething. No shame for Zed—he's fiftysomething, bald, out of shape. Classic Hells Angels—fuck the world and fuck you too.

As soon as I sit, he orders a round of rakija, the Serbian national drink. This is a sweet fruit brandy usually distilled from plums or grapes, but it's strong—80 or even 100 proof.

At 1700 on the dot, in walks Sonja with five scantily clad girls. She knows everyone, everyone knows her. The girls take seats throughout the lobby and get straight to work. Zed introduces us, then he and his arm candy bounce.

Sonja sits in a high-backed chair across from me. Early thirties, emerald eyes, raven hair, full-on Instagram model. Face, teeth, cheeks, ass—all have had work done. Fake tits the size of party balloons. She looks like Jessica Rabbit on steroids—in other words, she looks ridiculous. She wears an impossibly short miniskirt, a black tube top hanging on for dear life, a fur shawl, Louis Vuitton bag, Dior shades, and knee-high Louboutins.

"Daniel," she says slowly, pulling on a single white glove. "I know you don't want to talk to me to meet girls." She places a cigarette between her gloved fingers and lights up. As you know, SEALs occasionally live cinematic lives—but this moment stands out as the most movie-like of any I've experienced so far.

I'm tempted to ask how she knows this, but she beats me to it. "You are good looking, you have Rolex, you have blue passport. It is clear what you want is information, no?"

"You're correct. I'm trying to find out if a certain someone is a connoisseur of your goods."

"Ah, not what I was expecting. But you must know that discretion is very important for my business."

"Of course. But is it more important than money?"

She smirks and takes a long drag off her cigarette before saying, "Nothing more important than this."

I figured this would be the case—I've come prepared. I discreetly slip four €500 bills from my inside pocket and hold them behind my phone while I tap my target's name into the Notes app. I then pass both phone and bills to her. "Do you know this man?"

She places her cigarette in a pedestal ashtray and takes my phone with her gloved hand while she discreetly palms the cash with the other. "Yes," she says.

"A client?"

"No." She takes one last drag off her cigarette and then mashes it out.

"Well, Sonja. Thank you for your time. It's been a pleasure meeting you."

"The same, Daniel," she says, removing the white smoking glove and stuffing it in her purse. We both stand and shake hands. "Sorry I could not be more help," she says.

"On the contrary. Your answer is as informative as any other. Maybe I'll ask some other ladies."

She has been all but expressionless to this point, but at this a little twinge of annoyance passes over her lips. "Don't bother," she says in a low tone. "I tried to get him on as a client, and with the girls and prices I gave him, he would have to be an idiot to pass up. He is—how do you say—incorruptible on this matter. He is very religious." She gives a small shrug. "It is all the same to me."

"Also good to know. Thank you, Sonja."

"Ciao, Daniel." She spins and sashays away to talk to one of her girls.

"Ciao," I call after her. But she's already gone.

33

SVETI SAVA

BACK TO SQUARE ONE. I GO TO RESTAURANTS HIGH AND LOW, TO BACK-ALLEY clubhouses, to more hotels, to nightclubs. I ride in nice cars and not-so-nice ones. Girls sit on my lap, men clap my back as they shake my hand. I learn that Serbia is a wild place. The football hooligans are way more than thugs, they're straight-up Mafia, involved in drugs, prostitution, business, and politics. They fall into two basic camps: men who root for Red Star, and men who root for Partizan, both Belgrade teams. The Red Star hooligans are hardcore Serbian nationalists, the Partizan hooligans are harder to pin down politically. When these teams play each other, the city goes on lockdown. It's not an exaggeration to say that the Third Balkan War started in a Belgrade soccer stadium. I learn that everyone is scarred by this war, on all sides, and that Serbians have a *long* memory that dates to the Crusades and even earlier. I learn that nearly every Serb hates America. I learn that the place is hopelessly corrupt. I learn that their contract killers don't merely shoot their victims, they torture them. They tie them up and smash their heads with sledgehammers. They wrap them in chicken wire and shove screwdrivers into their ears. They beat them to death, chop them up, and feed them to their friends on skewers.

Wild.

As for the job, I put eyes on my guy's house, but there's nothing interesting about it. Certainly there's nothing about it that lends itself to blackmail. I think about how I might get inside the house. But I'll need clearance before I do that—from Malachi and from Al in Abu Dhabi. I learn a little Serbian. "Koliko?" "Gde je kupatilo?" "Da li ste ikada bili u Americi?" I further refine the skill of sizing people up using nothing more than their wardrobe and whatever bottled scent they dabbed on their wrists and behind their ears that day.

Everywhere I go, I see portraits of Vladimir Putin. This country is technically in central Europe and nearly seven hundred miles from Moscow, but if you didn't know better, you'd assume Putin ruled the place. To build trust, I tell people I'm a SEAL—most don't know what that is, so I say I'm in the US Navy—and all they want to know is why "we" bombed "them" during the Kosovo War in the late 1990s. My pat answer is, "That was before my time, brother. Besides, I'm a soldier, not a politician." Then I buy a round of rakija and we move on. Overall, I feel more like a Cold War spy than a mercenary. It doesn't hurt that during my entire time there I haven't once touched a gun. For a mercenary, it's a strange gig.

One night I make a new friend: Nikola. Well off, went to Boston College, speaks perfect English, very connected. I take his number and start working him, gathering intel on his network. Not only is Nikola a useful source, I also enjoy his company. We start working out, he takes me around Belgrade. After a couple of weeks of hanging out, he invites me to a dinner party at his apartment. "It will be small. There will be plenty of girls too." He pulls out his phone and scrolls through his Instagram, showcasing his pretty friends. One woman catches my eye—not because of how she looks but because the image shows her at my target's firm!

"I'll be there," I tell Nikola.

The next day, Nikola takes me to Belgrade's main church, Sveti Sava. I'm early. I stand next to the towering white walls, the giant green copper dome rising over two hundred feet above. It's an Orthodox Christian church, but something about it reminds me of the grand mosques I've seen in the Middle East and Turkey.

Nikola arrives, leads me toward the entrance, promises that the inside is even more stunning than the outside. And he's not wrong.

"They say that Saint Sava, the founder of the Serbian Orthodox Church, is buried underneath. The Ottomans burned his coffin at this very location in 1595."

I barely hear any of this and only respond with a whispered "Wow."

I crane my neck, trying to take it all in. The marble and granite walls are covered in golden depictions of Christ and the saints. The place looks ancient, but Nikola tells me they broke ground in 1935 and only finished in 2004. Hanging from the center dome is a tiered chandelier at least sixty feet across. As we walk around, I get a closer look at the paintings on the walls—only they're not paintings, they're mosaics.

I point this out to Nikola, he nods proudly. "Every single one is a mosaic. Fifty million pieces of pure gold and gems in total."

It's almost too much to take in.

"Wait until you see the crypt," Nikola says. "Follow me." He leads me down a set of stairs to a room under the nave. The ceilings are low and arched. As above, everything is covered in gold.

Nikola makes his way over to one of the small podiums scattered all around. On top of the podiums are small figures or cards. An old man slips by us, kisses one of the cards, says something private, and moves on. When he's gone, I ask Nikola what they are.

"Ikona. Little saints. Every family has their own patron saint. Kind of like you all have St. Nicholas—and you celebrate Christmas for him—but we each get our own. Our saint's day can come any time of the year, even in summer. And on that day we all get together and party, have a feast, you know?"

"Cool."

"Yeah. It is pretty cool."

I follow him across the crypt and he shows me his family's saint. Then I step back, out of respect. He kisses the image, says a prayer, returns to me. "So, what do you think?"

"I'm blown away, man. Thank you."

"One last stop." We head out of the crypt and back outside to a small gift shop. He pays for something and hands it to me. "Here you go, Daniel." It's a black hand-woven bracelet that has an image of the church stamped on a plastic bead.

"Thanks, Nikola. I really appreciate it."

A couple of days later, I'm back at Nikola's, helping him get ready for his party. We cook, he takes a call, dips out for a bit. I'm there alone. I watch TV, fiddle with my phone, put a call in to Mom and Dad. I stir the lamb stew every now and then and have a taste. It's great. Right before people are due to show up, I strip out of my hoodie to put on some nicer clothes.

And then Nikola's door crashes open. Nikola falls inside, followed by four cops. Nikola's hands are cuffed in front of him. I'm standing there, shirtless and confused. My first thought is that this a prank.

But then I notice the pistol.

The pistol pointing directly at my head.

34

DANIEL CORBETT NUMBER THREE

I'VE BEEN AROUND A LOT OF GUNS IN MY LIFE, BUT NEVER HAS ANYONE LEVELED one at me at point-blank range. I turn to the weapon. My eyes adjust past the gun and I see the terrified face of a kid no older than twenty-one. He starts yelling in Serbian. I have no clue what he's saying. My eyes adjust back to the gun. His finger is on the trigger. He's trembling. I can hear the gun rattling.

When you learn to shoot, one of the first things you're taught is that you never put your finger on the trigger unless you intend to pull it.

Fuck me.

His finger on the trigger means one of two things. One, this kid may actually *want* to shoot me. Or two, this kid is so poorly trained that he doesn't know one of the first rules of using a gun.

I don't want my face blown off, so even though I don't understand a word this young man is stutter-yelling, I do what I think he wants me to do. I slowly raise my hands. Someone else pulls my arms behind my back, the handcuffs get ratcheted down on my wrists. I'm pushed to the floor face-first and shirtless.

The three other officers search the house, taking turns yelling at me in Serbian. I say nothing. After an eternity—probably only three minutes—a fifth person enters the scene. Cheek to the floor, I crane my neck and eye him surreptitiously. Everything about him is different. He's in civilian clothes, he's calmer. He walks to me, takes a knee. Says something in Serbian.

I say nothing, but he persists. Finally I say, "Anyone here speak English?"

The room goes silent. It's the equivalent of scratching a needle on a record in a packed nightclub. The four uniforms quit searching and form a semicircle around me. The plainclothes cop asks, "American?"

Before I can answer, another person comes screaming into the room. I can't see her, but she is beside herself. She throws herself on the floor and bursts into tears. Nikola immediately begins consoling her. It's his mom, who lives in the flat on the ground floor.

Two of the uniformed cops get Nikola's mother to her feet and lead her out.

The plainclothes officer pulls me up and sits me on the couch. "American?" he repeats.

"Yes."

"Do you live here?"

"No."

"Do you have passport?"

"Yes."

"What are you doing here?"

I'm fairly sure he's asking what I'm doing in Serbia, but I answer, "I am here for a dinner party."

"You like guns?"

I have no idea why he asks this, but I answer, "As much as the next guy, I guess."

He stands. Huddles with the rest of the cops in the kitchen. I look at Nikola, who still sits on the floor. He nods and gives me a wink. I have no idea what this wink means, but if it's meant to be reassuring, it isn't. Quite the fucking opposite. Has Nikola been playing me? Have I been a fucking idiot?

The plainclothes cop returns. "Where is your passport?"

"In my bag." After spending about two days in Serbia, I realized that the hotel safe was not in fact safe—I've been carrying my passport and cash with me ever since.

One of the uniforms hands him my backpack. He rummages through it, pulls out my passport, flips it open to my ID page.

"Excuse me, am I being arrested?" I ask.

Plainclothes looks from the passport to me to the passport and back to me. "You are now, Daniel Corbett Number Three."

35

VUČIĆ, AKA THE WOLF

YEAH, I *HAVE* BEEN A FUCKING IDIOT.

This is my main takeaway as Nikola, two of his friends, and I are driven across town in a low-rent paddy wagon that smells of piss and vomit. My only reassurance is that I've dealt with worse. This sucks, but Belgrade is not some desert hardship post. People are not shooting at me. I didn't do anything illegal. And I haven't been snagged for screwing up the contract. I'm fairly sure I'll be released by the end of the day, the next day tops. I'll come clean with Malachi and Al, I won't hold this development from them. Why would I?

As we're bumping down the road, Nikola says, "You can use my lawyer, Dan."

I give him a look that says I'll consider it, but my wheels are spinning. This whole thing stinks. Was there a bounty on my head? I was here playing spy games—did I waltz into an actual spy game? Why were Nikola's hands cuffed in front of him and mine behind me? Can I trust him? Who are these other two guys? Why, after flipping through my passport, did the cops decide to arrest me?

Whatever the case, I'm pissed at myself. I should never have gotten so chummy with Nikola. I'm here to work, not make friends.

After about twenty minutes, we arrive at the police station. We're marched out of the van and into the building. Crappy place with a real Soviet vibe. Old furniture piled on stairway landings. "No Smoking" signs on every wall, but all of them yellow with nicotine stains. I get strip-searched by an overweight, graying cop. That's a new experience. After making me spread cheeks, he tosses me my clothes and a tattered wool blanket. I'm separated from the others, who share a cell, and locked up alone. Not a good sign.

My cell is eight feet square. The walls are painted pea-soup green. There is a small bench against one wall, a hole in the ground that serves as a toilet, and a tiny window. Directly outside the window is a bright industrial-strength flood-light that prevents me from knowing the time of day. But I caught a glimpse of the guard's watch as he handed me the blanket. It's a little after 2100. They probably won't question me until tomorrow morning. I curl up on the bench and try to get some sleep.

It's cold and uncomfortable. I toss and turn before moving to the floor. At least there I can fully extend my legs.

Just as I'm drifting off, the cell door opens. Two plainclothes officers enter, both young and well dressed. They look confused or even concerned that I'm lying on the floor. They motion for me to stand and throw the cuffs back on. I'm escorted up a flight of stairs and taken down a long hallway to a room off to the right. The wing of the building is more of the same—half-broken chairs litter the hallway, lights flicker on and off. Another glimpse at another watch: it's 0530. I'm put in a plastic chair, one desk in front of me and another off to my right.

At the desk to the right is a uniformed police officer behind a 1990s computer. He's in his mid-thirties with chestnut hair. He looks pissed. Behind the desk directly across from me is a woman straight out of a movie. She's built like Ursula the sea witch and dressed like Cruella de Vil. Has their charm too. She's surrounded by a permanent cloud of cigarette smoke.

"I make translate for you," she rumbles in English.

Even though I'm not too concerned, I know this is a serious situation and I need a better translator than Ursula. Since Serbia is a Slavic language, I figure I might have better luck communicating using Russian—and thanks to Svit-lana, I know it well enough. So I answer in Russian, something to the effect of, "Maybe it's better if we don't speak English."

Everyone in the room freaks out. Two people say, "On je špijun!"

Translation: "He's a spy!"

Shit. I should have kept my mouth shut.

It takes a few moments for this commotion to die down. Then the man behind the computer asks me to type my name in. No one can understand the "III" at the end of my name. Whatever. I get pushed back into my chair. Two men in paramedic uniforms enter the room. The two plainclothes cops grab my shoulders. "DNK," says the one to my right. He also grabs the back of my neck. Sure, whatever the fuck that means.

One of the "paramedics" grips my jaw while the other points a cotton swab near my mouth. Ah, DNA. Don't know why they'd want that, but I have no say in the matter. The officer to my right chomps his teeth in an exaggerated motion, then waves his finger. My God, this guy is telling me not to bite off the paramedic's finger!

I open my mouth with a good amount of unnecessary assistance. They take two samples, maybe three—I can't tell.

The paramedics leave. Ursula pushes two sheets of paper toward me. Both are in Cyrillic. If it were Russian, I could read them, but it's all Serbian. "Do sign here," she says, indicating a line at the bottom of one of the sheets.

I lean forward. "Nope, can't do that. I don't know what this says."

"Do sign here," she says again.

"Sorry, I can't do that." I turn to one of the plainclothes guys. "Hey, is anyone going to notify the US embassy?"

The officer at the computer blurts, "Call embassy tomorrow."

Ursula ignores this exchange and pushes a different paper toward me. "This says is gun and bomb. You have gun and bomb. Sign."

I stifle a laugh. "No way!"

She pulls it back, looks at the cop to my right, they both shrug. This one little exchange says, "Hey, it was worth a shot."

She pushes a third paper forward. "This is passport and Rolex. We keep safe." I look closely. Because I know the Cyrillic alphabet, I can make out the words "passport," "Rolex," and "Daniel Corbett."

"OK," I say. I sign it. Then the cops stand me up and march me back to my cell. I guess that was processing.

Just before the door closes, I'm tossed a sandwich. It's mostly bread. It has a pathetic-looking slice of baloney and dab of butter. I eat half of it and use the rest as a pillow. I'm whipped, and this time I fall asleep quickly.

An unknown amount of time passes. I'm woken by the sound of my cell door opening. The same two faces as last time look down on me. I stand, present my wrists, get cuffed. I'm led upstairs and placed in a different room. Another glance at a watch: 12:50, but I haven't seen outside so I don't know if it's a.m. or p.m.

I'm deposited in a chair. Sitting nonchalantly on the desk is a massive plain-clothes cop—six-three, well over 250 pounds, bearded. He's rocking a black beanie, a gray puffer coat, tan tactical pants, and tan combat boots. "Daniel Corbett?" he asks.

"Yep."

"I'm Uros. Are those necessary?" He points to my handcuffs.

"No."

"Yeah, I didn't think so." He crosses to me, produces a key, removes my cuffs.

"Thanks."

"Coffee? Cigarette?"

"Yes to both, please."

He hands me a cigarette and lighter, then yells something into the hallway. Moments later, two cups of Turkish coffee arrive. OK, we have a "good cop" situation going. He'll try to build rapport and trust and get something out of me, even though there's nothing to get. I'm well rested, so I'll dance.

"American?"

He already knows the answer. "Yes, sir."

"What is your job?"

"Private contractor."

He frowns.

I explain. "I've ridden cargo ships as a security guard against pirates."

"Ah. Professional soldier. A mercenary."

"Sure."

"So you are former military."

"Correct."

"Are you here for work?"

"I told you, I used to guard cargo ships."

"That's not an answer. You were not arrested on a cargo ship."

"I'm not here to hurt anyone, if that's what you mean."

"Then why *are* you in Serbia?"

"Why not? The women are beautiful, the people are nice, and I just visited Sveti Sava." For some reason, they haven't taken the little bracelet that Nikola gave me. I hold it up. "It's gorgeous."

"You went to Sveti Sava?"

"Yep. Even went down to the crypt to look at the icons."

"Are you CIA?"

"No."

"DEA?"

"No."

"What did you do in the military?"

"I was a SEAL."

"Ah. Special forces."

"Yes. I see you have some tactical pants, and those are some high-end boots. Oakleys. I ran those once, although they were soft and I went through them too fast." I can build rapport too.

He lights up. "Yes! These are my third pair!"

We go back and forth like this for a couple of hours. His pattern is predictable—small talk, jokes, personal story, then he either throws me a pointed question or asks a previous question in a different manner. I ask questions now and then—Why are they holding me? Why was I arrested? Am I being charged? Why did they need my DNA?—but he never answers. Eventually we come to an impasse. This is going nowhere.

Then I hear Nikola's voice in the hall. He must be next.

"OK, that is all the questions I have for now," Uros says. He stands and dangles the cuffs. I hold out my arms. He puts them on, thankfully loosely.

A well-dressed blond woman walks in—modest heels, full-length plaid skirt, white blouse, reading glasses. She has a quick exchange with Uros.

"Ah, Daniel," he says, sitting back on top of the desk. "She is asking about a lawyer. Do you have one?"

"Uh, no."

"Of course. She says your friend Nikola is offering you to use his lawyer. That or you can choose to have Serbia appoint you a lawyer."

I briefly weigh this. Nothing about this country is impressive, and since public defenders get a bad rap everywhere, I assume they have an especially bad rap here. If you're a good Serbian lawyer, there is no way you'd take a public defender gig. I figure that if I accept the public defender, I'll be found guilty one hundred times out of one hundred. Provided Nikola isn't setting me up—still a big if—I give his lawyer fifty-fifty odds. This is probably too generous, but I have to hold on to hope. "I'll go with Nikola's guy."

Uros nods and translates for the young woman. She leaves, Uros walks me downstairs, hands me off to a guard, I'm taken to my cell. I finish the second half of my smashed sandwich and lie back down. I have no idea what time it is or how long I've been here—forty-eight hours, maybe seventy-two. I think over this situation. It's not good. I've been swabbed, I haven't been charged, I haven't been able to speak with a lawyer. No sign of an embassy consul or any other American. Did I misstep? Did I walk into something or just get unlucky? Is Nikola behind this? Did my target find me out somehow and put the screws on me? Have I been sloppy on this, my first real humint gig? Am I out of my depth on this job?

An indeterminate amount of time passes. My cell door opens. Uros again, and the old man who strip-searched me. "That can't be comfortable," Uros says, pointing at the bench.

"It's not."

He laughs, I get cuffed, back upstairs. This time to a different room. Bigger. A desk with two men already there. I'm sat in a chair across from them. Uros sits next to me. No one looks happy to be here.

Here comes bad cop.

Uros says, "Daniel, these men are from the organized crime unit. They have some questions for you. I will translate."

Organized crime? "OK," I say.

The men bombard me. They speak over each other, cut each other off, yell. There is no chitchat, no cigarettes, no coffee. I'm sleep deprived now but can't fuck up. I don't want to lie to them about anything, I don't want to give them any more than they need. I don't want to reveal why I'm in Serbia. I can have no tells.

When you're in the Teams, you train for interrogations in case you're ever captured by the enemy. You get questioned by people who are better at it than these amateurs. I've watched video of my performances in mock interrogations. I know what I do when I'm bullshitting. My tells are self-grooming, repeating questions, long pauses. I cannot do those things now.

It's easier than I expect. The two bad cops yelling over each other and Uros translating make for a lot of nothing time. The tension eventually melts away and is replaced by something close to humor—this is a silly situation. We all know it.

After a few hours, Uros gets upset. Not at me, but at the other cops. He pulls them out of the room for about ten minutes.

When they return, only one bad cop talks. Again, Uros translates.

"Are you here for Vučić?"

"Vuk, like a wolf?"

"No, Vučić, the person."

"I don't know who that is," I say.

"President."

"Of what?"

"Of Serbia!"

"Oh. Oh—no!"

"You *are* here for Vučić. To kill him."

"What?! No. I told you, I'm just a tourist."

Then the bad cop says in halting English, "And you already make kill on politician in Kosovo."

I look to Uros. "I have no idea what this guy is talking about."

I'm not lying. The idea is insane. If this had been a kinetic gig, we would have turned it down. Serbia is an afterthought for many people, but it's still in Europe. Besides, mercenaries never move against heads of state—it's extremely complicated and expensive, not to mention extraordinarily illegal.

But at least I know why they think I'm here—to assassinate their president. I silently pray that Nikola's lawyer is halfway decent. He's going to have to be.

After a few awkward moments, bad cop says something to Uros. But his tone isn't as grave—it's lighter, inquisitive.

Uros turns to me. "Are you willing to take a lie detector test?" Then, in a voice quieter than a whisper, he says, "Say no."

"No," I say. God, I hope that wasn't a mistake.

The bad cops look defeated. They talk for a minute, then throw a bunch of paperwork in one of their bags. This train wreck is over.

The other bad cop, who's barely spoken for a while, says something. Uros translates, "You are a former SEAL, American special operations. You are in Serbia for some reason. You are good, but everyone gives up something when being interrogated, whether they know it or not."

Uros is a bad bullshitter and I'm not buying it. Eventually the two men leave.

Uros lights a cigarette and passes it to me. I raise my cuffed hands to accept it—they never unshackled me.

"Finish your cigarette and I will take you back down to the cell," he says. "I'm giving you a warning, Daniel. You have been here for four days—"

I cut him off. "Four days?!"

"Yes. While you have been here, word has leaked to the media. Everyone is going crazy, you are all over the news."

"Why?"

"It is the story of the American mercenary in Serbia. You are famous!" He slaps me on the back, like this is something I should be proud of. Then he lets out a laugh and takes me back to my little cell.

His words ring in my head. "You are famous! You are famous! You are famous!"

Fuck me.

36

FAMILIAR FRIENDS, FAMILIAR FACES

I'M IN MY CELL FOR TEN MINUTES BEFORE I'M HAULED OUT AGAIN AND THROWN into another paddy wagon. Nikola and his friends are there. We barely say three words to each other.

A bumpy ride, maybe fifteen minutes, we pull to a stop. The cops open the van doors, daylight spills inside. I blink as my eyes adjust. We're pulled out. We're in a parking lot next to what appears to be a courthouse. As we're led inside, Nikola whispers, "Arraignment."

All right, at least I'll finally find out what my charge is. Maybe I'll even get to talk to a lawyer.

We're led though a succession of corridors to a wide hall where other accused mill around. We all look like shit and feel worse. At least I'm up and moving. Four days of sitting in interrogation and lying on a cement floor have done a number on my back.

As we wait, I'm struck by how disorganized it all is. The hall is full of about twenty people, and not just the accused. There are reporters, lawyers, clerks, all jumbled together. It feels unprofessional and ridiculous.

None of the reporters approach me, thank goodness. I'm cuffed, but given how tired I am, I don't know how I'd react to a string of questions. I'm glad I don't find out.

But someone does approach me. A perfectly groomed man wearing a sharp tailored suit. He even smells good. "I'm Milosh," he declares. "I am a colleague of Nikola's lawyer, Dragoslav Ognjanović." This name means nothing to me, but the way he pronounces it tells me he's important. Then Milosh leans close and whispers, "Mr. B and Mr. M sent me. They pass their regards."

Mr. M is Malachi, and I assume Mr. B is Branko, the president of the Serbian Hells Angels.

That's good enough for me. "You're hired," I say.

"Wise choice, Daniel."

The mention of Malachi means three things. One, the word is out and people know where I am. Two, Malachi has my back—not that he wouldn't, but it's still good to hear. And three, I made the right call by rejecting the public defender.

"When can we talk?" I ask.

"After this. I will come to you. It may take some time."

"Thanks, Milosh."

He nods and slips away.

Not long after that, the judge pulls the accused into the courtroom one by one. Some other guys are called in first, then Nikola's friends. Nikola and I stand there, not talking to each other. Once they're done, it's Nikola's turn. He shoots me another mysterious wink. As far as I can tell, none of these men are accompanied by their lawyers, all of whom—including Milosh—are huddled together in whispered conversation.

Finally it's my turn. A tiny cop who looks like Mr. Bean leads me in. The room is more office than courtroom. A heavyset, modestly dressed middle-aged woman sits behind a desk piled with paperwork. The arraignment judge. She looks exhausted and deeply bored. All she does, every day, is sort the accused. I'm plopped opposite her in a chair that's practically backed against the wall. Mr. Bean stands next to me. A translator is wedged into the corner of the room nearest the door.

The proceeding begins. I listen dutifully, but even though it's all being translated, the translation is rough and I'm fighting to stay awake. The only thing that sinks in is the translation of the judge's summation: "There is something going on here. You are US Navy SEAL, there were drugs, there were guns. I do not know what is happening, but you and your friends all going to jail while we figure it out."

I never saw any drugs or guns, but there's no way for me to object. I'm dismissed and led to the basement, where I'm put in a cell of my own. The other accused are down there too, also locked up. I don't know what's next.

The entire day passes. I try to rest, but it's useless. Then, around midnight, Nikola, his friends, and I are pulled from our cells, chained together, and shoved into another van.

"Where are we going?" I ask as the van sputters away from the courthouse.

"Centralni Zatvor," Nikola says.

"What's that?"

"CZ, Daniel…CZ is prison."

37

CENTRALNI ZATVOR

I'M FAIRLY SURE NIKOLA MEANS "JAIL," BUT THE DISTINCTION FOR GUYS WHO are actually headed to either of these places is academic. I'm headed to a cage inside a building full of other cages containing other men. I'm going to jail even though I haven't even been officially accused.

Our ride ends half an hour later. We hear the unmistakable sound of a large metal door swinging open. The paddy wagon pulls forward, then stops, and the sound starts back up again. We're inside.

As soon as the gate closes, two officers open the back doors of the van and we awkwardly shuffle out, our wrists all chained together. Each of us holds a large Ziploc bag containing our personal items sans cell phones (they impounded those). Nikola is first, I'm last. The klieg lights shining on the vehicle bay are blinding. We're led through a door and down a dark hall. I'm sure the walls were once white, but they have a sort of green tinge to them. The floor is gray cement with cracks webbing through it, the white metal doors to the left and right are covered with rust splotches. The weak overhead lights are caged, they flicker on and off. Each step I take feels like I'm moving deeper into a film or book—a story I might enjoy, if only I weren't in it.

We reach the end of the hall. A table staffed by six guards. One of the guards removes the chain tethering us together, but we're still cuffed. Nikola and his two friends hand over their stuff, get a bundle of something in exchange. It's my turn. I hand over my plastic bag—I can feel my watch, wallet, and passport inside—and I'm handed a wool blanket, a plastic bowl, a metal spoon. We get to keep our street clothes. Mine are disgusting, but they're comfortable—I've got my Lululemon joggers, my hoodie, a pair of Nike Metcons.

Before I'm led away, one of the guards says, "You are the American, yes?" He looks like he jumped off a caricature artist's sketch pad: five-five, bowl cut, menacing grin.

"Yes," I say wearily.

"Ah! Kosovo?" He holds up his hands and mimes firing an invisible rifle at me.

"No, dude. I was like fifteen years old in nineteen ninety—" I stop myself. What's the point?

Bowl Cut fires his air rifle some more and laughs. "Fuck America!" he says happily.

Whatever, man.

Another guard jabs a finger toward my feet. I look down. I look at him.

"C'mon, my shoes? Those guys didn't have to give you their shoes."

He shakes his head, makes an untying motion with his hands.

"Oh, my laces." No one else had to give up those either, but I can live without laces. I kneel and take them out, hand them over. The guard stuffs them into the bag with the rest of my belongings.

Bowl Cut points to my pants, another flash of the junk and spread of the cheeks it is. At least they're not putting us in jumpsuits—I soon learn that Serbian prisons are so poorly funded they can't afford them.

After this I'm taken to an eight-by-ten holding cell. The place is a shit box. There's a sink, a stained hole in the ground, a bunk bed—and someone already sleeping on the bottom. A tall, bald, round man. He's snoring. The guards uncuff me, push me in, and lock the door behind me. I rub my wrists. The cuffs were tight.

I soon learn that my roommate is Don, a Swede who speaks fluent English. He's a career petty thief whose latest scam entailed dressing like a traffic cop, setting up fake vehicle checkpoints, and shaking down travelers. He gives me the lay of the land. This is not where we'll live, we're just being held here until they find a place for us in one of about twenty cell blocks. The blocks have roughly a hundred prisoners each—in all, CZ holds around two thousand prisoners. Men and women, always kept separate. We'll spend most of our time in our full-time cell, which will be much nicer than this one, we'll get to go outside every day, rain or shine or snow. There is no cafeteria, meals are brought to us. Soup, bread, a single hot dog, sometimes a scoop of jam in the morning.

That first night, our "soup" is some brown salty water with a few beans at the bottom. Because I'm American, I'll get treated differently, and not necessarily in a good way. Because I'm ex-military, they'll probably be even harder on me.

Three days pass. I manage—it's a lot like being on a really shitty SEAL Team deployment—but by day three, Don has lost it. I'm not threatened by him, he's just not fun to be around. He bangs on the door, grabs the metal sink like he's going to pull it off the wall, throws his pillow against the wall over and over, screams at the guards. At one point he hunkers down and takes a giant shit, mostly missing the hole in the floor. He just leaves it there. He probably does it on purpose so the guards will have to clean it up later.

We're transferred at the end of the third day. I'd say bye to Don, but he's not even acknowledging me, so fuck it. They take him away.

The guards look me up and down. I haven't showered in a week, I haven't had access to toilet paper, I haven't brushed my teeth in what feels like a year. One guard lets out a low whistle. He doesn't need to say it—I look and smell like dog shit. "Come on, let's go," I say, almost ordering them. They don't care. One leads, one follows, I stay in the middle. The guards are a little rough, probably because they're scared. They're just normal guys doing their job—I make more in a good week than they do all year—so I cut them some slack.

We go down a hallway, bang a left down another hallway, down a flight of stairs, bang a right down another hallway. This floor is like another planet. The walls are clean and freshly painted. The metal cell doors show no rust. The cells have windows that look outside. It's daytime, the sun is shining. Best of all, there's life on this floor. I hear TVs, radios, people talking and even laughing.

We turn another corner and stop. One of the guards indicates a cell door. We're next to my new home. Just past this cell is another that's being cleaned by a custodial worker and two prisoners on what I assume is some kind of work program.

They're mopping up blood.

A *lot* of blood.

38

THEY CALL ME FOKA

OVER THE COURSE OF MY LIFE, I'VE SEEN LOTS OF BLOOD ON FLOORS (AND ON dirt, and on rock, and on walls, and on you name it)—it is unmistakable. This blood on this Serbian cell block has that familiar viscous look, that slightly metallic smell. It's everywhere. Whatever happened in the next room was fatal and extremely violent.

Meaning I have to be ready for violence.

One of the guards chats with one of the inmates on the cleaning crew. They're chummy, maybe they were friends on the outside. The other guard spins me from the crime scene to the door of my cell. He moves to unlock it. I steel myself.

I briefly think, *All right, Dirty. You may have to take off your human mask while you're in here. I know you're good with that, but don't forget to put it back on when you get out. The world has enough monsters.*

The outer cell door swings open—there's an inner door that's already unlocked and opened into the room. As Don promised, this room is much nicer. I see a proper toilet and makeshift shower in a bathroom to one side. There's a metal mirror screwed to the wall over a sink. There are two bunk beds lined up against the left wall. Above the farthest top bunk is a large window. On the right are a table and two benches. At the far end is a stack of metal cabinets, and above these is a thirty-two-inch flat-screen TV. The cabinets contain toilet paper, playing cards, a few books, some magazines, and Tupperwares full of things like cookies and cigarettes.

There are three men inside. Two are at the table playing a game of dice. Both stop their game to size me up. One man is in his mid-thirties with black hair and matching dark eyes. He looks to be about four inches taller than me and at least thirty pounds heavier. The other is a kid—can't be older than twenty—with light-brown hair and light eyes. He's about my height and fit.

The third man is lying on the bottom rack of one of the bunks. He's old, small, with long gray hair and a beard. He takes one look at me, then rolls back over.

I head to the back of the cell and put what little I have in the one empty cabinet. Without saying a word, the guards close and lock the inner door. The two men at the table slowly stand. The kid grabs a pile of folded clothes from the top bunk under the window and shoves them in an overflowing cabinet. He's clearly annoyed that his extra storage space will be taken up by me.

I give him a quick nod and throw my blanket on the bed. The kid and the dark-haired man shoot each other a look and move close to the bed where the old man is lying down. The three have a whispered conversation. I don't know what they're saying, but I keep hearing the same word over and over: "foka, foka, foka."

Now I hear it coming from…*the TV*?

I turn around. One of the men has used a remote to unmute the television. It's a news show. Talking heads, my name in Cyrillic scrolling across the bottom. Foka…is *me*.

I turn back to the men, they continue to eye me. I take a seat at the table and face them. "Foka, Foka." I have no idea what it means.

The kid sits directly across from me, the old man stays in bed. The large dark-haired man rises to retrieve something from his cabinet, which is behind me. I don't like strangers to my back in any situation, especially in prison.

I turn around. The dark-haired one is advancing toward me. He has a wicked smile. In his right hand is a small homemade knife.

39

ROOMIES

I GET READY TO FIGHT.

This guy is big, but he's not in great shape, though most fights happen so quickly that fitness level doesn't come into play. Strength and experience are what count, and I have both in spades.

But before anything happens, the dark-haired man stops cold, looks at the blade, looks back at me, and laughs.

"No, no, Foka. Is OK! No scared!"

He puts the small blade—a sliver of metal melted into a plastic BIC pen—on the table and turns back to his cabinet. He's still laughing, and the other two laugh also, although a bit uneasily.

What I'd taken for a wicked smile was in fact a genuine one. "Is OK," he repeats. He grabs a pack of food from his cabinet, picks up the knife, this time being careful to keep it away from me, and slides it into the packaging. He holds it out. "Cookie?"

I feel like an idiot, but considering the floor outside is a bloody Slip 'N Slide, not *that* much like an idiot. I take a cookie.

I bite into it. After a week of shitty sandwiches and watery soup, it's one of the best things I've ever tasted. I thank him and he offers me another. I take it.

We make introductions. My roommates are a Croatian terrorist—the young, fit guy; a kidnap-and-ransom specialist—the old, gray guy; a Serbian music producer who murdered his pop-star wife with a hammer—the dark-haired man. Like me, each is innocent. It's like *The Shawshank Redemption* up in here.

Of course, they know all about me. During my days at the police station, at the courthouse, and with Don, I silently hoped to be a gray man in this

168

place—someone who could keep a low profile, take care of his day-to-day, and get out ASAP. But I'd forgotten what Uros had told me—I'm famous.

To help me understand just how famous, the Kid changes the TV to Serbian cable news. Within what feels like only a few minutes, there I am. The Kid, who's halfway fluent in English, does his best to translate. (Hammer Murderer understands English fairly well but can only use a hundred words or so; the Kidnapper barely speaks English at all.)

"American Foka jailed in Belgrade," the Kid says, reading the titles. "Foka won't talk to police. Foka here for Vučić."

I take the remote and mute the TV. "What does 'foka' mean?"

The Kid smiles. "They are calling you animal."

"Like I'm some kind of monster, that kind of animal?"

"No, like animal animal. Here, let me draw." He grabs a pen and paper. I look over his shoulder as he sketches out a long blob with a pointed nose. I have no idea what it is.

Hammer Murderer yelps, "Foka! Foka!" clapping his hands in front of him, keeping his arms perfectly straight.

"Oh, seal!" I say.

"Yes, seal!" the Kid says, suddenly remembering the English word. He adds a few whiskers to his sketch. Now that I see it, the drawing isn't half-bad.

I laugh. "Guys, this is all bullshit. Yeah, I was in the navy, but the rest? No fucking way."

"Not what news says," the Kid insists.

"Obviously. That's why I am saying it's bullshit."

"But Foka, look." He points at the TV—and right on cue, there's my picture—"It is the TV. It is true."

Hammer Murderer hands me a cigarette and lighter and waves his hand at the TV. I light the cigarette and inhale. It's strong. My mouth feels like a sewage pipe. God, I need a toothbrush.

"Kurac," Hammer Murderer mumbles. I don't know what that means, but he clearly shares my disdain for the Kid's faith in TV news.

I watch as the show juxtaposes me with Vučić. This can't be good. I say as much, Hammer Murderer rattles something off, the Kid translates. "He says no, is fine. Not to worry. No one likes president. Everyone hates. If anything, people, they will like you!" The Kid smiles and claps me on the shoulder.

We'll see about that.

The first night in my new room is difficult. Everyone seems to be doing drugs of one kind or another, so "lights-out" is more a suggestion than a rule. The Kid and the Kidnapper play dice and chat until one or two in the morning and then pass out. Hammer Murderer, whose rack is directly below mine, talks to himself and scribbles furiously in a notebook, all while listening to the radio. At one point I hop down to turn it off. He doesn't like that, but he doesn't turn it back on either.

The doors open at 0700 with a bang. My roommates pop to their feet, I follow suit. A guard does a quick head count, then closes and locks the outer door. I lie back down. Ten minutes later, a prisoner pushes a dolly with a white five-gallon bucket on top. We line up with our bowls. One by one, the inmate ladles a heap of red jam into each. No bread today, just jam. I sit at the table and eat. Breakfast of champions.

At 0900 the guards are back. I look at the Kid. "Walk," he says.

"Outside?"

"Yes."

I struggle to contain my joy. I haven't really been outside since the morning of my arrest. This was fewer than fourteen days ago, but it feels like a lifetime.

I throw on my laceless Nikes, the guard leads us down the hall. I count cells as we walk. Including ours, there are seven. Our room is in the middle of the hallway, so multiply that by two—there are fourteen rooms on this block. Most rooms hold four men, but two are larger and they hold as many as twenty. I do some quick math—there are about ninety men on this block. Close to what Don said. We hit the stairs and head down two flights, bang a right down another hallway. Two guards escorting a prisoner pass us going in the opposite direction. "Hajde, Foka!" the prisoner says with a smile. He raises his cuffed hands and…salutes me?

Then one of the guards does the same, sans words.

What in the actual fuck. The media coverage can't help my legal situation, but it sure is working out so far in CZ.

We come to a stop in front of a blue metal door, the guard pops it open. We walk down three cement steps to a twenty-five-by-fifty cobblestone courtyard. It's littered with cigarette butts, trash, pigeons, pigeon shit, and solitary pieces of grass fighting to find sunlight. The prison itself serves as the courtyard walls.

Castle-like, these reach five stories into the sky, the barred windows of the cells looking down on us. At the end of the courtyard is a wall with another blue door, and through a fence I can make out an identical courtyard on the other side.

Aside from the guards, we're the only ones out here.

My three roommates immediately begin power walking. I follow. I'm in step with the Kid. "Where are the other prisoners?"

"They walk different time," the Kid says.

"Because…?"

"Because we are the special ones. Because of our crimes. Because you are American Foka—and here for Vučić!" I don't contradict him. There's no point. "And also, that was cool!" he says, saluting me like the guard and the prisoner. "You are cool, Foka."

"Thanks, Kid." I don't mean it. We take a few steps, turn around. "Why does everyone hate Vučić?"

"I don't know—I am Croatian!"

The Kidnapper, who's behind us, overhears the word "Vučić" and starts talking quickly, the Kid translates.

"Ah, OK, OK. Foka, he says the president is totally corrupt. There is no money. The guards make three hundred euros a month. He says Vučić's brother, he is big gangster. He says Vučić is gangster. He is a hooligan. He is biggest hooligan! Bigger than Red Star or Partizan, he has fingers with both. He has beat people when he was young, he talks about this on TV like he is proud. He controls security service, press, courts, everything. Corruption everywhere. Everyone hates Vučić. Right now there is assassin in CZ who works for a man who works for Vučić. The Butcher. But the Butcher—he hates Vučić too!" The old man bursts out laughing at this.

What a mess.

Thirty minutes later, a guard pops out and we're led back inside. The Kid tells me that the other inmates get two whole hours in the yard. And that the other yard has some exercise equipment. We switch yards every day, which means that tomorrow I'll be able to do some pull-ups. I can't wait.

I grill the Kid as we head back to our cell. He tells me it's Wednesday. He tells me that we get to use showers on Monday, Wednesday, and Friday. I *need* a shower. He tells me that before we head to the showers, we go to the cantina.

If my lawyer put any money in my account, then I can buy food, deodorant, soap—a toothbrush!

At 1100 a guard comes to the room and takes us to the cantina, which is just down the hall. The room is divided in half. It looks like the checkout counter of a liquor store you'd see in the hood. A woman behind a thick sheet of plexiglass takes orders and barks at trusted inmates working in the storeroom.

I step up to the window—Milosh has put €300 in my account. Thank God. I buy a toothbrush, toothpaste, deodorant, toilet paper, soap, a towel, a couple of cans of tuna, and a small bucket on the advice of the Kidnapper. (I also notice that they sell things like safety razors and pencil sharpeners, which makes no sense to me.) From the cantina we head to the showers. There are three cement partitions on either side of the room, so six stalls. I disrobe and head to the first station. I turn on the tap. Piping hot water blasts from the showerhead. I'm so happy the water is hot, but it's scalding. I fiddle with the tap, the temperature mellows. I count how many days it's been: twelve. Unfortunately, as soon as I dry off, I have to throw on my filthy clothing. I skip the underwear and go commando. It's too disgusting.

When we get back to the room, my cellmates have a quick powwow. Hammer Murderer gifts me two pairs of clean basketball shorts, the Kid throws me two clean shirts, and the Kidnapper tosses me four pairs of clean socks. "Foka, you stink, take these, they are yours now," says the Kid. I thank them. Lunch is wheeled up to the door at noon—yellow water today, along with a loaf of bread for each of us. I eat one of my cans of tuna. It's amazing. I lie back in bed, enjoying the full stomach, fresh shower, and clean clothes. Dinner shows up at 1900, a solitary hot dog for each of us, individually wrapped in Saran Wrap. We sit around after dinner—more dice, more mysterious drugs, more music from Hammer Murderer's little radio—and it's lights-out at 2300.

It plays out like this day after day. Like the military, prison life is built on routine. I learn where the pills—pinks and blues, little powdery whites—come from. Some are courtesy of the guards—most likely downers, since these keep everyone chill. The others come from the affable junkie with a smashed nose who pushes the lunch cart. His name is Gile. Everyone in my room encourages me to partake, everyone is disappointed that I don't. I will not ever do drugs in here. They're not my thing on the outside, and they sure as shit won't be my thing inside. Way too risky.

I also learn that the blood being mopped up on my first day came from a man who was killed by his cellmates, although the official line is he did himself in by slicing his neck open with the edge of the metal mirror mounted to his cell's bathroom wall. But apparently he was an evil asshole who got what was coming to him. The guards hated him too, so no big deal—except for all that blood, I guess.

I only bring this up to say that there are nights when I come awfully close to doing something similar to Hammer Murderer. Yes, he gave me cookies on that first day, and yes, he shared some clothing with me, but he's hard to put up with. He's high twenty-four hours a day, is writing some kind of prison manifesto in his diary, and plays shitty pop music late into the night, every night, bouncing along with the beat. Since we share a bunk, this cuts into my sleep a lot. And one thing I need in this situation is sleep.

If I don't get enough, I'm liable to hurt someone.

I need to be careful.

40

THE STATE DEPARTMENT

On day twenty-two at CZ, a guard pops open our cell door and says, "Foka, advokat."

My vocabulary is limited, but I know "advokat" means "lawyer."

I put on my shoes—I've fashioned some laces with strips of black trash bags—and pull my hoodie from our ad hoc drying rack at the back of the room. Then the guard cuffs me loosely and jerks his head toward the hall. I follow.

We pass the cantina and then go down a long hallway I haven't been in yet. At the end is a desk, and behind the desk is a female guard in a crisp blue uniform. To her left are large rooms labeled by number. Inside the nearest room I see what appear to be a wife and child visiting an incarcerated man.

These are the visiting rooms.

The female guard sends us to room four. We stop outside, the guard uncuffs me, I enter.

Milosh is already there. He's a picture-perfect lawyer: three-piece suit, tie, Italian dress shoes, matching belt, rimless reading glasses, styled yet modest hair, impeccable hygiene. I move toward him with a little pep in my step. I don't expect good or bad news, I'm just glad my lawyer is finally here.

"Hey, Milosh!" I smile and reach out my hand.

"Sit," he says.

I'm almost offended, but then he taps the face of his watch. This meeting is timed, and he doesn't want to waste any. Fine by me. I sit.

"You OK?" he asks.

It's obvious he means "Is anyone fucking with you, have you had any fights, has anyone tried to hurt you?" and not "How is the food, how are the guards treating you, is your bed comfortable, are you cold at night?"

"Yeah, I'm good," I reply.

He looks at a piece of paper. "I see they put you in the cell with—" he mimes swinging a hammer forcefully.

"They did. He's not great."

"I think they will move you soon," Milosh says.

"Fuck, I hope so."

Milosh grabs his briefcase and places it on the desk and leans in close, almost like he's hiding behind it. Maybe he knows the location of a hidden camera. "Daniel," he says, "we still don't have specific charges, but it is confirmed they are treating this case as organized crime."

"What does that mean?"

"It means this could take a long time."

"Like what—a couple months, six months? A year?!"

I jokingly say this last part, but Milosh doesn't bat an eye. "Probably longer."

"Really." I strangely feel nothing. Must be shock. Milosh nods. "Why so long?" I ask.

"There are many reasons. For example, the court has up to six months to formally charge you, and I promise they will take the full six months. Then, if and when any of you get charged, any of you can appeal individual charges. Each time this happens, add at least another three to six months."

"All right." It's not all right. "Is there any way for us to request that the organized crime case be dropped and they charge us individually?"

He gives me a look of approval. "Very clever, Daniel. Yes, there is, and we may go this route—but many things need to happen first. Many things that do not happen quickly."

"Nothing here happens quickly, does it?"

"No. Everything is very slow."

"What about house arrest? I can rent a flat and wear a bracelet for as long as they want."

"This is a possibility. Nikola and one of the others are already home, wearing trackers."

"No shit! What about the other guy?"

"He has been arrested twice before, so no chance." I raise my eyebrows and point at myself. "I know, you have also never been arrested here," Milosh says. "I've already started the paperwork, but don't get too hopeful. You are the

American, the Foka, you're very dangerous." He makes spooky hands on either side of his face and laughs a little.

I don't laugh.

Just then, the guard pops in. "Vreme." Time's up.

Milosh grabs his briefcase, stands, and shakes my hand. "Daniel, have you been to the cantina?"

"Yep. I got the money. Thank you. Truly."

"I will continue to put three hundred euros in there every month. Let me know if you need more."

"Thanks."

"I will see you next month, and the month after that, and so on. Don't worry. This will be OK in the end, but you need to be ready to be in here for a long time." He exits the room and leaves.

A few days later, a guard pops open our door again. "Foka, ambasada." Finally the Americans are coming.

The Kidnapper jumps out of bed, beaming. "Foka go home! Foka go home!" Hammer Murderer and the Kid say the same thing but with less enthusiasm—they must have taken the pink pills today.

I damn near skip to the door and present my wrists. The guard cuffs me and escorts me to the visiting rooms. While we walk, he says, "You go home."

"You think?"

"Sto posto." One hundred percent.

I'm taken to room one and sit. Directly across from me is a man, late thirties, curly brown hair, glasses, nervous as hell. To his right is a woman, mid-forties, blond, short, modestly dressed. She's calm, and she even looks concerned for me.

Yes, Milosh warned me about how long this could take, but now the cavalry is here! I've been wrongly accused and falsely arrested and I carry a US passport and I'm a SEAL reservist with Team 17. Uncle Sam will come through.

"Daniel, I'm Eric Roth. I work at the US embassy here in Belgrade."

"Nice to meet you, sir." I move to take his hand, but he hesitates before reaching across the desk and giving me a limp-wristed shake. It feels gross.

Is that a tremble I hear in his voice? This dude seems scared to be in CZ, that or maybe he's scared to be sitting across the table from me, the American Navy SEAL. He nods to his right, indicating the woman.

"Hello, Daniel. I'm Ana." She confidently sticks out her hand, I shake it.

"Nice to meet you, ma'am." She looks nothing like my grandma, but she has that grandma vibe. I half expect her to take my hand between both of hers and whisper, "Pobrecito mijo." (My grandma on my dad's side is full Mexican, from Chihuahua.)

She continues, "I'm a Serbian national who works in the US embassy. We have been assigned to your case."

"Well, thanks for coming." *Took you long enough*, I think.

Roth asks, "Daniel, are you OK?"

"No, I'm not. I haven't done anything wrong, I haven't been charged, I broke no laws. I'm stuck in a room with a guy who killed his wife with a hammer. My lawyer says I'm going to be fine but that it could take years to deal with my case. So no, I'm not OK."

"Yes, well, about your, uh, situation. The news is saying some pretty bad things about you."

"The news?"

"Yes."

Is this guy serious? I've yet to get angry, but in only a few minutes, Roth from the State Department has me close to losing it. I take a breath. "Yeah, we have TVs in here. I've seen the 'news.' It's all bullshit, so it doesn't bother me. Or I try not to let it bother me."

"Good," Ana says kindly. I give her a nod of thanks.

Roth then asks about the food. "The food? It's fantastic!" I answer. "Fillet every night, fried potatoes, lobster on Fridays. What do you think? It's awful."

He jots something on a legal pad. I don't understand how the quality of the food is going to help me get out.

"Mr. Roth, what is the official purpose of this visit? Are you going to get me out of here?"

Roth seems to suppress a nervous laugh, I nearly jump across the table to slap him. I grab the arms of my plastic chair to stop myself. They creak audibly in my fists.

Roth's face gets serious again. "We're not here to get you out, Daniel."

Fuck this guy. "Mr. Corbett," I correct him.

He then explains I had been arrested in a nonofficial capacity, and like any American, I was bound by the laws of the country I was visiting—in this case, Serbia.

"But I didn't break any laws. I was in my friend's apartment literally doing nothing when I was arrested."

"We've read the reports," Ana says. "They don't reflect well on the police."

"I guess that's good?"

"Listen, Mr. Corbett." Roth slides a form across the desk, a ballpoint pen on top. I scan it as he speaks. "We've been in touch with your parents. This says you will allow us to speak to them about you and your case."

I sign it. "A legal document in English. What a revelation," I joke. Ana laughs, Roth doesn't. I slide the form back to Roth. "Tell them I'm fine. Everything's good. I'm not scared." And I'm not. Not just because I'm a SEAL, but more because I know that I'm loved, by my parents and many others. Just like Mom used to say, "Love is the antagonist of fear." That might be truer in prison than anywhere else. Guess I'll find out.

I say none of this to Roth or Ana. Mom and Dad will know.

"I'll relay the message," Roth says.

Just then the door opens, the guard comes in. "Vreme." Time's up.

Roth stands and moves quickly toward the door. Wow. I guess he really *is* scared.

"Hey, Roth, don't forget. Tell my folks I'm good, got it?"

"Yes, of course." Roth doesn't shake my hand. He then steps out of the room and disappears into the hall.

Ana steps up to me. "I'm sorry this is happening to you, Mr. Corbett." She offers her hand, I shake it. "One of us will be back, every month, to catalog your detention. We will try to work diplomatic channels for your release, but I can't make any promises."

"I appreciate it, Ana," I say.

"Remember. Next month." Then she disappears down the hall too.

The guard steps in and stands there. After an awkward silence, he says, "Go home?"

I shake my head. "No go home."

"Ah, Foka. Jebi ga." He pats me on the back and puts the cuffs back on.

I walk back to my room feeling completely abandoned by the United States. I'm on my own. I'm going to have to persevere here in CZ for as long as it takes.

That night, long after lights-out, Hammer Murderer's radio plays the worst music I've ever heard. I can't take it. I jump down from the top bunk, grab his radio, and smash it to pieces on the floor. Hammer Murderer does nothing. I think I can hear him crying quietly, but it's too dark to be sure. I get back into bed. Love may be the antagonist of fear, but it doesn't always work against anger. Soon I fall asleep.

The next morning, the Kid tells me it was his wife singing on the radio when I destroyed it. I almost feel bad, but then I remember: he killed her. With a hammer.

That afternoon, I'm transferred to a new cell.

41

ROOM 311

My new home is room 311. My roommates are Aussie Dave, junkie Gile, and tattooed Luka. I recognize Gile as the drug dealer who pushes the lunch cart. Right away, I can tell that things are better in 311. The cell is clean, the men are too. No one seems high. No one in here is accused of hammer murder. There's a TV near Luka's bed, and he holds the remote.

They all know who I am, and like everyone in CZ, they call me Foka. Once again, I get the top bunk near the window. I don't know why I keep getting the best bed in the house, but I'm not complaining.

Luka—mid-twenties, six-two, 220 pounds, tattooed—speaks passable English. Dave and Gile are here on drug charges—I have no idea what Luka's in for. Whatever it is, he's clearly the boss. He lays out the rules: Lights-out by 2300, no noise or smoking after that. Lights on at 0700, nothing before that. Keep your stuff in order. Take regular showers. No bitching. Absolutely no drugs. (Luka doesn't drink or get high, and I'm thrilled about it.) He also asks me directly if we're going to have any trouble. "Not at all," I answer. I appreciate everything Luka says, and he can tell.

This room is arranged differently. The cabinets are lined up along the wall to the right as soon as you enter. The table is off to the left just past the bathroom and parallel to the wall, which makes for back support on one side. There's a chessboard on the table, the pieces already set up. The two bunk beds are across from each other at the end of the room. Gile cleans out the overflow cabinet. To my surprise, he does it with enthusiasm, not like the assholes in the previous room. I can tell they're not thrilled to have a fourth roommate, but apparently my celebrity status has some pull in CZ and these guys are happy to have me join them.

Once I'm settled, Luka asks if I play chess.

"I know how the pieces move," I say, lying a little. I played tons of chess on my phone when I was in the Teams.

"That's a yes. Let's play."

Just as I'm about to sit, a guard opens the outer door. "Foka, paket."

I look at Luka. He says, "You have a package."

The guard pushes a clear plastic storage container into the room. There's a small piece of paper with the date, Milosh's name, and a large "B" signed in ink. I thank the guard, he doesn't respond. He and Luka are chatting like old buddies. Clearly Luka is connected.

After the guard leaves, Luka leans over my shoulder to read the note. "Who's it from?"

Besides taking a shit, there's no privacy in CZ. "My lawyer."

He points to the large "B." "And this?"

"I have an idea, but I'm not sure."

"What is your idea?"

"Someone from the Hells Angels."

Luka doesn't respond. Hopefully, he's not in a rival club.

I tear off three layers of tape and pop off the top. I pull everything out and put it on my bed: four pairs of boxer briefs, three pairs of Champion sweatpants, five T-shirts, five pairs of black Nike socks, two gray Slazenger sweatshirts, one pair of black knockoff Crocs, four pairs of Nike basketball shorts, one full length military-style canvas field jacket for winter, and books. There's *Crime and Punishment*, *The Gambler*, *The House of the Dead*, *The Mysterious Island*, and *Sherlock Holmes: The Complete Collection*. I'm stoked for the books, but also a little bummed: I hope I don't have the time to read all of them.

I put my stuff away—tossing *Crime and Punishment* on the bed for later—and then sit so Luka can kick my ass at chess.

I quickly learn that Gile is a prime source of entertainment. He's got a great sense of humor and constantly bullshits, using sound effects and theatrics. On my first night, with Luka translating, he tells about how he won a gold medal diving off Mostar bridge into the Neretva river. Luka and I sit at the table and Dave watches from his bed as Gile stands in the middle of the room and goes through his dive routine, including two forward rolls on the floor while making whooshing sounds through labored breaths. Luka and I cry laughing. Dave just calls bullshit the whole time.

A few nights later, over a game of chess, I ask Luka about his case. "Gile tells me that you're here for murder," I whisper.

He shrugs a little. "Murder for hire, but yes." The distinction between simple murder and professional killing is important for him—and for me. It just makes me like him more.

"You've been locked up before, I assume?"

"Yes."

"For what?"

"The same as now."

"You must have a good lawyer."

"I do. I am also good at what I do, plus if I go down, I bring important people with me."

Mutually assured destruction is always a good bargaining chip. Wish I had some. I'm over ten years older than Luka, but I feel like he has things to teach me, not just about life in CZ but also about the trade. Time will tell if my intuition is correct.

Aside from the improved company, the best thing about being in room 311 is that I get two hours a day outside with the rest of our block. Before my first walk, a guard comes by for a quick conversation with Luka. It's obviously about me. As soon as the guard leaves, I ask for details.

"They're worried about you having some problem."

"I told you, I'm not going to make any trouble."

"I know. But you are famous, and famous people are good measuring sticks. Maybe someone else wants to use you to make trouble."

"That would suck. Mostly for them."

"I don't doubt it. But it would also not be good for you. I tell you now what I told the guard: If someone makes trouble, you will handle it. And if things get out of control, I will stop it."

"Thanks, Luka."

"No problem, Foka."

We go outside. Everyone forms into cliques and, like a giant clock, we all start walking slowly around the perimeter, moving counterclockwise. Whispers here and there, quiet conversations, not-so-sly exchanges of contraband, almost everyone smoking.

I quickly discover that Luka is a celebrity—in fact, he's the Butcher the old man mentioned. Everyone goes out of their way to say hello. It's like some of them are kissing the ring—which makes sense if he works for a man who works for Vučić.

At one point I jokingly ask Luka if *I'm* going to have any trouble with *him*—since I'm Foka, the presidential assassin, and he's the Butcher, the president's assassin. He just hisses, "Vučić!" and spits on the ground, then wraps his arm over my shoulder. "No trouble, Foka." He means it.

I'm glad for that.

It takes me around two weeks to get introduced to everyone. I meet Gypsies, hard criminals, street kids, white-collar guys, drug addicts, gangsters, racketeers, rapists. I meet football hooligans from Red Star and Partizan. Their rivalry isn't Yankees/Red Sox or Man City/Manchester United—it's Crips/Bloods, Montague/Capulet, Gambino/Bonanno. They've divided Belgrade and the surrounding area into their own fiefdoms, controlling everything. I even hear a rumor that the Partizan hooligans keep a meat grinder in the bowels of their team's stadium to grind the bodies of their victims. Fun!

For the most part, though, these two gangs put their differences aside in CZ. One, everyone in here is either on trial or awaiting it. If they get in trouble, it just complicates their cases. Two, there is an overriding sense of us vs. them in CZ—us being inmates, them being everyone else.

If I'm not using the pull-up or dip bar, I mostly walk around with Luka. I quickly get treated like his sidekick. Fine by me. "Foka, Foka, Foka!" That's all I hear. Everyone insists I'm a career criminal, and while I don't see it that way, I also concede they have a point. I killed for the US military, and now I'm a jailed mercenary (though I don't tell anyone about the mercenary work, not even Luka). The street kids ask me how American prisons are and what kind of cocaine is the best. I tell them I haven't been to prison in America and I had no idea there are distinct types of cocaine. My answers are brushed aside with sly grins: "Yeah, sure, Foka. Whatever you say. We are all angels in here."

One day Luka calls me over to join him and two others. I finish a set of pull-ups—I'm up to four sets of eighteen by now—and head over. "Foka, this is

Mozza. I've known him for a long time." Mozza towers over all of us at six-five, weighs well over 250 pounds, has close-cropped black hair and a baby face.

I reach out my hand, preparing for a crushing shake, but he just wraps me a bear hug. "Foka, drago mi je!"

His hug catches me off guard, but it's a good hug so I don't fight it. "Nice to meet you too!" I manage as he squeezes the air out of me.

Mozza releases me, Luka points to the other guy. "This is Bulgi. He is the barber of the block. He cuts my hair twice a week." Bulgi is about five-ten and looks like Uncle Fester. He eagerly shakes my hand. "Statham! Jason Statham!" he says, pointing at me. "He is the best! You look like him!" His English is good.

"Nice to meet you, Bulgi. Why haven't I seen you out here before?"

"Ah, too cold. I like summer. And too many people in my room. They all go, and I get the room to myself."

Smart. Luka takes off and the three of us get to know each other, Bulgi translating. Mozza is a high-ranking Red Star hooligan, locked up for beating two guys with a baseball bat. Bulgi is a Bulgarian national and professional thief specializing in luxury watches. I tell him about Malachi's collection. Over the following days and weeks, we group together. Me, Bulgi, Mozza, and sometimes Luka. Regardless of why he's in here, Mozza is a big softy, and Bulgi is hilarious. They ask me if any of the guards have fucked with me, especially the older ones. I tell them no. At one point Mozza gets really animated, talking fast, running his hands over his head. Bulgi says, "He's angry. It's so unfair how the news talks about you. He says he had a dream that you go free. I hope you go free too."

I thank them. Everyone wants to see me win my case—if and when it ever begins. If I can beat the system, they can too, right?

This is my first glimpse into how hope is traded among prisoners. Of everything that gets passed among us—rumors, drugs, cigarettes, chocolate, coffee—hope is the most precious commodity.

42

CZ99

At the end of April, the cell door opens. "Foka, advokat."

I'm cuffed and escorted down the hall to room four. Milosh is already there. I'm uncuffed and take a seat.

"How is everything?" Milosh asks.

"Much better. I'm in a new room."

"I heard. Did you get your package?"

"Yes. Thank you, and thank Branko for me, please."

Milosh nods. "I will. Now. The investigation is underway. They found your DNA on a gun."

"DNA? A gun? What gun?"

"When Nikola and the others were arrested, he had a CZ99 with him. That gun."

I know the make and model—it's a knockoff of a SIG Sauer P226, the standard sidearm for the SEAL Teams. "Milosh, I've never touched a gun in Serbia. Never. Not a CZ99 or any other."

Milosh shrugs. "Still, they have your DNA."

I think back. "It must have gotten there from all the swabs they took during my interrogation."

"Maybe. But it doesn't matter. We can't just deny that you touched it and blame the police. That won't work as a defense. In Serbia, DNA is king."

I clap my hands suddenly. "Wait—was this gun used in a crime?"

"No. They are not saying that. They are saying you ordered Nikola to get you a gun, and he did."

"I've never asked anyone in this country to get me a gun. No one. And if I did, I wouldn't ask some spoiled kid who went to Boston College. I'd ask... someone else. Fuck, almost *anyone* else."

"Nevertheless, there is a gun with your DNA on it."

I ignore him. My mind is spinning. I continue, "Besides, if I had asked him to get me one, and he did, and I'd touched it, then wouldn't *I* be the one with the gun when we were arrested? Not Nikola? This shit makes no sense!"

"This argument is logical, and it may work in court, but it cannot remove your DNA from the weapon." Once again, Milosh places his briefcase on the desk and leans behind it. I meet him there. Very quietly he says, "We need to come up with a plausible explanation for why you touched the gun."

I think for half a minute. I whisper, "OK, what about this. As you know, I'm a Navy SEAL. When people find this out, they show me all kinds of different guns. Their grandpa's hunting rifle, their shotguns, their pistols. I've even been shown antique muzzleloaders." Whenever it happens to me, I usually disappoint my host. I'm not a gun nut and only know the weapons I've used throughout my career—if they start talking about ballistics and different kinds of bullets, forget it. I gloss over and check out.

I continue. "So he had a gun, and he thought it would be cool to show it to me. I humored him, took it, and checked to make sure it was clear and safe. And then handed it right back."

Milosh asks me to carefully explain "clear and safe." I walk him through it.

"I like this idea," he whispers. "We are going to say Nikola bought the weapon to impress you. He then showed it to you and you handled it once—doing this 'clear and safe' thing—and that was it. Yes. This is good. Detailed, logical. I will talk to Nikola personally."

"OK. So we have a plan then?" I lean back in my chair now that this part of our discussion is over.

Milosh leans back as well. "Yes, for this part of the case at least."

"Speaking of—when the hell is it going to start?"

"Ah, you've beaten me to my next topic. You—along with Nikola and his friends—will get a chance to make your statement regarding the gun in a few days in 'small court.' This is where they decide if there will be charges."

"Wait—'*if* there will be charges'?"

"Yes. There's a decent chance you won't be charged at all. You could be out of here as early as next week."

Suddenly I feel like I'm floating. "Milosh, why didn't you start with that? Your fucking bedside manner sucks, man."

Milosh shrugs, starts going through some papers.

"What about the State Department?" I ask. "Have you talked to them?"

"Forget the State Department," he says. "They are worthless here."

Just then the guard enters the room. "Vreme," the guard drones.

Time's up.

The guard hustles me out of there faster than before, not allowing me or Milosh to say anything else. With no help from the embassy, it really is just going to be me and Milosh.

Fine by me.

43

A FLASH OF SILVER

I'M A LITTLE SHOCKED BY THE LIGHTNESS IN MY STEP AFTER THIS MEETING. For what it's worth, Luka agrees with Milosh. He's seen it before. The Serbs love to arrest people, sit on them, and then just let them walk. When I ask him why, he says wisely, "Making the system unpredictable checks behavior." He pauses. "Sometimes. Still, I think you will go free, Foka."

The takeaway from my sudden sense of hope: I have been pushing down a lot of shit as I've adjusted to life in jail. And this one bit of good news releases some of that pressure. It feels good.

That night, I'm all over the news. All the "reporting" is completely fabricated. In addition to my interest in Vučić, they say I'm in Serbia to kill the minister of trade, tourism, and telecommunications. They quote the minister of defense saying, "He isn't here to shoot fish in the Danube with that gun." They call me the "najopasniji čovjek"—"most dangerous man"—in the history of Serbia. I laugh out loud several times. This is a country full of dangerous people, a country that fought a bloody war not thirty years ago. A country whose former president was tried for crimes against humanity. And I'm the most dangerous? Really? It's like they don't even know who they are.

The next day, a light drizzle is falling as we're walking the yard. Like most days, I'm with Mozza and Bulgi. It's only May, but it's already hot. I begin to suspect Serbian summers are sultry. If I get released, I won't stick around to find out. (I've had no contact with Malachi or my client, but at this point I know the job is dead and I have no obligation to hang around.)

Since boredom is endemic in prison, news about me travels like wildfire. Everyone is desperate for something to be excited about and it might as well be me and my "small court" date.

About an hour into our recess, the blue metal door opens. A new guy appears. Early twenties, tall, lanky. I look to Mozza and Bulgi, they shrug. No one seems to know him. Maybe he got transferred from a different block, because he doesn't have that new-fish look. He peers around, exuding a real junkie vibe. He shuffles in the same direction as everyone else, scanning, scanning, scanning.

After a few moments, he breaks the prime unspoken rule of the yard—he leaves the circuitous march around the edge and makes a beeline diagonally across no-man's-land. Mozza, Bulgi, and I are on the far side of the yard. It quickly becomes obvious that the junkie is coming for one of us.

Judging by his fixed and empty stare, he's coming for me. I'm not excited about this. My small court date is imminent—I can't hurt anyone.

Only it looks like I'm going to have to hurt someone. I get ready.

He's six feet away. He's four feet away. He pulls his hands out of his pockets. A flash of silver. Great. Another man walking toward me brandishing a knife.

One thing's for sure: unlike Hammer Murderer, this guy doesn't want to share his cookies.

44

SMALL COURT

IN THAT BRIEF INSTANT, I'M TRANSPORTED TO MY ASSIGNMENT IN THE PHILIPPINES with SEAL Team 5. Short version: As part of building rapport with the partner force, I got involved in cockfighting. I knew nothing about cockfighting. Another SEAL and I bought a small, pugnacious rooster we named Flex. We trained him— basically by starving him and getting him to try harder and harder to reach food just beyond his reach. We went to cockfighting night, and when the locals saw us—two white Americans posted to a jungle on the other side of the world— they tried to figure out how to make money off us and our little Flex. One guy approached, called himself the Blade Man. Apparently the roosters had little knives tied to their legs. Who knew? Blade Man liked Flex. Flex got hooked up, he went into the cockpit, the fight began. The locals went crazy, yelling, waving money, taking and making bets on the fly. Flex had four-to-one odds against. He was smaller and weaker than the other bird, not as pretty either. But Flex didn't give a shit. After thirty seconds or so, he launched at his opponent, flashing his silver, slicing the other rooster's stomach. Feathers flew, the other bird ran off, the crowd went wild. Flex peacocked around like he was Manny Pacquiao. The fight was over, and we were four times richer.

This zombie crossing the yard with his little knife reminds me of Flex.

Here we go.

Just as I'm about to move on him, I'm blindsided by Mozza, who shoves me into the wall. He then full-on tackles the Zombie, lifting him off his feet and throwing him onto the ground. There's a pronounced crack as his head bounces on the pavement. The knife falls from his grip, Bulgi kicks it away. Mozza pins him by stepping on his face, leaning into it. The Zombie squirms to get free but it's no use. Bulgi leans over him and belts out a string of expletives and spittle.

He makes a point of ashing his cigarette into the guy's eyes. I try not to laugh. Two guards show up and take him away. They saw the whole thing, and Mozza isn't in any trouble. I thank Mozza for looking out. He knows I wouldn't have had any problems with the Zombie, but he was still protecting me.

That night I try to piece together who would send a half-assed knifeman for me and why. I can't come up with anything solid. I can only assume it has to do with my small court date. Maybe that will reveal something.

Just after breakfast the next morning, a guard comes into our room. "Foka, sud." Court.

I'm cuffed and escorted downstairs. Five others dressed in their Sunday best are headed to court too. We're marched to the vehicle bay. I'm last in line. The other guys pile into the paddy wagon, I follow. But just as I'm about to step in, a guard grabs my arm and yanks me back. The paddy wagon's doors shut, it takes off. Another pulls up, its doors open. I'm getting the Foka treatment. I'm getting my own ride.

I'm put in the back, the guards load up in the single cab, packed shoulder to shoulder like three teenagers in the front of a pickup heading to homecoming.

The fact that none of them are with me makes no sense. I could pick my cuffs, kick the door open, and run. I could disappear, sneak around, and get the hell out of this country. Of course, I'd be leaving my passport behind, which would complicate things, and I'd technically be a fugitive, which would *really* complicate things, but it's still possible.

Also, they have my Rolex.

Ah, it's pure fantasy and I know it. Escaping would be worse than beating some junkie into the infirmary, or even killing one. Escapees are guilty. No other explanation.

As we drive to court, I become aware of a small crack in the side of the van. I scooch down the bench and peer through it. I get little snapshots of daily life. People grocery shopping, families headed to the park, a young couple kissing on a low wall under a leafy tree. Jesus, it's spring. I haven't seen a tree in months, and certainly not one with leaves on it. Then we pass Sveti Sava. Seeing it feels like getting backhanded.

Being in CZ has been a full-time game for me, one that I didn't completely realize I was playing. It's on this van ride, when I'm alone, that I fully grasp the fact that I've been separated from society. No one outside cares about my paddy wagon, and they certainly don't care about me, no matter what the media says. I feel like a pawn in one of my chess matches with Luka. Worse, because if I am a pawn, I don't even know where the boundaries of the board are, or what game is being played.

A short while later, we pull into the courthouse's vehicle bay. The three guards slide out, pop open the doors, and hand me over to three court officers. These guys are rough. They grab my arms with kung fu grips and physically drag me to a holding area on the ground floor. There are about a dozen cells, and I'm taken to the last one on the right. While we're walking, I hear "Foka!" I crane my neck. It's some kid I've never seen before, locked away in a cell. He smiles and waves like we're long-lost friends.

I'm shoved into a four-by-six cell, cuffs still on. One of the guards sits on a small bench in the hall and stares at me. I try to ignore him.

An hour later, two of his comrades arrive. They manhandle me, drag me down the hall and up some stairs. The other prisoner yells, "Foka!" again as I pass.

We come to a landing and step into a hallway. It looks familiar—this is the same courthouse we were brought to after leaving the police station! Same people are here too—there's Nikola, his two friends, and Milosh.

Milosh crosses to me and says something to the guards. They release my arms and step away. Blood rushes to where their hands gripped me. Milosh leans in. "Nikola is going in first to make his statement. On the day of the arrest, before he left the apartment, he showed you the gun. You picked it up to make sure it was not loaded and gave it back to him. OK?"

"Got it." I'm not eager to lie to a judge, and I don't like that we are literally getting our stories straight in the hall outside the courtroom, but what can I do?

The guards inch toward us. They don't like us speaking. "One more thing, Daniel. Important. I can't be in there with you. Only answer the questions they ask. Keep everything short. 'Yes,' 'No,' 'I don't know.' All of those are good. No unnecessary explanations. Do not give opinions. Stay on target."

I can do that. I've been doing that my whole life.

The guards step next to us before I can respond. Milosh gives me a nod and steps away. The court doors open. Nikola—on house arrest, not cuffed, not guarded—waltzes in, shooting me his trademark wink. The doors close. Everyone else waits.

I go over Milosh's statement over and over. It's not a hard script to remember, but it's essential I do not fuck it up. Thirty minutes later, Nikola exits, another wink. I nod. We aren't allowed to talk, so this is all we've got. I'm led in. It's the same cramped office and the same judge. I assume this is all she does, day in and day out. Like a one-stop grand jury.

To the judge's left is a woman, mid-thirties, light hair pulled into a tight ponytail, reading glasses. She speaks first. "Good morning. I will be your translator today. If you don't understand something or need something repeated, please speak up."

"Thank you," I say. "And will do."

The translator gives the judge a nod, the judge wastes no time. "Name?"

"Daniel David Corbett the third." I have a tough time figuring out whom to look at, the translator or the judge, but settle on the judge.

"Date of birth?"

I answer truthfully.

"Tell me what happened the day you were arrested."

"I was at Nikola's house, we were getting ready for a party."

"What kind of party?"

"A dinner party, I think. It never happened." Fuck. I'm already talking too much. I can't screw this up. "I don't know what kind of party."

"What were you doing there, in his apartment?"

"We were cooking, cleaning, hanging out. At one point he left, and I stayed at his place."

"Why did he leave?"

"I don't know."

"Tell me about the gun."

"What do you want to know?"

"How did you come to possess it?"

"I never possessed it, Your Honor. I only held it."

"This is what I mean. Tell me how you came to hold it." Then she tilts her head and gives me a funny look. "What is 'Your Honor'?"

"That's how Americans address judges, uh, Your Honor."

"You can just call me 'Judge.'"

"OK, Judge."

"How did you come to hold the gun?"

"Before Nikola left, he showed me a pistol. I took it and made sure it wasn't loaded."

"Did he show you the pistol? Or did he hand you the pistol?"

"Yes. I mean, both."

"Did you ask him to show you the pistol?"

"No. He just showed it to me."

"Why?"

"I don't know." I resist talking about how people like to show SEALs their firearms. No unnecessary explanations.

"How did you determine if the pistol wasn't loaded?"

"I cleared and safed it."

"What is clear and safe? Walk me through that process."

"Sure. First I removed the magazine. Then I racked the slide three times, locked it to the rear, and did a visual inspection of the chamber."

"So you admit to handling the gun?"

"Yes." A pit forms in my stomach. I don't like lying, and I'm pissed I'm in this situation in the first place. I think back to interrogation training. To how they made us lie, and made us good at it. I think about my tells. I bottle them all up—hands in lap, steady breathing, no fidgeting, keep my eyes forward and on the person I'm talking to.

I'm as cool as a snowball in summertime.

"Why didn't you tell the police this at their initial questioning?"

"They didn't ask."

"Did you ask Nikola to buy you this gun?"

"No."

"Then why did you inspect it?"

"I inspected it to make sure I knew the condition of a gun that was being shown to me."

The judge wrinkles her brow. "Is this a normal thing people do?"

"Yes. In fact, it's encouraged. In the military we call it 'standard operating procedure.'"

I catch the guard to my right nodding in agreement. The judge takes note of this too.

"At any point, did you ask Nikola to buy you a gun?"

"No."

"Why were two of the gun's serial numbers scraped off?"

"Excuse me?"

"Why were two of the gun's serial numbers scraped off?"

"I don't know. I only held it once. I had no idea that was the case."

"At any point, did you ask anyone to buy you a gun?"

"No. Never."

The judge makes a series of notes on a form of some kind. An awkward silence fills the room. If that's all there is, I think I did well. No curveballs, stayed on target. Milosh would be proud. The only concern I have is whether my account jibed with Nikola's. Did he say I racked the slide once or three times? Did he say I checked the chamber? I have no idea, and no way of finding out.

Finally the judge signs the form. She looks at me as she speaks. The translator says, "Congratulations, Mr. Corbett. You are very smart. The judge sees no reason to press charges. The court apologizes for your inconvenience. You are free to go."

"Excuse me?" Did I hear that correctly?

The judge says it this time, in English. "You are free, Mr. Corbett. Thank you for your time."

45

MILOSH'S NEWS

I'M HUSTLED OUT OF THERE, NO SIGN OF MILOSH, BACK TO THE PADDY WAGON. I have to go back to CZ to get my stuff and sign some papers. They don't even cuff me.

As soon as we're back, the guards take me to my cell. Luka and Gile stand to greet me, Dave stays on his bed. I stop in the doorway and hold out my arms. "Free as a bird, brothers!"

Luka and Gile laugh, they give me big hugs. "I told you, Foka!" Luka says. Gile rips a black trash bag off the roll we keep by the sink and hands it to me. Black trash bags are the carry-on luggage of CZ. I throw in my notebook and two stacks of newspapers, all of which feature articles about me. I tell Gile he can have my clothes. None will fit him, but he can trade them for coffee, cigarettes, or drugs. He's happy for the windfall.

Just then a guard opens the door. "Foka, advokat."

Roger that. I grab my trash bag and head to the door. The guard shakes his head and motions for me to leave my things in the room. I drop the bag and head into the hallway. But the guard places a hand on my chest. He holds up a pair of cuffs. I guess he didn't get the memo. Whatever. I offer him my wrists, he cuffs me lightly, we head to visiting room four.

I'm uncuffed and ushered inside. Milosh is there. He's sweating and breathing heavily, like he raced over from the courthouse.

I beam at him. "Milosh! We did it!" He doesn't smile back. "What's up?"

"Please." He points at the chair. I sit. "They're not going to let you out, Daniel."

"*What?!*"

"You can't leave today. After you left small court, an order came down."

"From who?"

"Someone high, but I don't know. Maybe the justice minister, maybe even the defense minister. The order is direct. 'The American must be charged with something.'"

"What the fuck! Seriously?"

"Yes. I'm sorry. I tried—"

I cut him off. "Can we appeal?"

"Not until you are charged, no."

"Jesus Christ, Milosh. What kind of fucking system is this? Why is this happening to me?"

Milosh puts a finger to his lips very briefly. I guess I shouldn't be asking these kinds of questions. Fuck me.

I lean back in my chair and gather myself. There's no point getting mad at Milosh. "I've been here three months, so, what, worst-case scenario, they charge me in another three months. Am I doing the math right?"

"You are, yes."

"And then we can appeal?"

"We can appeal the rescinding of today's order. We can't appeal your charge—we have to wait for a guilty verdict before we do that. If you are innocent, there is obviously no reason to appeal."

"What's the conviction rate here again?"

"Let's talk about something else."

"High, then."

"Let's talk about something else," he repeats.

"OK. What about me getting house arrest like Nikola?"

"My first request was denied, but I have appealed this."

"So is there a chance—and before you answer, please don't bullshit me. You got my hopes up before, and in a way you were right. For a little while today, I was free. But from now on, just level with me. Good, bad, ugly. I need to know."

He takes a deep breath. "Fine. No, you will never be granted house arrest."

"Why?"

Again he places his finger quickly to his lips. What I'm asking is unanswerable within these walls. Still, he says, "You have been and you will continue to be looked at and treated unfairly for the entire process."

But why? I want to yell.

I don't.

He can see that I'm unsatisfied with his nonanswer. "The media coverage is killing you."

"But why is there so much media coverage? Milosh—I'm nobody. You know that." I'm sure he knows the basic contours of why I'm here—Malachi is presumably paying his bills—but if he does, he doesn't let on. He also doesn't answer this question. He can't. Not here.

"I'm sorry, Daniel. As I've said, you're going to be here for a long time."

I take another series of deep breaths, lower my heart rate, get collected. "All right. You know I'm fine in here. I'll be fine. Know that I'm not angry with you. I see you're doing the best you can."

"Thank you. I completely understand your frustration."

I'm not sure that he does, but I'll take him at his word.

The guard comes back in. He doesn't need to say anything. Time's up.

46

FUCKING SERBIA, MAN

WHY IS THIS HAPPENING TO ME? I DISCUSS IT QUIETLY WITH LUKA IN THE yard—talking seriously in our cell feels too risky, it could be bugged for all I know. Milosh's paranoia is rubbing off on me. Probably a good thing.

The primary conclusion is that the Serbs must think I'm a spy. If I were them, I'd assume the same. The downside to this is that, well, they think I'm a spy. The upside is that they don't seem to know why I was really here.

At least I didn't fuck up the contract. Good mercenaries don't get arrested in the first place, but if they do, they don't let the contract slip. Hopefully, I get some credit for that; hopefully, someone else is working my target by now, and Al down in Abu Dhabi is getting some good dirt on him.

Hopefully.

I tell Luka over and over how pissed I am that I screwed up, but Luka shakes that off. Mostly he thinks the arrest was blind luck. Good luck for the Serbs, bad luck for me. I was simply in the wrong place at the wrong time. Compounding my bad luck, Nikola had recently bought a pistol with the serial numbers scraped off. For all I know he *had* bought it to impress me. He might be a fucking idiot, but at least he didn't set me up. Anyway, once the Serbs had me, ran my passport, and saw my military career, they assumed I was some kind of assassin. Then the wheels started spinning. Law enforcement created evidence. Someone in the Ministry of the Interior tipped the media and told them to run with it. Who knows, maybe Vučić himself thought, *A US Navy SEAL! What good fortune. He can be here to kill me. He can be the man who killed that politician in Kosovo. Why not? And the Kremlin will love that we have him. I can tell Putin personally that we have a jailed American spy. Jailed American spies should never be wasted. Never!*

It had to be something like that. Whatever the real reasons, it fucking stinks. For the next few days, I have trouble sleeping. My mind won't turn off. I'm angry, I'm confused, I'm homesick. I don't feel sorry for myself—like I said, I don't do self-pity—but I am angry at myself. I should never have spent so much time with Nikola. I shouldn't have put myself in that position. It was a rookie mistake. I lie there, on my two-inch-thick mattress, getting eaten alive by bugs, fucking seething.

Oh, and about those bugs. Now that it's getting into summer, I finally understand why I keep getting the top bunk by the window. It's because I'm the first stop for every goddamned vampiric insect that comes alive between May and October. The "best" bed is actually the worst.

I have another meeting with Milosh that week. It comes to nothing. He just drills into me—again—that I'm going to be here for some time.

After this I decide, fuck it. When in Rome, right? If I'm going to be in prison indefinitely, I might as well make the most of it.

I get a Serbian-English dictionary from the library and make flash cards. I practice them every night in bed. During the day I practice with Luka and Gile. In the morning we read or talk quietly, and then, around lunch, the three of us play a dice game called Yamb that's a lot like Yahtzee. Luka gets tired of Aussie Dave stealing his Snickers bars, so Luka has him moved to another cell. (The best thing about this is that I move from the window bed—aka the bitch bed—to a lower, less buggy bunk.) Luka and I play chess every evening. Whenever I move a pawn, I think of my situation. What a joke. Luka and I work out every day in the cell, and also on the yard. When we go to the cantina, I buy sudoku magazines, rolling tobacco, papers, coffee, canned tuna, and salted peanuts. These last two are my go-to meal. I mix the peanuts with the tuna, right in the can, and eat it with my spoon. If they have mustard in the cantina (they often don't), I top it with that. I also buy the unofficial national snack, something called Plazma—a vanilla wafer. I elevate my cigarette-rolling game. It becomes a little meditation. A quiet moment when I can concentrate on doing one thing well as I try to let go of what surrounds me: my dark cell, my cellmates, the single bathroom the three of us share, the guards, the flatulent reminders of a prison diet that consists primarily of bland soup, cold hot dogs, and stale bread. Smoking centers me too. The cigarette dangles from my lips. I inhale. The ember glows. Blue smoke curls from the tip. The foul odors of CZ are pushed aside. The tobacco is George Karelias and Sons, a blend of brown and blond strands that smells like a Yankee Candle shop. Gile admonishes me: "Foka, why you smoke this champagne? I quit yesterday!" He's learned a little English. He laughs, a big belly laugh. I smile at him. I pass him a cigarette. He's always quitting yesterday. He lights it and smiles back.

In the evenings we watch game shows, trivia shows, football. If Novak Djokovic is playing, we watch his match. Everyone in Serbia has a crush on Djokovic, aka Nole. We also watch the news. I remain all over it. Luka assures me this won't last. "Some other crazy thing will happen and the news will go there. Some murder, some scandal. They will leave you. Once that happens, things will get better. You will see. This is Serbia. Understand?"

I understand. But this scandal never materializes. Everything is still "Foka, Foka, Foka." Killer, spy, bomb maker, criminal, American—I'm all these terrible things and more.

I'm the national bogeyman.

I tune it out.

Fucking Serbia, man.

47

DRAGOSLAV

At the end of July, I'm taken to visitor room four for my monthly chat with Milosh. He informs me that we're on our fourth request for house arrest. I tell him to drop it. But he says, "No, I am your lawyer. Serbia has a strange system, but everything must be well documented. We love bureaucracy. This injustice must be well documented as well."

"OK," I say, not really caring.

"Besides, it is easy," he says. "All I have to do is change the date and refile." A pause. "Daniel, do you remember me talking about my associate Dragoslav?"

"Sure. Nikola's lawyer, right?"

"Correct."

"What about him?"

"He's joining us. He wants to officially represent you alongside me. He is convinced of your innocence and feels you're getting severely mistreated."

"Milosh, I told you not to bullshit me."

"This is not bullshit. It is true."

"Imagine that. Truth! In Serbia!"

Milosh laughs. "I know what you mean, though. You said good, bad, and ugly. This is a good thing. It is meaningful. Dragoslav is one of Serbia's best defense lawyers. Maybe *the* best. It won't make things faster for you, but it does increase the odds of a good outcome."

"That is good, I guess." Milosh really is trying. "How much is this going to cost me?"

"It will not cost you. He will help you gratis."

I thank him and tell him to pass my gratitude on to Dragoslav. "I can't wait to meet him," I say. Just then the guard appears. "Vreme." Time.

When I tell Luka about this development, he jumps up and down. "Foka, this is amazing! You will be free. I don't care what Milosh says—sooner than later. You will be free. Dragoslav Ognjanović is a fucking killer, Foka. A killer." Coming from Luka—an actual killer—this is high praise.

He can see I'm not convinced, so he explains why this is so amazing. Dragoslav doesn't just have an excellent acquittal record (no small task in Serbia), but he also helped defend Serbia's former president, Slobodan Milošević, for crimes against humanity at the International Criminal Court. Now, in a normal situation, having a war criminal as a former client might be disqualifying—but this *is* Serbia, and it counts for something. Mostly, it means Dragoslav isn't afraid of anything.

I ask Luka why he thinks he's taking my case. "He must believe you are innocent. Also, if I were him, and I was able to get the notorious Foka an acquittal, then this will help me get more clients in the future. It will be a feather in his cap, my friend."

I climb up on my bunk and roll a cigarette. I light it, close my eyes, inhale. It's hot in our cell. There's no AC, not here or anywhere on the block. Rumor is even the warden doesn't have AC. The thick inner door of our cell is wide open. The outer barred door is closed and locked. Some feeble air moves through the room from the window to the door and out into the hall.

I close my Tupperware smoking kit, stuff it under my pillow, and hop off my bunk. I stand at the door, threading my arms through the bars. I continue smoking. One of the friendly guards nods as he strolls by.

Gile rattles out a snore behind me, even though he isn't asleep. Luka is silent, reading on his bed.

Dragoslav fucking Ognjanović. Maybe after everything, I have some reason to hope.

The next morning, we're woken abruptly by the guards. They yell and make a big fuss just outside our cell. Then the outer door swings open and five guards swarm inside. They pull us from our bunks, have us strip nude, and toss everything. Luka, Gile, and I stand in front of our bunks, our hands cupped over our groins, looking at one another with resigned confusion.

I don't understand everything the guards are saying, but the main thing they yell over and over is "Foka."

Not good at all.

They confiscate my tobacco and a small baggie of marijuana hidden under Gile's mattress. As they leave, Luka asks a question. For an answer, the tallest guard just sneers at me and points at our TV. The door closes, the lock is engaged. Just like that, they're gone.

As we pull on our clothes, Luka turns on the news.

Dragoslav Ognjanović has been gunned down in the street.

The headline in the main daily tabloid, *Sprski Telegraf,* says it all: "Advokat Ubijen Zbog Foka!" According to reports, he was assassinated—and I ordered his hit.

From here. From my cell. From CZ.

Well, I guess this is the next big scandal Luka promised. Unfortunately, I'm right at the center of it.

48

THE DOLDRUMS

LIKE EVERYWHERE IN EUROPE, SERBIA SHUTS DOWN FOR THE MONTH OF August. Normally court business would resume in September, but following Dragoslav's murder, the entire legal profession is planning to stand down in remembrance. Milosh tells me that this will last the whole month. I gather that this is some kind of protest against a corrupt law enforcement system that can't even protect its own lawyers, prosecutors, and investigators—but I have a hard time figuring out whom this is supposed to punish. It's not going to punish the justice minister, or the president, or the judges. It may cool off regular graft payments and bribes, but it isn't going to change anything. The people who will suffer most are us poor accused.

A month of vacation plus a month of legal sit-outs means nothing will happen on anyone's case for two months. Two hot and humid months. In a prison. With no AC and hardly any fans.

By mid-August, tension within the walls is at an all-time high. Fights become frequent, especially in stairwells, where there are no cameras.

One day Gile is up on the bitch bed talking to one of his boys from a different block who's out in the yard. I'm getting better at Serbian, but I have no idea what they're talking about. A big commotion erupts outside, and Gile gets excited. Luka is on his bed and I'm at the table making flash cards. Neither of us is interested in whatever is going on out there, but Gile starts barking, telling us to come look. Luka waves his hand—he's seen it all, doesn't feel like seeing it again. I get up.

Gile scoots over, I climb next to him, I look out on the yard. A man is lying in a growing pool of blood. He's moving, but just slightly. His hands are on his neck. Nearby, three guards are kicking the shit out of another man. He's balled up in a defensive position, arms covering his head, his torso taking a beating. Another set of guards is loudly ushering what remains of the other inmates back into the building, where they will be herded to their rooms. I'm sure none are happy that their daily walk has been cut short.

Gile says that the man being beaten attacked the other man with the lid of a tuna can. We watch as he continues to bleed, no one helping him. He stops moving. He's dead. The guards clean up some of the blood, but we're in a dry spell, and the rest stays there, staining the ground, for weeks.

During those weeks, Gile gets antsy. He's not good in the heat and no one likes the holding pattern all of us have been placed in regarding our cases. At the end of August, on the hottest day of the year, we're lying on our beds watching *Baywatch*, the movie. Luka had a thumb drive full of American films smuggled in. It's been a good distraction.

While we're watching, Gile lets out a snort and says, "Foka, American women. All ružna." This is the word for "ugly."

"Really?" I say, turning to face Gile.

"Yes. Sto posto!"

"Jennifer Aniston is hot," Luka interjects.

I ignore him. "Which country has the most beautiful women, Gile?"

"Italy, Mexico, France…Serbia!"

"Gile, you know America has people from all over the world, right? Do you mean Native American women?" Luka helps me translate this last part.

"No. I mean *all* women in America are ugly."

"You're fucking crazy, man. If you ever get to America, you'll see. California girls, New York in the summertime, fucking Miami. You wouldn't know what to do with yourself."

"Of course I would!" he says, grabbing his crotch and sticking out his tongue.

"I doubt that. Talk about ugly! Look at you. I bet you don't have to worry about women at all."

Luka starts laughing, I laugh too.

Gile sits up in his bed and points at me. "Fuck America. I hate America. You guys bombed us to protect fucking Muslims!"

That's enough. I get out of bed and grab all of Gile's American shit—Snickers bars, Nikes, Coca-Cola—and climb up to the bitch bed to throw everything into the yard. There's another group out there on their daily walk. They start giggling and jostling for the bounty.

Gile's ranting changes to a low rattle of protest, but he doesn't stop me. He knows better.

A pair of guards arrive. Luka is in tears laughing, Gile is fuming, I'm holding a Nike shower slipper.

"Foka, what are you doing?" a guard yells.

"Gile says he hates America, so I'm throwing all of his American shit out the window!" I answer in Serbian.

They look from me to Gile and back again—and then they start laughing too. I throw the slipper out the window. Before leaving, they tell Gile, "You should know not to upset Foka." Gile shuts up about hating America after that.

Not long after this incident, I begin to turn drastically inward. It's not lost on me that if I do hurt someone, it will most likely be someone with whom I share a cell. Probably a friend, like Gile. And if I hurt someone, the media will run with it. I will become the monster they describe so gleefully. I cannot let that happen.

49

CHANGE OF COMMAND

AUGUST CRAWLS INTO SEPTEMBER, SEPTEMBER MORPHS INTO OCTOBER, AND the Serbian legal system slowly churns back to life.

Of the three of us, this break has been hardest on Luka. His final court date was scheduled for September, but it got pushed back. But then, in early October, he heads to court.

We'll know soon.

Gile skips the morning walk to watch the news—he wants to see the verdict as soon as it's announced. When I return from the yard, I ask if he's heard anything. He's chain-smoking and glued to the TV. "Nothing yet."

I hop into bed and start a sixteen-by-sixteen sudoku. An hour passes. Then Gile pops up. "Foka! Foka! Look!"

Luka, my best friend in CZ, is innocent. They had some DNA evidence against him, but this "disappeared," and he can no longer be tried.

Mutually assured destruction in action, no doubt.

As soon as we get the news, Gile's eyes begin to well up. I don't know if he's sad that Luka will be leaving or if he's overjoyed that Luka will be free. I just feel happy for my friend.

Another hour and Luka is back to get his stuff. Gile wraps him in a big hug. I congratulate him and hug him too. He's smiling from ear to ear. The guard waits impatiently while Gile tears four garbage bags from the roll, doubles them, and helps Luka pack up. While they're working, Luka steps past the guard and yells into the hall. The block erupts in cheers, Gile breaks into tears again. It's strangely all very moving.

Luka is ready to go in under ten minutes. When he's about to leave, he comes up to me. "Ciao, Foka. Maybe our paths will cross again. I'll be following your case. If I can put in a good word, I will."

"Ciao, Luka. Thank you. For everything."

"Don't mention it. Even if you didn't have me, you would have been fine. You don't need me telling you that."

We hug one more time. He passes me the TV remote. "You're in charge now, Foka."

Luka speaks quietly with Gile, and when it's finally time for him to leave, Gile almost tackles him for one last hug. Then Luka grabs his trash bags and, after sixteen months in CZ, leaves room 311.

Later that night, Gile tunes our handheld radio to 89.4—Boom Boom Radio. The program at 2100 is dedicated to loved ones in prison and recently released inmates. We listen to it regularly. At one point the hyped-up DJ's voice announces, "This one's from Luka! 'This song goes out to my all my brothers in CZ: Mozza, Bulgi, Pera, the list goes on. And a very special shout-out to my brothers Foka and Gile in three-one-one!'" Luka's dedications take over an entire one-hour block—he must be having a great night. We get multiple shout-outs over the course of the show. Every time Gile hears his name, the tears start flowing again.

Over the next few days, I take charge of the cell. I continue enforcing Luka's rules. I maintain control of the TV remote, there will be no late-night smoking, and everyone (though it's just me and Gile for now) must be quiet by 2300. I understand by now that democracy doesn't work in CZ, especially with bunk-mates like Gile.

Just like that, Foka, the American Navy SEAL, is running a Serbian prison cell.

And it's a good thing too. Over the next few weeks, Gile and I get some new roommates.

The first arrives one evening. He's clean cut and well dressed, early forties. He stands just past the threshold, bowl and spoon atop his neatly folded blanket. "Hello, gentlemen. My name is Goran. This is my first time being arrested, nice to meet you."

He's terrified. I silently commend his courage for introducing himself.

Gile jumps out of bed and gives Goran the lay of the land. When I introduce myself, he looks confused. "American?"

"Yep."

He stares for a moment, then his eyes go as big as saucers. "*Foka?!*"

"That's me."

"My God...It's an honor to meet you."

I can't tell if he means it sincerely or if he's saying it because now he's even more terrified and is desperate to make nice with the dreaded Foka. Either way, I put him at ease. I tell him I'll look out for him. His shoulders loosen up and fall an inch. I can see (and smell) that he hasn't showered or brushed his teeth in days. I give him a brand-new toothbrush and ask the guard to fill my bucket with hot water so Goran can rinse off. Over the course of the next month, we become friends—but just as quickly as he arrives, he leaves. He'd been accused of petty theft by his father-in-law and is released with no charges. Must be nice.

After Goran is Zoki. Early fifties, average height, barrel chested, thin comb-over. He's a transfer from another block and therefore has considerably more shit than a new guy, mostly jumpsuits in every color. He and Gile know each other, they start chatting as soon as he comes in.

He then turns to me. "Ah, the Foka. I am happy to share a room with you." He offers his hand, I take it.

"What are you in for?" This is kind of a prison faux pas, but I don't give a fuck anymore. Everyone in the entire country knows my story—or thinks they do—so I might as well know theirs.

He starts talking extremely fast in a mumbling monotone, I can't understand much. Gile conveys that Zoki owns a textile factory and is accused of dumping toxic sludge into the watershed. Fittingly I find out in the middle of the first night that he has a colostomy bag.

So now our room always smells like shit.

After Zoki, Ryko arrives. He's young, tall, good looking, and the heir to some kind of real estate fortune. Basically, a spoiled rich kid. Like many spoiled rich kids, he got bored with life and started dealing drugs. In his case ecstasy. He thought of himself as a true criminal, and now that he's in CZ he thinks he's moved up even higher. None of us care enough to straighten him out. Neither Zoki nor Ryko is very interesting, which in prison is a good thing.

A few weeks after Ryko arrives, Gile goes off to court. Each time he leaves, he says, "Foka, today's the day!" But it never is.

I pay him no mind when he returns. He stands in the middle of the room, turning little circles, not saying anything. Then he grabs a trash bag and starts throwing his stuff in.

I hop off my bed. "Holy shit. Gile, are you free?"

He looks numb, even sad. "Yes and no."

"Bro, what do you mean yes and no? You're out of here!"

"They gave me house arrest."

"That's better than this, right?"

"It is, but it won't last long. One condition is that I get drug tested once a week. If I skip it or fail, I go straight to Mitrovica"—this is the big prison for people who've been convicted—"on a three-year sentence."

"Dude, you can—"

He holds up his hand. "I'm a junkie, brother. Believe me, I will be in Mitrovica next week."

I try to say something to cheer him up, but it's no use. Before leaving, he gives me a dead fish handshake and a weak smile. "Good luck, Foka."

"Good luck, Gile." He turns. "Hey, I'm sorry I threw your American things out the window that day. That was shitty of me. I shouldn't have done that."

"It's all right, Foka. I was being an asshole."

"Sometimes we all are, right?"

"Right." He turns to leave.

"See you around, Gile."

He pauses, shakes his head. "No, you won't." Then the guard takes him away.

So long, Gile. I'm going to miss you.

50

COURT DATE!

In early November, nearly ten months after my arrest, Milosh visits. It's the first time I've seen him since July. As soon as I walk into room four, he stands, a smile on his face. "Daniel, you've been charged!"

Great news, I guess.

I'm being accused of gun possession and the manufacturing, distribution, and possession of explosives. When I ask how that is even remotely possible, Milosh explains, "They mean bullets."

I don't know how they think I was making bullets, but I suppose I'll find out at trial.

Except that Milosh tells me there's still no trial date.

"Why not?" I ask.

"Because no judge is willing to take your case."

"Jesus. And why is that?"

"You're too hot. As you know, there are no juries in Serbia. So everything comes down on the judge."

"I don't see how this matters. I'm Foka—shouldn't judges be clamoring to put me on trial?"

"This is precisely the problem—you're Foka." He can see that I'm not following. "The judges look at your case and they see that the evidence is weak. But you're Foka. If they find you innocent, they would have to deal with a disappointed Serbian president. If they find you guilty, it would be obvious that they'd been instructed to do so by the Serbian government. The judge is in a bind. You understand?"

"Yeah, I get it. I'm a lose-lose proposition."

"Yes."

"Milosh—am I ever going to get out of here?"

"Yes, just—"

"Yeah, yeah. Just be patient."

But who would have guessed? I don't have to be *that* patient. A couple of weeks later, a judge accepts my case. I'm headed to court soon—November 18.

Milosh drops by for a powwow on November 17. I go to room four, he's there pacing, looking down at the floor. Here we go. Another delay. Maybe the judge was killed. Maybe they just decided I'm guilty, no trial necessary.

I sit in the chair. "What's wrong?"

He stops pacing and stares at me. "It is terrible. The judge—the judge is a woman."

I frown. "So? What's wrong with that?"

"Nothing, except that women are no good at adjudicating male crimes."

"Milosh—what's a 'male crime'?"

"You know, ones with guns."

Putting aside the fact that this is sexist, it sounds totally asinine. I'm happy to have anyone take the case, and I feel like Milosh should be too. "Well, I'm stoked. Hey, maybe she'll think I'm cute!"

I think it's funny. Milosh doesn't. Before leaving, he lays out the ground rules. It's not like court in the United States. I'll be sworn in once at the first hearing but not again. I'll never take the stand, but I will be asked questions, sometimes by the judge, sometimes by the prosecutors, and sometimes by Milosh. In all cases, I'll be expected to answer. As with the small court hearing, short answers are best: "Yes," "No," "I don't know." Unlike that hearing, I will be asked to elaborate. Still, keep it short.

"The most important thing: don't lie."

"Wouldn't dream of it," I say, knowing full well that I'll have to lie at least once.

I wake before sunrise the next morning. My clothes are clean, I get dressed. It's the same outfit I wore when I was arrested—hoodie, Lululemon joggers, Nike Metcons with my DIY trash-bag laces. I'm not nervous, I'm excited. My entire life has been bent toward action—high school sports, the navy, BUD/S, the Teams, training, hustling on SEAL Team 17, working with Malachi—and now, after ten months of monotony and uncertainty, something is finally happening. Win or lose, I can't wait to get started.

The guards arrive after breakfast. I'm cuffed, taken down to the vehicle bay, given the Foka treatment. The other prisoners headed to court that day pile into one van, I get my own. I peer through the rear window. We drive through Belgrade, taking a different route this time, but we still pass Sveti Sava. As we do, I'm overcome with a sense of ease. I don't know why. Does it have some spiritual meaning for me, does it bring me closer to God, does it represent justice somehow, or freedom? Is it just something familiar and easy to pick out? I can't tell. We round a corner, it disappears. But I know it's still there. That means something.

Courthouse, more guards, same cell at the back on the right. A solitary guard watching over me, just to make sure I don't vanish into thin air. I'm Foka! I'm probably a wizard too.

An hour later, I'm dragged upstairs. I'm taken through a large door into a waiting pen. It's packed. I spot Milosh, he gives me a nod. I'm not there for three minutes before a set of double doors swings open and the guards push me inside.

The courtroom looks like a miniature church. Two rows of six pew-like benches facing an elevated dais, a desk on either side jutting into the room. I'm taken to the front bench and seated. Three women walk by me and ascend the dais. All sit. The one in the middle is the judge, an attractive woman in her mid-thirties. She looks ambitious and no-nonsense. Fine by me. Flanking her are the other two women. They could pass for twins: fifties, heavy makeup, mean looking. Throughout the proceeding, neither says a word. They are silent sentinels of justice.

The room fills behind me. The energy is slightly electric.

I turn and see Nikola; naturally he winks. A guard yanks my hoodie, I face forward again. Other than Milosh, the only person here for me is Ana from the US embassy. She and Eric Roth have continued to come visit me, and their visits have continued to have no substance. I assume she has to be here for her job.

Milosh is in front of me. He's in an expensive navy suit. He has a Montblanc pen and a stack of leather-bound notebooks. The prosecutors wear clothing that looks decades out of date. The judge starts the proceedings. There's a translator, so everything takes twice as long. Despite this, one of the first questions directed at me is, "Do you speak Serbian?"

I answer, in English, "Well, after ten months in prison I can count to ten and say every bad word imaginable."

Laughter throughout the courtroom, including from the judge. She clarifies, "Did you speak Serbian at the time of your arrest?"

"No, ma'am."

She makes a note of it and moves on. Those are the only questions I'm asked. The hearing drones on for another hour or so, all of it in Serbian. I only understand about 20 percent of what they're saying. As quickly as it began, it ends. Milosh tells me that we'll reconvene at CZ. I'm hustled out of there, downstairs, into the paddy wagon, back to prison. As I sit in the van, I'm totally confused. It seems like nothing happened. Was that good or bad?

Milosh is already in room four at CZ. As soon as I enter, I ask, "Well, how did it go?"

"I think good, even with the judge being a woman."

"Great! What's next? Court for the next week or so and we're done?"

Milosh shakes his head. "Didn't you hear what they said at the end of the hearing?"

"I heard it, but no one was translating."

"She said the next date would be after the holidays."

"Which holidays?"

"Christmas. New Year."

I raise my eyebrows. "Two months from now?"

"Yes. We'll have opening statements then."

"*Two months from now?*" I repeat. He nods. I've never been on trial in America, but every TV show, movie, and true crime podcast I've ever come across depicts constitutionally required "speedy" trials in which court days occur one after the other until everything is over. "Why so long?"

"I'm sorry, it is not like America. Typical trial days in Serbia occur one month apart. Our system is always stressed; bailiffs, translators, stenographers, lawyers, and even judges have to be meted out. Justice moves slowly here."

Justice my ass. A case that consists of twelve trial days could easily take a year. Really more than a year, since no one works in August, over Christmas, on New Year's, or over the May holidays. I'm not happy about it, but what can I do? Nothing.

I go back to my cell, and I wait.

51

THE STENCH

Just before Christmas our cell door opens and in walks a skeleton of a man with reading glasses hanging off the end of his nose. He's six-three, rail thin, shaved head, fingers stained yellow from nicotine, blackened fingernails. He wears a filthy hooded jacket that used to be white, black sweatpants with holes in them, and off-brand shoes with his toes sticking out the sides. I can smell him from across the room. He smells like literal shit.

All he has is the spoon, bowl, and blanket, so he must be new. The bowl is full of prescription pill bottles. The door closes behind him, but he just stands there, mute.

"Hey, who the fuck are you?" Maybe not the best way to start, but who cares.

"I'm, uh, I'm M-M-Mille." His stutter isn't fear induced, it's like he had to remember his name.

"OK, Mille. I'm Foka. Why are you here?"

"Uh, I, well, I had problems in another room and got moved. This is actually the third time it has happened." All of this is in English, no hint of an accent. Weird.

"No—why are you in CZ?"

"Oh. Yeah. My dad wouldn't give me money, he didn't want to give it to me because it was for drugs, so I beat him with a coat hanger."

Fuck me. At least he's not a liar.

"Put your shit in that cabinet," I say, pointing to the empty one. He does, but in slow motion. It's like watching a sloth put away groceries.

"Don't touch anything, especially anything that isn't yours."

"OK."

Thankfully, Ryko is already in the rack above me. Mille throws his blanket on the rack above Zoki. Zoki rolls his eyes. I barely acknowledge this. Mille smells like shit, Zoki has a colostomy bag—they can make it work on their side of the room.

It doesn't take more than a day to learn that Mille doesn't like showers. He likes filth. He likes surliness. He likes stench. He doesn't wash his hands after he uses the bathroom or before he eats. He doesn't use toilet paper. On his first shower day, he sleeps through our turn.

On his second shower day, I shake him. I prod him with a Coke bottle. I turn him over and grind his sternum with my knuckles as hard as I can. I know this hurts, but all he does is groan. He's completely zonked on drugs. Ryko calls for a guard. We tell him Mille won't shower and that it's becoming a hygiene issue. The guard says, "No one is required to shower."

I say, "If I drag his ass out of bed and into the shower, are you required to stop me?"

"Do what you have to do."

So I do. I grab his hood, yank him out of bed, drag him seventy-five meters down the hall. He doesn't protest or fight back. I've never met someone who could care less. Just as we reach the stalls, he starts to move under his own power. He takes his clothes off, I make sure he rubs all over with soap, he dries off. Of course, he has no choice but to get back into his filthy clothes. I could give him some of mine, but fuck this guy.

Back in the room, he gets high. He lights cigarettes and forgets about them. He farts and says nothing. He sleeps twenty-three hours a day. He never goes outside. All he eats is drugs. He gets them from his prescriptions, from the guards, and from the new dealer who took over after Gile, another junkie who pushes the lunch cart. Fuck, I miss Luka. He'd know how to stop this guy. He'd know how to get rid of him. If Luka were still here, they never would have put him in our cell. I'm sure it's all part of the Foka treatment. Now that my Serbian guardian angel is gone, I'm getting the dregs. The fuckups. The testers.

That's what Mille is. After all this time, if I'm going to hurt anyone, it's going to be Mille.

52

HAPPY BIRTHDAY TO ME

Just before Christmas, Goran, the petty criminal who was in 311 for only a few weeks, sends me a care package. Cured meats, French and Swiss cheeses, fancy mustards, a baguette, raw milk butter. A fucking Toblerone wrapped in foil so none of my cellmates will notice it. It's some of the best food I've ever eaten, and I don't share it with anyone.

Christmas comes and goes. New Year's comes and goes. No one cares.

That month I "celebrate" my first birthday in prison as I stand trial for a crime I did not commit. I'm not a criminal, I'm not a mercenary, I'm not a SEAL. I'm a prisoner, and I'm trying to survive, and that's about it.

Happy birthday, Dan.

Another month passes, court day. "Foka, sud." Paddy wagon, I find Sveti Sava on the way, the courthouse guards treat me like I'm a criminal mastermind. I enter the courtroom. There's Milosh, there's the pretty judge, there's Ana from the State Department.

Once again, the room is packed. All here for Foka. For some reason the judge kicks off with a weird kind of roll call. She points at random people, asking them to identify themselves. "I am Nikola's mother." "I am a journalist from *Blic*." "I am Goran."

Goran! What's he doing here? I perk up, look around, the guard bops me on the head, I look forward and listen.

"And why are you here, Goran? Do you have any relation to the defendant? Do you have a professional obligation to be here?"

"I am not a journalist, Judge, if that's what you mean. But yes, I have a reason to be here. I am a friend of Daniel Corbett and I am here to support him." All of this is in Serbian, but I'm able to follow.

Wow. Fuck it. I don't care if the guard tackles me to the floor. I want to see Goran. I want to see my friend.

I turn my head as far back as I can, and no shit, there he is on the last bench. He smiles and waves, I wave back. The guard yanks my hood, I wave some more, he yanks it harder, I face forward. Milosh looks back and forth between me and Goran, then rolls his eyes. Whatever, dude. I have a friend. A real friend. And he's here. For me. I haven't disappeared, I'm real, I exist. So fuck everybody.

The judge accepts Goran's explanation and gavels in. We're supposed to have opening statements, but as soon as things get underway, there's a small commotion on the prosecutor's side. I look to Milosh, he's looking past me at the double doors. It's then that I notice the translator is AWOL.

I whisper to Milosh, "What's happening?"

He holds up his finger and addresses the judge. After a brief exchange, the judge gavels again. The room begins to buzz. I turn to Milosh.

"What the fuck. That's it?"

He's already stuffing a legal pad into his briefcase. "For today, yes. There's no translator."

"You can translate for me."

"I just suggested that. It's not possible." He seems upset with me, like this is my fault.

The guards stand and pull my arm. "Give me moment," I say in Serbian. I turn back to Milosh. "When's the next date?"

"Next month."

"Fuck, man, another month? Can you ask again?"

"No, Daniel. I can't. She said it's not possible without an official translator. In fact, she said it would be illegal to continue without one."

"Fuck that! You speak better English than any translator I've had to date."

"Be that as it may, we have to wait for the next date."

"And when's that? Next year?"

"No. Next month." He still seems angry with me. What the fuck?

"Oh. Fucking wonderful! Thanks, Milosh."

Just then, the guard pulls me away and marches me toward the exit.

53

NEW FISH

As I'm walked out of the courtroom, Milosh approaches Goran. They have a hushed and urgent conversation. I have no idea why Milosh is pissed at Goran, but he clearly is. Then I'm pulled out of the room.

I'm transported back to CZ and taken to room four. This time I beat Milosh there. Only a few minutes later, he hustles in.

"Dude, what was that all about? Are you fucking mad at me?"

"I'm mad at the situation, like you."

"Not as mad as I am, I promise."

He takes a deep breath. "I'm sure. I'm sorry, Daniel. The translator thing is infuriating. But really, I was mad at Goran."

"Goran? Why? I was glad he was there. I've been here almost a year. It was nice to see a friendly face."

Another big breath. "I know. I'm sorry. But the fact is, he should not have come. He had no business being there. Any presence by any Serbian national will only complicate your case and worsen your chances. You cannot be associated with someone who was recently in CZ, even if it is someone as timid and harmless as Goran."

Now it's my turn to let out a sigh. I see his point. "Sorry I snapped at you."

"You have every right. It's just that, while you're in here, while we're doing this, you can have no actual Serbian friends. Can you imagine how it would look if Luka had shown up? He wouldn't do that to you. That is what I told Goran, in so many words. You must be a nobody, with few connections, a phantom who was in the wrong place at the wrong time. Your friends must help convey that."

I concede that he's right. And so begins another month of waiting.

A week later, Zoki, the colostomy-bagged toxic-waste dumper, is sentenced to twelve years. We say goodbye, but it's not like when Luka or Gile left. Shortly thereafter, Ryko, the wealthy wannabe molly dealer, takes a plea deal. He's gone too. Both are sent to the Big House, Mitrovica. The place we're all trying to avoid.

Now it's just Mille and me. From the instant Ryko leaves, I need to be on point. If I kill Mille, I'll also kill my chances at freedom.

It's not easy. For twenty-two hours a day I'm stuck in 311 with his stench. You'd think that someone who sleeps as much as he does would be tolerable, but you'd be wrong. He won't play chess, he won't do Serbian flash cards with me, he won't help clean the room. He is the personification of someone who has given up. He is like a black hole of resignation. I can't be sucked in. If I am, I'll never get out.

Mille is on every pill CZ offers. Pinks, whites, cupfuls of blues. Usually he swallows them, but sometimes he crushes them with the butt of a lighter into little piles of powder. He snorts this, or rolls it into cigarettes, or rubs it on his gums. Once I catch him trying to shove the powder up his ass. Of course, he doesn't wash his hands.

Most of the pills are downers, but by the middle of February, he manages to score some amphetamines. This would be fine if he got jacked and went on a cleaning tear, but instead all he does is pace up and down the middle of the room, talking to himself, rubbing his head, picking his nose and ears maniacally. I move the table so that he can't come back by the beds without climbing over it. Instead of pacing, he starts turning in circles.

Every night, I fantasize about how I'm going to kill him. Mostly I want to beat him to death. I've never done this to anyone, but I bet it would be gratifying to do it to Mille. I imagine stabbing him in the neck with a nonexistent buck knife, inserting it into his muscles, pushing it forward to sever the jugular. When I eat my tuna, I catch myself gazing at the curled edge of the metal lid. It would look good coated in blood, wouldn't it? But usually I dream up less violent ways to make him go away, ones that might not be so incriminating. He's a drug addict—what do drug addicts do? They overdose. I imagine making nice with him for a bit. "Hey, man, we don't like each other but we're stuck here together, so let's make the most of it." I imagine getting a little morning coffee routine going with him over a couple of weeks. Then, once he trusts me to make the coffee, I'll crush up twenty blues—which I now know are opioids—and stir them into his cup. Then he takes a nap and doesn't wake up. Problem solved!

It takes everything I have not to do any of these things.

Finally, sometime in February, we get new cellmates. One is a die-hard Red Star hooligan called Nole, since he's a dead ringer for Novak Djokovic. Nole is in for selling cocaine. Just after Nole, Kiro arrives. He's huge, six-four, 230 pounds, all muscle. Kiro—who speaks excellent English—is in for beating the shit out of a patron at a bar he was bouncing. I quickly learn that he's spent a ton of time in Iraq as a mechanical contractor for KBR. Of course, I'm Foka, so he knows all about me. With a wry smile he says, "I bet you're a bad mother-fucker, but there's no guns or night vision in here, Foka. Don't get any funny ideas. I can squash you like a gnat."

"No shit," I say, punching him in the arm. "You're a monster!"

As with Luka, Kiro and I become fast friends. We work out in the room every day. Burpees, planks, air squats, you name it. Like me, he's a neat freak who's totally offended by Mille. During our walks outside, we conspire about how to defeat him and his stench. He also knows a few of the guys I'm friendly with in the yard, and best of all, he's a great chess player. So we also start playing chess, and by day three he promises to make me into some kind of junior grandmaster.

And then, only a week after Kiro arrives, it's determined that Mille is not mentally fit to stand trial. He's transferred to a psych unit. Thank God and good riddance. I won't be killing anyone anytime soon.

The day after Mille's departure, the three of us scrub every inch of the room, but it's Kiro and I who do most of the work. It takes a week for the smell to clear out. Then Petar arrives. He's a fat street kid, not affiliated with any gangs, but he's a rabid fan of Partizan, the sworn rival of Red Star. He and Nole do not like one another.

They try to force me to pick a side, but I'm not an idiot. I refuse. "OK, Foka," they say, "but you better pick before derby day in May!"

I look at Kiro. "That's the day Red Star and Partizan play each other," he explains.

"Ah, got it. I'll still be neutral," I promise them.

They refuse to accept and continue arguing with each other. Hopefully, by May I'll be guilty or innocent, and in either case I won't be here.

54

THE GLASSES

WHO KNOWS, MAYBE I'M A PSYCHOPATH. LOW EMPATHY, HIGH FUNCTIONING, dissociative, able to make and carry out hard calls. In my opinion the world needs people like that. Not just special forces operators, but also lawyers, surgeons, EMTs.

Who knows.

During that break between court dates, I begin a new bedtime routine. Kiro has helped reestablish order in our cell, so it's lights-out at 2300 and total silence. Every night from 2300 to 0100 I lie in bed, thinking about the things I've done. The mistakes I made that led to my arrest. The people I've hurt over the years. The horrible things I've done with my own hands. I let guilt ball up in my throat and weigh on my chest. It doesn't feel good exactly, but it feels... *right*.

You might be thinking, "Oh, here is where we learn about all the things he did in the SEAL Teams!" Sorry, that's not what I'm talking about. I don't have feelings about the things I did in the Teams. That was my job, and I did it well, and that's that.

I'm talking about all the human things any person does. Let's go way back.

One of my earliest memories is of playing with friends in a sandbox in Germany. I'm probably five. At one point a boy shows up, heavier, wears glasses. He plays for a while nearby, removes his glasses and puts them on the edge of the sandbox, then runs off to the swings. For whatever reason, I sidle over to the glasses, pick them up, walk to the other side of the sandbox, and bury them. Then I go back to playing with my friends. None of them see me do it, or if they do, they don't say anything.

I don't know what a prank is at the time, but that's how I think about what I've done. It's funny.

The boy comes back from the swing set and looks around. He gets more and more agitated as it dawns on him: he's lost his glasses. He starts to cry. He drops to his hands and knees and digs, looking all over for his glasses.

This is my first memory of guilt.

Five-year-old me doesn't think it's funny anymore. The guilt makes me stand up, walk to where I think I've buried the glasses, and start looking for them too. Only I can't find them. They're gone.

The boy has no idea what I'm doing, but now I'm getting agitated too. As I sit there, clawing through the sand and trying to keep my cool, a large pair of boots appear in front of me.

Not a kid's boots. Military boots.

I look up, craning my neck all the way back to find a large man standing over me.

"Did you bury my son's glasses?" he asks in an American accent.

Guilt quickly changes to fear. "Um…yes," I whisper.

"Do you remember where you buried them?" This is rhetorical. He can tell I don't remember.

"Um, no, sir," I reply.

"Why don't you try over there? He points his toe to a far corner of the sandbox.

I run over and start digging. Almost instantly I have the boy's glasses in hand. I walk back to the man, head bowed, and hold them out.

"Those aren't my glasses," he says. I look up. He gestures toward his crying son, who's suddenly standing right next to the giant man.

I hold them out to the boy, he takes them.

"Thank you," he says through whimpers.

I'm so mixed up, I don't know what to say. So I say nothing.

Then the dad leads the boy back to a bench, where he quietly scolds him for not being responsible for his things.

I'm not a dad, but I'm pretty sure this guy was one of the good ones.

I go through this kind of exercise every night. I remember throwing away Christmas cards from Mom the moment I got them, not because I didn't want a card from Mom but because I didn't understand or appreciate the sentimental value of things. I think of fights I got in, of nights spent in the drunk tank. Some of those fights qualified as assault, no question. But they didn't lead to me getting charged with anything, and certainly not to me getting convicted. I think about how, at a certain point when I was in the Teams, I didn't take life seriously. I was all business at work, but once I was off-base it was the Me Show and nothing else was a priority. It wasn't that I didn't take ownership for my actions so much as that I had a "What's the big deal?" mentality. This eventually led to an early transfer off that Team and onto another.

After fifteen or twenty of these self-audits, I come to realize that CZ is probably one of the few places they can happen. Prison is clarifying like that if you have enough self-awareness to use your time this way. I am bored and aimless, living in a pre–World War II prison with other bored and aimless men. For some reason people remember the bad more easily than the good, and this is the setting I need to go back through and catalogue all the bad. Still, I try to remember the good things too. The thing that keeps coming back, like a mantra, is Mom wandering around the house when Dad was sick, saying, "Love is the antagonist of fear." I repeat it over and over. It's not just useful in my situation, it's true. In any situation.

A night or two before my next court date, I feel particularly heavy. I've voluntarily dug up thirty-plus years of guilt and shame and plopped it all on top of myself. I'm alone, in a foreign country, behind thick concrete-and-steel walls, with no way to communicate. Most of the people I need to apologize to, like that boy from Germany, I'll never see again. What am I going to do?

And then it hits me: it feels impossible, but I have to forgive myself. It's my only choice. In order to absolve myself, to keep moving forward, to be of clear mind so that I can continue to survive and fight for my freedom, I forgive myself for all the wrongs I've done to people I will never see or know again.

If you're reading this and you happen to be one of the many people I've wronged and you can't forgive me, no worries. I understand and respect that. I'm still sorry for what I did. But there in CZ, I had to forgive myself. It's the least I could do. I'm pretty sure this is true for everyone.

55

TURNS OUT I AM FLUENT

FEBRUARY 19, 2019. IT'S BEEN ONE YEAR AND TWENTY DAYS SINCE MY ARREST, and I'm only on my third court date. I'm whisked from CZ to the courthouse in my rusted blue chariot. I see the people outside, living their lives. We pass Sveti Sava. I am completely unfree.

I look at the judge as I enter the courtroom. Maybe it's the lack of exposure to women, or maybe I'd never noticed how great looking she is, but she has it going on. I sit, the courtroom is relatively empty. She looks at me and greets me in English. "How are you doing?"

Without missing a beat, I say, "I'm fine. Your English is fantastic!"

"I've been practicing," she says, blushing.

Are we flirting? "I've been practicing my Serbian."

"Oh? Let's hear it," she says, smiling.

"Dobro jutro," I say in my best accent. Good morning.

"Wow, very nice," she says, tossing her hair. We are 100 percent flirting. This has got to be a good sign, right?

Just then the two Sentinels of Justice walk in and take positions on either side of her. She transforms, immediately becoming all business. The courtroom doors open, the room fills. The prosecution arrives, Milosh takes his seat near me. He reminds me that today we'll be doing opening statements, as if I need a reminder.

The translator appears and takes a seat on my right. "Thanks for showing up," I say. What I really want to say is, "Where the fuck were you last month?" but I hold my tongue.

She grins and nods quickly. Either the joke went over her head or she didn't understand me. Either way, not a great sign.

The judge gets things going, the prosecution goes first. I catch a few words here and there, but my specialty is prison Serbian, not legal Serbian. I lean over to my translator, but she doesn't speak in sentences. She barely speaks at all, instead just giving single words like "house" and "phone."

I lean in the other direction and ask Milosh what they're saying. He seems mildly annoyed—his job is to listen carefully and make adjustments as needed, not to tell me what's going on. "Nothing much," he says, jotting some notes. "I'll tell you later."

I try to keep up as best I can, watching the prosecutor's body language for any clues. More than anything, he looks bored. After five minutes or so, I give up and tune out, nodding sporadically to give the impression I'm paying attention. But I'm not.

The prosecutor wraps, Milosh gives our statement. We've been over this a few times, so I know the gist: "My client is innocent. This is a miscarriage of justice and we shouldn't even be here. But since we are, we concede that my client touched the weapon, then checked to make sure it was safe and not loaded, then gave it back to his friend. There was never any crime nor any intent to commit a crime. Thank you." Even though the exact language is lost on me, I nod along, catching some words here and there. My "translator" makes no attempt to translate for Milosh. Great job, lady.

At one point I completely zone out. I remind myself to nod now and then, mainly so I can stay awake. Falling asleep at my own trial would be a terrible look. At one point I daydream of Outback Steakhouse—which is weird, because I don't even like Outback Steakhouse—and Red Bull vodka slushies at Shore Club. And going on long runs. And women.

In the middle of my reverie, the translator taps me on the shoulder. I snap out of it. "Yeah, what is it?"

"The judge is asking if you understand that the next court date is for March twenty-second and that we will be going over text messages pulled from your and Nikola's phones."

Fuck—this lady speaks perfect English. What the hell?

"Yeah, I understand."

She tells this to the court, the judge gavels out.

On the ride back, I think about my phone. There's no way they can access the encrypted app I use with Malachi, so I'm not worried about that. What I am worried about is what's in my regular messaging app. There's not anything incriminating in there, but there will be ambiguous stuff in there, and probably some distasteful stuff too. Like every person's messaging app in every corner of the world.

I have a pointless debrief with Milosh and head back to my cell. Kiro's at the table, the chessboard is waiting for us. I shake him off. I've been a pawn all day, I don't want to move them around the board right now. I also don't want to lose—Kiro always beats me, and it's not always fun. He's disappointed, but he'll have to deal.

I fall asleep early that night and sleep like a rock. The next morning I turn on the TV while Kiro and I exercise. I'm wiped out from the court day, but I have to move or I'll just lie in bed all day doing sudoku.

In the middle of a long plank, the news turns to my trial. I get out of the plank and sit cross-legged on the floor.

Kiro turns it up. I catch a few Serbian words, but mostly I hear "Foka," "American," "Corbett." "What are they saying?"

"They're saying you are a liar."

I think back to the day before. "How can that be? I didn't say a fucking word."

"They are saying that in your first court appearance you said that you didn't understand Serbian."

"I didn't. I barely do now."

"They say that multiple reporters saw you nodding your head in court yesterday. They say you are fluent. They say you understand."

"Fuck me. I was trying to stay awake!"

"Foka, don't yell at me, brother. I'm just telling you what the news says."

Wonderful. So now I am a liar too. Milosh won't be happy. I'm not happy either.

56

FOKA LEGENDE!

MARCH 22. CUFFS, PADDY WAGON, SVETI SAVA, HOLDING CELL, COURTROOM. As before, I get there when it's relatively empty. The judge is there. I say hello and ask how she's been.

"I've been better," she says curtly. What can I expect—it's not like I'm her friend or anything. Maybe some personal issue, a jilted lover, a sick mother, financial woes. Any of it, all of it.

"Sorry to hear that. Me too." She smiles, I smile back. The room fills, she gavels in.

Milosh warned me in our prehearing meeting that text messages are always problematic. From discovery, he has a list of "evidence"—specific messages between me and Nikola—they will ask about. I will be expected to clarify everything and do so quickly and convincingly. I'm dreading it.

The prosecution dives right in. My phone and its many messages are introduced as evidence. Things seem to be going as expected, but then the translator says, "Please tell us about these 'fifteen things' you asked Nikola to buy for you."

If I were in the United States, I might plead the Fifth here. Not because these fifteen things were contraband or illegal, but because, well…

"Viagra," I say flatly. Like the words "Hollywood" and "coffee," "Viagra" needs no translation.

A murmur goes through the room. Some people stifle laughter.

The prosecutor's expression is so amazing that my sails immediately fill. In an instant, at least for this one day, I feel vindicated.

"I see, well, um, Mr. Corbett…do you suffer from erectile dysfunction?"

More laughter. The guards nudge each other and point.

"Sure, sometimes."

A few guffaws. This is comedy gold. I can picture headlines already—"Limp Seal." "Seal Needs Help." "Trouble in the Courtroom—and the Bedroom!"

"By 'sometimes,'" the prosecutor asks, "how often do you mean?"

"Whenever I drink."

"And how often do you drink?"

"Often."

The courthouse erupts, even the judge is getting in on it. I start laughing too. Not because I'm funny, but because this whole situation is absurd. If I need to be the punch line, then so be it.

The prosecutor abandons this line of questioning, we move on. Milosh gives me an encouraging nod. At the end of the hearing, the next date is set: April 18.

I'm completely wiped out the next morning. I get up late, I don't exercise with Kiro, I have a tin of tuna for breakfast. I don't let anyone turn on the TV, I don't want to deal with it or think about it. I need a minute.

The guards arrive, we head out for our daily yard time. Hallway, stairwell, blue door. I move into the yard and take my place in the line of prisoners for our daily circumnavigation.

Before I take three steps, someone grabs me from behind and lifts me into the air. It's not threatening, though. Whoever it is, he's happy.

"Ah, Foka, ti si lud, brate!" It's Bulgi. He releases his grip, I turn around. He's beaming, he says it again. Translation: "Oh, Foka, you are crazy, brother!"

Mozza rushes toward me yelling, "Foka legende! Foka legende!" Other men start yelling it too, it echoes through the yard. I see faces in the windows above me. They're yelling too. Some throw makeshift confetti out of their windows. Everyone points at me, claps, stamps their feet. Even the guards join in. Everyone is happy. I've never seen anything like it.

Somehow, I've cheered up all of CZ.

When things die down, I ask Mozza what it's all about. "It is the Viagra, Foka. It was so funny. They thought they had you! But no! You had them. Viagra!" He folds over laughing. "Fucking classic, Foka. You're just like us!"

And that's the heart of the matter. Overnight, I go from Foka—a super-powered Navy SEAL American spy-assassin—to just another dude who can't get it up. Like countless other dudes on the block and out in the world. This one little turn has done more for my reputation in CZ than anything I could have done with my fists or physical prowess. It's amazing.

I ride the wave all morning in the yard. I do extra pull-ups and dips, I joke around with anyone who wants to chat with me. When we get back to the cell, I turn on the TV. Sure enough, there I am—Foka, the Spy Who Didn't Love Me. (Not an actual headline, but it captures the spirit of them.) As with my fellow prisoners, my Viagra quip in court has done the unimaginable: it's made me sympathetic. Maybe even a little pathetic—a trait not typically associated with Navy SEALs.

Fine by me! Who knows, maybe it'll help my court case.

I kill time over that month by trying to learn the inner working of chess from Kiro. He's a good teacher, but the undertaking is humbling. Like the SEAL Teams, chess has its own language. Sicilian Defense, Ruy Lopez, French Defense, Evans Gambit, fianchetto, en passant, Alekhine's Defense, Queen's Gambit—the list is endless. Kiro teaches me all of these and more.

There's a former champion in CZ now, and one day in the yard I watch him make an opening I've never seen with white. When we get back to the room, I set up the board. "Kiro, chess?"

"Sure." He sits, grabs one white piece, one black, and puts them behind his back.

"Actually, can I play white?" I ask. "I want to try a new opening."

"Really? You barely understand what I have been trying to teach you."

"C'mon, man. Let's play. Just for fun."

"Chess is war, and war is never for fun, Foka."

"Fine! Let's go to war. Just let me be white!"

Kiro's face tightens, but he agrees. He puts the two pieces back, we begin. I can tell that there aren't going to be any hints, takebacks, or "Are you sure you want to make that move?" in this game.

I start a pawn to c4. He wastes no time and plays a pawn to e4. I play a knight to c3. Kiro laughs. "Foka, you are playing the English?" I shrug. "You are going to learn a lesson today."

I shrug again, we play. I finish my opening sequence with my light-square bishop in a fianchetto on g2. Kiro closes the center and starts picking me off one by one. I try to fight back, but it's useless. All of Kiro's pieces are developed and my dark-square bishop is locked up.

"Mate!" Kiro says extra loudly, slamming his knight on a new square. "Quit fucking around, only play e4 like I taught you."

"OK, I will only play e4 like you taught me," I say, staring down at the board.

I replay the game in my head that night while lying in bed. I have a decent head for chess, but not a great one. No matter how many variations I make, I don't see how to win.

As I'm drifting off, images from my life drift over an imaginary chessboard. I've been moved around like a chess piece for a long time. Certainly that was the case when I served in the SEAL Teams. And before that, when I played football, I was used like a chess piece. And now, in CZ, I'm absolutely being used as a pawn by players far beyond my perception—the system is using me for some game, President Vučić himself is probably taking meetings about me. It's insane.

In this Serbian game, I have no control, no agency. But it dawns on me that before, when I was free, I had choices. Yet out of a sense of duty, I was willing to take orders and instructions without question. I begin to wonder: Why have I accepted that?

Kiro and I play a lot of chess over that month. I only ever manage to beat him once. In time I resolve not to be a piece on a board anymore. Obviously each of us is bound to other people, and sometimes we have to do things because others ask us to or because we have no control over our lives. Regardless, I promise that if I ever get out of prison, I will no longer be a piece, but the player himself.

I will become my own master.

57

DERBY DAY

A WEEK LATER, I'M TRANSPORTED TO THE COURTHOUSE FOR MY NEXT DATE. The guards there know me by now, so they lighten up. They don't grip me as hard or treat me like shit. This time we go straight up to the courtroom, no holding cell.

The judge flashes me a smile on the way in. "Srećan Uskrs," I say. Happy Easter.

"Happy Easter," she replies in English, also smiling. I've come to love our back-and-forth—not just because it's fun, but because she alone will determine my fate. (At least she will deliver the news of my fate—someone else is most likely deciding it.) Back in SERE school—Survive, Evade, Resist, Escape—it was drilled into me that I have to humanize myself with any captors. Create a kind of reverse Stockholm syndrome where they come to like me as much as possible.

I take my seat, the room fills, she begins. The prosecution goes first. As promised, all they do is talk about DNA. They bring in an expert, a cop who talks about DNA. DNA, DNA, DNA, DNA! We get it. You're the fuckers who put it on the gun.

The judge asks me to stand so I can answer questions. She seems just as impatient as I am with the prosecution's broken-record "reasoning," which amounts to, "His DNA is on the gun, therefore he possessed it, and therefore he was intent on committing a crime." I feel like I'm in that movie *Minority Report*, and I'm being judged for precrime.

The questions begin, all through the translator just to my right.

"Did you touch the gun?"

"Yes." This is the only time I lie in court. I do not like it, but it's Milosh's plan, and I trust him.

"So you possessed the gun?"

"No."

"But you held it?"

"Yes." I catch the prosecution team looking at the judge. The looks on their faces say, "See? He did it! Case closed!"

"Where did this take place?"

"At Nikola's apartment."

"When?"

"I don't know the exact date. Sometime before you arrested me."

"Why did you hold it?"

"Nikola showed it to me and I wanted to make sure it wasn't loaded."

"Why would you do that?"

"Whenever someone hands you a gun just to look at, it should never be loaded. It isn't safe."

"Did you shoot this gun?"

"No."

"Did you try to scratch off the serial numbers from the gun?"

"No." The question is ridiculous. I've never removed or tried to remove a gun's serial numbers, but I imagine you need a lathe or some kind of special grinding tool. Maybe even some kind of acid.

"So you don't know why the serial numbers were removed from this weapon?"

"No. To be honest, I didn't even know they were." True—since I never touched the fucking thing.

This kind of questioning goes on for at least ten minutes. They often repeat a question, hoping to trip me up. They don't. When I'm finished, they question Nikola. His answers are spot-on and perfectly corroborate my answers.

Milosh asks basic questions about responsible firearm handling, and that's it. The judge thanks everyone, gavels us out, and announces the next date: May 16.

Another month comes and goes.

The guards appear on May 16. I'm in my freshly washed Lululemon getup, ready for court. Except that I'm not taken to the vehicle bay, I'm taken to visitor room four. The guard doesn't uncuff me for some reason. Milosh is there, looking like someone stole his lunch. "I'm sorry, Daniel. But there's no hearing today."

"What? Why?"

"No reason was given. The next day will be June eleventh."

Fuck this clown show. I'm promptly marched back to 311.

Thus begins my second summer in CZ. The heat returns. The mosquitoes. The humidity, as if the Danube flows through our room. The bedbugs. It's miserable.

A week later, the news spreads through all of CZ that Gile died at home. Overdose. We have a little memorial for him on the yard. Poor, poor Gile. At least he didn't have to go to Mitrovica.

Before my next court date, derby day arrives. This is when all of CZ—and Serbia—is treated to a Red Star/Partizan football match that every God-fearing Serbian man under the age of seventy must watch. The place comes alive. Brawls break out across the yard, the guards work hard to keep the hooligan bands separated. Inmates sing their teams' chants from the windows. Everyone wants me to pick a side, but I won't—I'm an American. If I'm going to cheer for a football team, it's going to be the Raiders. Every TV is tuned to the game, including ours.

Petar is in rare form: from the coin flip, he struts around like a cokehead on the best Saturday night of his life. He incessantly talks shit to Nole. Nole counters, but he's a real hooligan, not some casual fan. His banter is relatively light. Kiro and I ignore the children as we play chess.

A foul is called on one of the Partizan players, Nole claps. Petar is livid, he throws a full water bottle at Nole, it hits him in the face. Just like that, it's on.

Nole jumps down from his bed, so does Petar. Nole swings and catches Petar on the side of the head. Kiro and I watch, hoping that Nole will put Petar on his ass. Nole swings again, Petar jumps back, then bull-rushes him. Both go to the floor.

"Prestani!" Kiro yells, standing up. Stop! Nole is on his back, he releases Petar. Petar throws a cheap shot, but Nole checks it.

Then Kiro leans over and grabs Petar by the back of the neck, pulls him to his feet, and slams him against the bed. Kiro says something to the effect of, "Knock it the fuck off and shake hands." They do, everything is back to normal.

For a few minutes, at least.

After a controversial noncall on a Red Star midfielder, Petar goes off. He speaks—no, yells—about how shitty the refs are. Nole looks at Kiro for permission to shut him up, Kiro shakes his head. Petar continues, transitioning from football to all the pussy he gets to all the drugs he sells. The whole time he's walking back and forth, pointing at the TV, at Nole, at me, at Kiro, his bare feet clapping the cement floor. Partizan scores an early goal in the fourteenth minute to go up one–nil. He's amped. "You bitches need to show more respect," he yells into the hall at one point to no one in particular. "I'm the biggest cocaine dealer in Serbia! I make this whole fucking city high!" He spins to us, not really looking at us, and says, "And you guys need to show more respect too! I do everything in here and it's bullshit." *Oh boy*, I think. "Kiro, I've never seen you clean up in here once!"

Kiro stands.

Let's go! Where's the popcorn?

Kiro walks up to Petar. The veins in Kiro's neck are popping. He gets inches from Petar's face. Petar stops talking. I half expect Kiro to grab Petar by the wrist and pull off one of his arms. But no. He just says, "If you speak again, I will beat you until you stop moving."

Petar starts shaking. He doesn't say much of anything after that. Not that day, not ever.

Even after Partizan manages to hold on and win.

58

CLOSING ARGUMENTS

June 11 arrives. I go to the court, taking a route that does not pass Sveti Sava. I hope this isn't a bad omen.

I spend an hour in my holding cell and am then ushered into the courtroom, the guards only gripping the sleeves of my hoodie.

I look to the judge as I'm brought in. She busies herself with some papers on her desk, taking pains not to look at me. "Dobro jutro," I say, trying to catch her eye. She glances at me for a split second but doesn't say anything.

Another bad omen? If she pretends like I'm not here, then it'll be easier for her to send me to prison for something I didn't do, right? Is this the rule of three—the same rule I was so cognizant of on that first job with Malachi—finally coming to get me? First no church. Now the judge is ignoring me. Closing arguments are today, but maybe they don't matter. Maybe I'm already guilty.

Then it hits me: if I followed my gut way back in Yemen, would I even be here now? Probably not.

Milosh arrives. The hearing begins. The prosecution goes first. Its argument, delivered like the sermon at some Texas megachurch, amounts to: "This American ex–special forces soldier came to Serbia, our beautiful country, and instructed Nikola to buy him a pistol! Why? So he could commit a crime. Thank God he was arrested before he could commit such an act! As we have stated before, his DNA is on the gun. And he himself admitted to handling it."

The judge thanks the prosecution for its time and its work on the case. The state rests.

Milosh goes next. Speaking calmly and never raising his voice, he says, "This case against my client, Daniel David Corbett the third, should never have gone to trial, but here we are. This was a simple instance of one young man showing off to his American friend, who, yes, just happens to be a reservist with the US Navy SEAL Teams. Nikola, the young man in question, took Daniel aside one day and said, 'Hey, check out my gun.' He thought Daniel was cool, and Nikola was trying to impress him. Daniel, who is responsible and highly trained in the handling of firearms, took the weapon, ensured it was safe, and gave it back. 'Cool gun,' he said. That was the extent of his so-called crime. That, and the fact that he is an American with a military background. For over a year, Mr. Corbett has been grossly misrepresented by the media, going far past farce to the point of slander. During this time, he has been detained by the government in Centralni Zatvor. And for what? Simply for touching a gun and not even committing a crime, as the prosecution has just admitted. I know the honorable judge will look past Daniel's mistreatment by the media and the prosecution and only look at the facts. In so doing, there can be no conclusion other than the one that says Daniel is innocent."

If the judge is convinced, she shows no indication of it. She thanks Milosh and sets a final court date when she will read the verdict: June 18.

Only seven days away.

59

THE VERDICT

THOSE SEVEN DAYS ARE INTERMINABLE. I TRY TO PICTURE MY LIFE IN A WEEK'S time. Will I be found innocent? I still remember what it was like to be free, and I'll slip right back into life, I have no doubt. Go back to San Diego, see my family, return to SEAL Team 17 and catch up on a lot of lost weekends. Be the best and happiest SEAL reservist the navy has ever seen. Maybe get back with Malachi, or maybe give up on mercenary work altogether. Maybe write a book, maybe work with my friends in Hollywood as a consultant. Maybe get a fucking desk job, or (perish the thought) finally go three-letter. Whatever happens, it will be because I choose it. Because I will be free, and I will exercise my freedom. It will be…wonderful.

But what if I'm found guilty? Ironically, I have an even better idea of what my life will look like in that case. The upside is that I know I can survive in a Serbian prison. No—I know I can *thrive* in a Serbian prison. Maybe I'll just become what they call me: Foka, the criminal, the assassin, the bogeyman. I'll go Keyser Söze on everyone. Maybe I'll get with Luka's people. Maybe I'll pick a side in the never-ending Red Star/Partizan feud.

I'd be pretty good at all of it.

I hope for freedom, but as the days crawl by, I become resigned to captivity. I have to be real: this is Serbia, and there's no way I'll get out.

Finally June 18 arrives. I go through the same trip in the same van with the same guards. This time I catch a glimpse of Sveti Sava.

I'm taken straight from the van to the stairs. No holding cell today. We go to a different floor and then a different courtroom. It's huge, more auditorium than hearing room. When I get there, it's empty. Instead of benches there are plastic chairs, and the dais looks like it was just wheeled in. Everything feels temporary.

Over the next fifteen minutes, the room fills. Aside from Milosh, the only other friendly face is Ana from the State Department. No sign of my compatriot, Eric Roth. Fuck him.

The judge begins. Everyone is told to sit—except for me. She's very pretty today. As she speaks, she barely looks in my direction. Like I'm already gone. Milosh stares blankly into space. The prosecutors hang on every word. They're smiling.

Fuck.

My court translator is someone I've never seen before, and she's horrible. Of course I get the worst translator on the most important day. I catch a few words here and there, but that's it. The translator asks for clarification on something. The judge nods in my direction and speaks quickly. The translator asks her to repeat what she just said. Milosh stands ramrod straight, practically at attention. I lean past the translator. The prosecutor is slack-jawed.

The translator turns to me and says, "You can go, you can go."

Milosh makes a low whoop. I turn to him—he's beaming. To the judge—she's just looking at me blankly. And then back to the translator.

"I'm done? I'm free?"

"Yes, you can go."

"Under what conditions? I need to know exactly what the judge said."

The translator and the judge speak some more, and then the judge turns to me and says, "You are innocent of all charges, Mr. Corbett. The court is terribly sorry this has happened to you. On behalf of the Serbian government, I hope that your ordeal has not ruined your perception of Serbia. Our government will pay any and all legal fees, as well as restitution for missed wages and damages. Do you understand?" Turns out she spoke English this whole time.

"*Yes!* Yes, I understand."

"You will be returned to Centralni Zatvor, where you may collect your belongings. Then you must immediately leave Serbia, as your visa has expired."

I stifle a laugh at this final absurdity, but who am I to argue?

I am free.

60

BOWL, SPOON, BLANKET, KIRO

I'M TAKEN STRAIGHT TO THE VEHICLE BAY UNDER THE COURTHOUSE. ALL THE guards are struck with disbelief—not that I'm innocent, but that the judge actually said it, that's it's official, that I'm going home. They give me a lit cigarette and don't cuff me for my last ride back to CZ.

Instead of going to room four—I'll just meet with Milosh at his office, like a normal person—I'm taken straight to 311. Everyone is out on the yard, except Kiro, who stayed behind so he could be here when I got back.

I step into the cell.

"Well, what happened?" he asks.

I hold out my arms. "I'm outta here, brother!"

He doesn't say anything, just crosses the room and wraps me in a hug. He lifts me off the floor and jumps up and down a little. He's so strong, I can barely breathe.

When he puts me down, he says, "I'm so happy for you, Foka."

I clap him on the shoulder. I grab a trash bag and put some books and newspapers inside. Kiro asks about my clothes, I say, "I'd burn them if I could. I never want to see them again. Give them to Nole, or to the next sorry fuck who ends up in here."

I tie a knot in the top of my trash bag and shake Kiro's hand one last time. "Goodbye, Kiro. I wish you the same outcome, and to make it quick."

"Thanks, Foka. We will see."

"Don't kill Petar."

He shrugs. "I'll try not to."

He gives me one last quick hug, then I turn and leave.

The guard is waiting for me. "One last thing," I say in Serbian. "Can I go down to the yard to say goodbye?"

"No."

"Come on, man. I have people here."

"No." He grabs my arm and pulls me forward.

As we're walking away, I hear Kiro. He's yelling down into the yard below, "Foka is free! Foka is free!" Then I hear a cheer go up from outside, and another. Then other parts of CZ start making noise, the guys still in their cells, as the news spreads.

I'm free. My acquittal has dropped a big deposit into the CZ hope bank—if Foka can get out, then anyone can! It feels really, really good.

The guard leads me to a room I've never seen. I turn in the bowl, spoon, and blanket. I sign a piece of paper, they give me my shoelaces, my passport, my wallet—and my Rolex. Somehow it also survived.

I'm quickly taken out of CZ, but unlike in the movies, where the jailbird is standing on the side of the road waiting for a bus, or where the whole legal team is there to greet the ex-con, they put me in a squad car and rush me into the road, avoiding a gaggle of press. I ask the driver where he's taking me. All he says is, "Immigration."

When we get to the other side of Belgrade, a new set of cops in different uniforms meets me and drags me into some kind of immigration police head-quarters. They take my passport and put me in an interrogation room. "Your visa is expired," one officer says, eyeing my passport. "Why have you been in Serbia for so long?"

"Are you fucking kidding me?"

"Answer the question."

"I'm Foka. I've been in jail for the last eighteen months. You just brought me here from there!"

"Why did you come to Serbia?"

"Sir, look. I've already answered these questions. I'm not answering them again."

The officer snaps my passport closed and slaps it on the table. "You must leave Serbia."

"No problem! Let me go, and I will. Might take me a few days to get my shit in order, though." I'm not having any of this.

"You must leave tomorrow."

"Dude, I don't even have a plane ticket."

"You must leave—"

Just then a larger, more senior-looking guy comes in. "How does seven days sound, Mr. Corbett?"

"Sounds wonderful. Thank you *so much*."

Finally they let me outside into the free air.

One upside of this unexpected detour is that no one knows where I am. CZ was crawling with reporters—but here there are none.

Milosh is waiting for me outside immigration, and he takes me to his office. We have a celebratory rakija, which goes straight to my head. I have to be careful after eighteen months of stone-cold sobriety, especially in a country as committed to alcohol as Serbia.

We finally have a proper debrief. I learn a lot. I learn that he put the chances of my acquittal at somewhere around 20 percent. Not good. I learn that the Serbs definitely thought I was a spy, and that it took them a long time to learn I wasn't. I learn that Milosh heard that the Serbs, working at the behest of the Kremlin, had suggested the Serbians swap me in a prisoner exchange for someone named Maria Butina, whom the Americans had arrested in 2018. I've never heard of this woman. Milosh tells me she's a Russian agent accused of espionage by the United States. I learn that when she received her sentence a couple of months ago, in April—a sentence of only eighteen months, one she would probably only serve a portion of—the pressure was off. She could do that amount of time. On a hunch, Milosh also thought that around that time, the US government—hell, maybe even Eric Roth himself—finally convinced the Serbs (and their Russian backers) that, geopolitically speaking, I was indeed a nobody.

"And as soon as you had no value, you could be freed," Milosh says, pouring me another shot.

It all sounds pretty cloak-and-dagger to me, but I'll take it.

Milosh only mentions Malachi once, to say that he passes his regards. I don't bring up the job that brought me to Belgrade in the first place. What's the point? The less Milosh knows, the better, and in truth he probably knows more than I do, so, again, whatever.

I'm fucking free.

A little while later, Branko, the president of the Serbian Hells Angels, as well as their treasurer, Ivan, show up. Both are in full colors. I thank them over and over as they give me big hugs and more rakija. We say goodbye to Milosh, we hop in Ivan's car, and they take me to a hotel where they've booked me a room. All my stuff from Square Nine is there. They give me a new phone and €1,000 in cash. They give me a paper ticket to San Diego, for a flight departing in two days.

Hells Angels, man. Good friends to have.

I take the longest shower I've ever taken. I dry off, put on my old clothes. They feel amazing. I open my new phone and use WhatsApp to make a video call to Mom and Dad.

Mom's face pops up, at first confused because she didn't know the number. But then she sees me and starts crying. "Dano, Dano," she calls to Dad. "It's our son!"

"The favorite one!" I joke, also tearing up.

We only talk for about ten minutes. Mom is too excited, and besides, she just wants to see me face-to-face, which she will in only a couple of days. Toward the end she says, "I was so worried someone would get hurt."

"I wasn't going to get hurt, Mom. It's me. Also, I had some pretty scary friends in there."

"I know that, Danny—I meant someone else!"

I laugh. "Yeah, I was worried about that too for a while. But it's all over now." Mom tells me they'll be in San Diego to meet me, along with my brother, Joe.

"I can't wait to see you guys," I say. "I'm free. I'm safe."

"We love you, Danny!"

"I love you too."

That night, sleeping in a bed in civilization doesn't feel right. I don't miss my bunk, but I don't sleep very well either. At some point I move to the floor. But I keep the pillow.

I forgot how much I like a good pillow.

61

HOME AGAIN, HOME AGAIN

THE NEXT MORNING, I DO SOMETHING DECADENT: I HEAD DOWN TO THE small hotel restaurant and order breakfast. Two sausages, three eggs, toast, butter, jam, coffee, juice.

It's the best food I've ever eaten.

After breakfast, I head upstairs to make a call.

I need to check in with Malachi.

He picks up before the line even rings. "Allô?" he says with that familiar and thick French accent.

"Malachi! It's me. I'm out."

His end of the line is silent for ten full seconds. I can hear him breathing, though. "Oh, Dirty," he finally says. "I am so super relieved to hear your voice, brother."

"And I yours."

"I know you are OK. So I will not ask."

"We'll talk about everything in person."

"Good. Hopefully that will be soon."

"Yes, hopefully."

Another ten seconds. "Brother, I am so sorry for this bullshit. I tell you that sometimes I was thinking of coming there with François and some other guys and getting you out!"

"Ha! A good old-fashioned prison break."

"Yes, just like that," he says. "Again, I am sorry that it happened. Maybe next time I come too. Or you have a partner."

I almost say, *If there is a next time*, but hold off. I'm very much in one-day-at-a-time mode. Instead I say, "No need to apologize. I fucked up, it's on me. What's important is that it's all over. Or it will be, as soon as I'm out of this fucking country."

"Do not stay there one second longer than you have to, Dirty. You never know."

Malachi's right. I'm not off the chessboard yet. I could get arrested again. I could get accused of something else. "I won't," I say. "I'm on a plane that leaves tomorrow."

"Bon. And Dirty! We will never work in Serbia again!"

"Never ever ever."

"OK. We will talk soon. Big hugs, brother."

"Big hugs."

We hang up. I sit there, the sounds of Belgrade outside my hotel window. A bird. A siren. Two people yelling. "Next time." Malachi's words ring in my head. If there is a next time, things will be different. For jobs like this, I'll have a different set of operating procedures. Be friendly, but don't make friends. Stay on target. Don't get distracted. Work efficiently. Be paranoid, even more paranoid than on kinetic jobs. Always keep an eye on the exit, and always have a plan for getting there, *fast*. Know my rights for whichever country I'm operating in.

And if I get arrested, don't answer any questions without a lawyer. If I'd only had Milosh at my side during my first interrogation, they might not have swabbed my DNA. And if they hadn't done that, I wouldn't have been in CZ for a year and half.

I turn back to my phone. I text my mom for a while, she helps me get my address book back together, sending me phone numbers for friends and guys in the Teams who reached out to her while I was locked up. I spend the rest of the morning checking in with these guys, letting them know I'm out and headed home. To a man, none of them ever worried about me. Their collective sentiment was, "It's Dirty. He's got this."

At noon Ivan swings by. "Let's eat!" he says. I'm not very hungry—I had a huge breakfast and am used to only eating sparingly—but I'm not going to sit in my room all day. I've done enough of that.

We jump in Ivan's car and hit a high-end seafood place. Branko meets us. We sit on old wooden benches on a lush lawn overlooking a small river. It feels so good to be outside in direct sunlight and surrounded by green. Branko orders for the table, and before I know it a flight of rakija is in front of each of us. Four stemmed miniature snifters, each filled with a different shade of fruit brandy. I know better than to try to keep up with the big boys, but it still hits hard. The waiter returns. Each of us has a whole fish, roasted with lemon and garlic and herbs, a chunk of peasant bread, a bowl of ajvar—a sweet relish of peppers and eggplant. After eating, Branko orders another round of flights. I'm still nursing my first one, so I give mine to the two of them. I order an espresso. It tastes incredible and goes straight to my head.

Branko asks for the check. While we wait, he jostles his phone. "Daniel, do you want a girl? Or maybe two?"

"Ahhh…going to pass for now. Not ready for that yet."

I get no pushback, which is nice. And a little unexpected, especially from Hells Angels.

We leave, I bounce around with the Angels for the rest of the day and stay up way too late.

Somehow, around midnight, I end up at Square Nine, my first home in Belgrade. Branko told me I was persona non grata at this hotel, which made no sense considering how much money and time I spent here.

So here I am, in the lobby, trying to find the owner. I want to ask why I'm not welcome anymore. The rakija flowing through my blood doesn't help. I glare around the room, but it's pretty dead. No one notices me, the dreaded Foka, the Most Dangerous Man in Serbia.

Certainly not the young cop thumbing his phone on a lobby couch.

I approach him. "You 'ere fer me?" I ask.

He looks up from a game of *Candy Crush*. An image of François, sitting on the base in Yemen, flashes before me.

The young cop is genuinely scared. "Y-yes," he stammers.

"An wha're you s'pposed t'do if I show up?" I manage to say, suddenly aware of how drunk I am. The sober part of my consciousness implores me: *Daniel, stop.*

The cop doesn't answer.

"Well?" I demand.

Daniel, stop. Get out of this country, like Malachi said.

"Make sure you leave?" he says, unconvinced he could do that, even given my inebriated state.

I take a step back. And then another.

Daniel, stop.

I'm not Dirty right now, and I'm sure as shit not Foka. I'm Daniel D. Corbett III, and I have to make my own decisions from now on.

"I'll leave wh'n I'm reddy," I say, though I've already dialed it down. We can both tell nothing is going to happen. A few minutes later, I'm gone.

———

I WAKE THE NEXT MORNING AT 0530. MY FLIGHT IS AT 0900. EVERYTHING hurts. I overdid it, but at least I stayed out of trouble.

Taxi, one more drive-by of Sveti Sava, airport, check-in. When I'm at the desk, I'm surprised to discover my flight itinerary. The check-in agent is surprised too. I didn't look at it before, just assuming I'd fly to Frankfurt or Heathrow or Schiphol and then off to San Diego.

But no. Instead it's Belgrade to Moscow, Moscow to Frankfurt, Frankfurt to Istanbul, Istanbul to Washington, and finally Washington to San Diego. I ask if I can be reticketed for something more direct, but the fare class is so bare-bones economy that I have no flexibility. Altogether, I'm looking at thirty-six hours of travel or more. Amazing. But it feels like the perfect coda to my time in this upside-down country.

Security, espresso, double espresso, gate. Despite the coffee, I sleep on all my flights. I don't drink. Thirty-plus hours later, I touch down in Washington. I have to go through immigration before my final flight to California. I steel myself for a steady grilling by the Customs and Border Protection agents. I regularly got questioned on the back end of jobs, my passport full of stamps from the Middle East, my beard long, my tan deep. This time my situation appears equally suspect, even though I have no tan to speak of. Abroad for a long time on an expired visa, just a backpack and my Rimowa roll-aboard.

I step up. The agent takes my passport, runs it, looks at me, looks at his screen. Then he looks back at me, smiles, stamps the passport, and says, "Welcome home, Mr. Corbett."

Shit. That was easy.

I clear customs and head to the domestic terminal and hop my last flight. Five hours later I'm home, at my most favorite airport in the entire world, San Diego International.

It's been too long.

I scan the faces as I ride the escalator to baggage claim—and there they are. Mom, Dad, brother Joe, all standing shoulder to shoulder.

I run down the rest of the steps, Mom hops up and down. She wraps me in a tight embrace. Dad sees that he won't be able to work in a hug right now, so he pats my back. Joe shakes my hand, grabs the back of my neck. We all laugh, Mom cries. The usual scene, the kind that never gets old.

We spend the next five days at my brother's two-bedroom apartment. We watch movies, we eat, we watch more movies. I'm blown away by all the new streaming services. They tell me that Eric Roth told them I was living in some kind of Club Fed penitentiary where everything was nice and nothing sucked. Fucking Roth. I tell them how it really was. Mom is angrier than me. We talk for hours, we play cards. It reminds me of our on-again, off-again tradition of renting a cabin at Lake Tahoe for New Year's. No agenda, no schedule, just good company.

Five days go by too fast. Mom and Dad get ready to leave, making the drive back up toward Sacramento. More hugs and kisses, and then, before shoving off, Mom grabs a full contractor bag out of their car. "I didn't want to give this to you right away and ruin the week. I figured it's been a couple years, what's a few more days?"

I take the bag. It's heavy. "What is it?"

"Mail." In other words, my life. Or what's left of it.

"Shit. OK. Thanks, Mom."

They leave, I stay with my brother until I can get my life back together.

And judging by my mail, it has completely fallen apart. I have no lease and no apartment. My cell phone has been cut off, my Netflix, my landline. My car got taken by the repo man. My bank account has a balance of $13.42. My credit rating has plunged to 580—the only cards I can get approved for have $300 limits. And to top it off, I have multiple notices from the IRS claiming I owe $80,000 in back taxes.

At night I try to forget the financial Armageddon lying all around me. I call my old buddies in the Teams. One Saturday night, I meet my friend Wyatt, we head to Pacific Beach. Shore Club, a line around the corner. It was never like this before. All I want is to get inside and have a vodka Red Bull slushy. "What the hell?" I ask, gawking at the line of people.

Wyatt pulls me to the side. "We can use the other entrance. I know the guy." We go around the corner, head up a flight of stairs. There's a bouncer there, but it's not Wyatt's guy. He's not having it and tells us to go back around front.

Just as we're about to give up, I hear someone call from inside the bar, "Dirty! Dirty!" An arm reaches out of the open door and taps the bouncer on the shoulder. It's Mike, one of my friends in the Teams and a Shore Club regular. He pushes his way outside and gives me a hug. "I heard you were back, Dirty! Great to see you, man."

"You too."

Mike vouches for us, we go inside. A lot of guys I know are there, and it quickly turns into a mini reunion. It was great to see some old friends, but as I'm standing there it hits me: my days of loitering in bars and drinking are over and done with. I stay out for a while, have a slushy and a fish taco or two, and head back to Joe's.

Every night, as I drift off, I say a word of gratitude for being out of CZ and back in America, back in a real bed, in a place where I can eat real food and see real friends.

I repeat that I will now make my own decisions. But the question remains: What the hell am I going to do?

62

YALLAH, BROTHER

A COUPLE OF WEEKS AFTER RETURNING HOME, I GIVE SEAL TEAM 17 A CALL. As a reservist, I want to get everything back online and make up all the weekends I missed.

My military ID is expired, so I arrange for Ops Officer Rivera to meet me in the dirt lot and drive me onto the base. He's there waiting as I pull up. I park, he waves me over, I jump in.

"Corbett! Good to see you, man. Sounds like you had a hell of a time."

"I did, sir."

"C'mon, man. You know it's Riv."

"I did, Riv."

"Welcome back!"

"Thanks, Riv. It's good to be back."

We drive down the road and through the gate, get out, head up to his office on the second deck of the outdated office building. We sit, he pulls a manila envelope from his desk and sets it in front of him. He rests both hands on it, fingers splayed.

"Well, Corbett. We extended your end of service as long as we could. As you know, it officially ended in June 2018. Considering your circumstances, we kept it going through May of this year. But that was as far as we could go."

"Understood, Riv. I really appreciate your extending it as long as you did."

"For you? No problem." He picks up the envelope and holds it out. "Here are your discharge papers. Of course, you received honorable, with an RE-1."

This means that rejoining the navy shouldn't be much more difficult for me than passing a physical.

"Great," I say, taking the envelope. "I guess I'll just call the office and schedule a physical before coming back to Seventeen."

Rivera's face changes, then he looks down at the top of his desk. "Yes, well... about that."

"Yes?"

"There's no easy way to put this, Dirt...The thing is, they pulled your trident."

"Excuse me?"

"They, uh, they pulled your trident."

"I, I...*what*?" No trident means I'm no longer a SEAL. "Why?"

"Well, an entire Team got popped for drugs last month on the East Coast."

"And?"

"And, uh, you've heard about Eddie Gallagher?"

"Yeah, I know Eddie."

"His final murder hearing is next week and, well, it doesn't look good."

"Of course it doesn't look good. The charges are complete bullshit. And besides, what does that have to do with me?" I ask, almost choking out the words, I'm so angry. "Is that what this is about? How things look?"

"I'm sorry, Dirty. It wasn't my call. I lobbied for you. But the higher-ups, they ordered the command to pull your bird. They didn't want another black mark on the brand." I can tell he doesn't agree with this and hates saying it. "Their words, Dirty, not mine."

I grip the envelope hard under the edge of the desk, nearly crumpling it. I take a deep breath. "I see. So they don't want a guy who was wrongly accused and spent time in prison in Serbia to join the ranks of some SEAL drug addicts and Eddie Gallagher? Because the navy has a brand to protect. So they're pulling my trident, but also giving me an RE-1 honorable. That it?"

What I want to say is, "Brand? Brand? Are you fucking kidding? This is my fucking life! The brand is not based on higher-ups or overweight officers. It's based on people like me who actually do shit! So don't piss on me and tell me it's raining, dude."

Rivera doesn't say anything.

"So what, I can rejoin the reserves undesignated, no rate? So I can pull guard duty for ten years or some bullshit?"

"Yeah. That's what they're saying."

I am beyond livid. I fought for my freedom without their help for eighteen months. When the Serbian media dragged my name through the mud, the navy didn't come to my defense. I didn't take a plea deal, I didn't pop pills, I stood my ground, I went to trial, I was acquitted and apologized to by the judge, and this is my fucking reward?

I ask Rivera if the commanding officer, master chief, and executive officer are in. They are, he takes me to them. They're all together, like they're waiting. They're horrified to see me.

"Who took my trident and why?" I demand. The CO does most of the talking, and it's just more bullshit. According to him, my only option is to get a congressional letter reinstating my status as a SEAL. That's it. No "Welcome back, glad you're safe." No medical, dental, or psych checkup.

Their horror isn't due to what they've done to me, it's due to my even being here in the first place. They just want me to go away. Life would be easier for them if I were still locked up.

After ten minutes, I've had enough. I spin around and march out of there. Rivera follows and gives me a ride back to the lot. We don't say much.

When he pulls to a stop, he says, "So what're you going to do, Dirt?"

"I guess I'm calling DC."

"I'm sorry I had to be the bearer of bad news."

"I'm sorry they made you do it, Riv."

I get in my rental car and drive away from the base for the last time.

Three days pass. I don't calm down. I talk to Joe, I talk to guys in the Teams, I talk to Mom. No one can believe it. During one of these conversations, Mom remembers that a DC staffer of some kind reached out to her while I was in CZ. I had Roth tell her not to talk to anyone while I was locked up, and she didn't, but maybe I should talk to this guy now?

She gives me his number and I call him up. First name Orson. I have no idea who he is, but he works for a congressman.

"So I heard Seventeen pulled your bird," Orson says.

"You heard right."

"They say why?"

"Not specifically. They just talked about Eddie Gallagher and some East Coast platoon getting in trouble."

"So PR ass coverage, sounds like. They give you any paperwork?"

I was so angry, I never even opened the envelope. "Yeah, they did." I find it, we go over it together. The official reason listed is "lack of confidence."

"That's it?" Orson says. "They give a reason for this lack of confidence?"

I turn the paper over, double-check it. "No. That's it."

"And discharge? General? Dishonorable?"

"No, man! That's the crazy thing. Honorable, RE-1."

"*What?*"

"I know."

"All right. Do me a favor and fax that over." He gives me the number. "I'll get this to the congressman ASAP. We'll get you sorted out."

Over the next couple of weeks, Orson and I exchange emails, but nothing happens. To this day I have no trident, all due to the fear-based decisions of a few people somewhere, people I'll never meet or get to plead my case to.

One day it hits me: I have been abandoned by the greatest organization on earth, one I still love, one that helped make me who I am. I gave it nearly seventeen years of service, following orders, hunting and killing America's enemies in every corner of the globe, and what did I get in return? Kicked to the side for public relations.

And so the question remains: What am I going to do?

I sure as hell am not reenlisting to work dead-end navy depot jobs just to get retirement. And I'm not going to use any of their dead-end veteran job-placement services. They'd do the bare minimum to help, and if they did help, it would be by placing me in some kind of soulless position not commensurate with my skills or interests. I'll say briefly that the US military can do much better at this. Perhaps ironically, given that it's so devoted to conformity and rank structure, the military creates go-getter creative types, especially in the special forces. We should be going into media or communications or the arts, but instead we're shunted into things like business or manufacturing. It's a damn shame.

I'm also not so sure I want to jump back into contracting. Do I want to endure all the absurdity, the false starts, the tough living conditions, the mercurial clients, the risk of getting blown up by an American Hellfire missile, the bad comms, the over-the-hill and eccentric operators who don't have half my skills? I'm not so sure.

During this time, a nonmilitary friend asks me if I want to join him in the exciting world of finance. He offered me a job on two occasions in the past, and

I turned him down. But this time he comes with an offer that's hard to refuse: excellent salary, four weeks' paid vacation, full benefits, matching 401(k), fully remote (even before COVID). I won't lie: I consider it.

"Finance"—whatever the hell that means—sounds boring, but boring won't get me arrested, maimed, or killed. I talk it over with my family. One day Joe and I FaceTime Mom and Dad. Mom holds the phone way too close to her face, Joe and I laugh at her. They want to know if anyone in DC has done anything. "No," I say. "And I'm not expecting anything there, Mom."

"It'll work out. I know it will."

"Maybe." I tell them about the finance gig. Dad thinks it sounds great. I mostly think he wants me to do anything, just to get back on my feet. Joe slips into frame at one point and shakes his head slowly.

"Your second-favorite son thinks it's a bad idea," I say. I already know Joe thinks sitting behind a desk would be spiritual suicide for me, and I agree. But I'm still unsure.

Dad goes outside to work on the yard, Joe goes to the kitchen to make lunch. I sit with Mom. We don't talk. I can see she's thinking, and I know her well enough to leave her alone when she's thinking. Mom has always been clear-eyed.

Finally she says, "Danny, stop."

"Stop what?"

"Thinking about this job. Why would you even consider a desk after all you've been through?"

"It's stable. No one will be shooting at me."

"Stable? When have you ever wanted that? You should do what you love, and what you're good at. You have to be safe—safer!—but I think you politely turn down that offer. Something will come up."

Another moment of silence. "Thanks, Mom. I needed to hear that."

"Do what you love" is a standard self-help book mantra, but it's standard for a reason. It's sound advice. What do I have to fear? I am loved, and love is the antagonist of fear. The next day I turn down my future in the exciting world of finance.

Not three days later, Malachi calls. I've chatted with him a couple of times since getting back, but our conversations were just friends talking, not business partners planning.

"Dirty, how are you, brother?" he asks in that low voice.

"I'm OK."

"There's talk of you retiring."

"There was some chatter of that, but it's a vicious rumor."

"Aha! This is super-fantastic news. I've got a good clean job. Should be quick. Just you and me. Your Spanish still sharp?"

"Sí, claro."

"How fast can you be in Central America?"

"As fast as you can send me a ticket—but first, Malachi, I have some questions."

"Let's hear them, Dirty." For the next forty-five minutes, I grill him on the operation. I won't put myself in a situation like Belgrade. Hell, I also don't want to sit around on some dusty black-site base with my thumb up my ass. I don't want to be a chess piece anymore, I want to be the player. I want to operate.

In the end I'm satisfied. If Malachi says it's clean, I trust him. "All right, I'm in."

"Fantastic. See you tomorrow, brother."

"Yallah, brother."

Yallah.

ACKNOWLEDGMENTS

THIS BOOK WOULD NOT BE WHAT IT IS WITHOUT MY WRITING PARTNER, NILS Johnson-Shelton. His ability to make my words come alive on the page, and his devotion during the past two years, have been indispensable. Through our time together we have become not just collaborators but friends. I consider him a mentor. Nils, thank you. You are truly a master of your craft.

I would have never been introduced to Nils if it weren't for my literary agent, Howard Yoon. Howard, thank you for connecting all the pieces and taking on this project. Thank you for your hard work through weekends and holidays to get this book into the right hands, and thank you for telling me hard truths when I needed to hear them.

Thank you to my editor, Alex Pappas, at Center Street for seeing this book's potential and letting Nils and me tell my story the way we wanted to. Thank you for not trying to change it into something it isn't.

Thank you to everyone at Hachette Book Group, from the marketing team to the unsung heroes behind the scenes who I never interacted with.

Thank you to all who have served—with me, without me, before me, after me. I see only so far because I've stood upon the shoulders of giants. I hope that one day I too can be a giant whose shoulders can be stood upon.

Lastly, to my family and friends. Words cannot describe the gratitude I have for each of you, nor can I express the depth of our mutual and unconditional love. Without you I would not be able to walk the path that I do. Thank you.

ABOUT THE AUTHOR

DANIEL CORBETT SERVED AS AN ELITE NAVY SEAL OPERATOR, PART OF SEAL Teams 5, 6, and 17. He's now an ex-military operator for hire. He joined the navy shortly after graduating high school in 2002 and was deployed to Iraq in the summer of 2005 with SEAL Team 5. He joined SEAL Team 6 in 2007, deploying to various locations around the world. In 2010, Daniel returned to the West Coast and began instructing at the Naval Special Warfare Basic Training Command (NSWBTC). Daniel ended his active-duty career after two years with NSWBTC and quickly fell into the world of private military contracting. Daniel joined the active reserves in 2014 and maintained his active reserve status until 2019. In 2017, Daniel made international news when he was thrown in jail in Belgrade, Serbia, for eighteen months after traveling there as a private contractor to track a terrorist financier. Daniel still monitors international news and continues to entertain phone calls and meetings with those who need unique solutions to unique problems.